DISCARD

PLANNING AND OPERATING A SUCCESSFUL FOOD SERVICE OPERATION

PLANNING AND OPERATING A SUCCESSFUL FOOD SERVICE OPERATION

William L. Kahrl

1973
CHAIN STORE AGE BOOKS
An Affiliate of Lebhar-Friedman, Inc.   New York

Printing 5 4 3 2 1

PLANNING AND OPERATING A SUCCESSFUL FOOD SERVICE OPERATION

Copyright © 1973 Chain Store Publishing Corporation, 2 Park Avenue, New York, N.Y. 10016. Printed in America. All rights reserved.
Library of Congress Catalog Number: 72-92136
International Standard Book Number: 0-912016-16-7

To my wife, Lois, for these many years of love, understanding, and patience

CONTENTS

Foreword   *xi*
Introduction   *xiii*

PART I. PRELIMINARY PLANNING

Chapter 1.	Why Start a Restaurant?	3
Chapter 2.	Choosing a Location 33 Considerations	19
Chapter 3.	Planning the Food Service and Layout For Productivity, Volume, and Profit	31

PART II. EQUIPMENT PLANNING

Chapter 4.	Food Service Equipment For Now and for the Future	49
Chapter 5.	Food Preparation Equipment How Much Do You Really Need?	66

vii

viii CONTENTS

| Chapter 6. | Warehandling
Do It by Machine | 79 |
| Chapter 7. | Miscellaneous Equipment
Efficiency Makers | 95 |

PART III. PLANNING FOR EFFICIENT OPERATIONS

Chapter 8.	Purchasing and Storage Plan for Control and Accessibility	111
Chapter 9.	Food Preparation How Much Is Necessary?	126
Chapter 10.	Food Service An Underestimated Factor	138
Chapter 11.	Sanitation Planning Can Reduce the Work	152

PART IV. PLANNING FOR GROWTH AND CHANGE

Chapter 12.	Moving Toward Automation Consider What's Available Now	165
Chapter 13.	Equipment for the Future What We Need	174
Chapter 14.	Remodeling and Expansion Points You Shouldn't Overlook	181

PART V. MAXIMIZING THE BENEFITS OF GOOD PLANNING

| Chapter 15. | Merchandising
Physical Elements | 189 |
| Chapter 16. | Meeting Competition
More than Price is Involved | 201 |

Chapter 17.	Employees	208
	Make the Most of Your Manpower	
Chapter 18.	Control and Profit	215
	Some Helpful Procedures	
Index		231

FOREWORD

This is about the most comprehensive book on restaurant planning I have ever seen. Anyone contemplating opening a restaurant and thinking it is a simple matter of location plus food equals profit will soon see that this is a most complex industry—one far removed from the diner of yesterday.

Our company, The Marriott Corporation, began as a single unit in 1927. There were no guides such as Bill Kahrl's book to assist you in those days. You worked on the trial and error method, keeping the good and rejecting the bad. You experimented constantly and, in doing so, built your experience a day at the time. Had this book been available back then, we could have moved ahead 20 years or more overnight.

Bill's book will be valuable to many in this industry. I envision it as a great help to those planning to open a restaurant, to those who want to improve their present restaurant, and especially as a training tool for new restaurant management. It is a most commendable work.

J. W. MARRIOTT, JR.
President
The Marriott Corporation

INTRODUCTION

The food service industry has long been troubled with many problems, and solutions have been slow in coming. Even though the industry is very large in total, it is primarily made up of many small and varied operations, and this has made it difficult to establish research, development, and lines of communication. Certainly food service has not kept pace with other industries owing to its major handicaps:

Wide variations in products and methods

Manufacturing and selling on the same premises

Long hours of operation

Operation nights, weekends, and holidays

Low productivity

Hard physical effort

The large supermarkets, in contrast, have standardized on products and methods, shortened their hours, and shifted much of the work to the customer. As a result, they have produced high sales per employee.

This book represents forty years of experience in the food service industry, during which answers to many problems emerged piecemeal as the author worked in all parts of the business and for many different companies. In testing, research, seeking ways to improve, and then evaluating by actual application, he found that solutions do exist which lead to greater productivity and profit for all types and sizes of operation. There is still no miracle solution, but many small improvements steadily applied can produce substantial gains—now.

The author's conclusion is that our industry is not as difficult as many have tried to make it, and that good planning and research direct us to some fairly simple courses of action. In the past, the manufacture of hundreds of items each day in the kitchen was a difficult and expensive process, but over the years methods have been devised to ease this burden. Automobile manufacturers make different cars and models, but they all employ the same efficient methods and systems. Food service operations must keep their individuality, but the entire industry can make better use of standard practices and systems. Any large task is easier to handle when it has been broken down into smaller parts, and this is one of the main reasons for *Planning and Operating a Successful Food Service Operation*. Once we can define and improve each basic phase of food service, we are on the way.

Part I
PRELIMINARY PLANNING

Chapter 1

WHY START A RESTAURANT?

The food service industry is large and complex. The hot dog stand at the beach, the drive-in hamburger joint, the neighborhood coffee shop, the industry cafeteria, the school lunchroom, the franchise fried chicken place on the outskirts of town, the toll road snack shop, the gourmet restaurant, the hotel dining room, the hospital kitchen, the airline catering service—all share some problems in common; each has some problems uniquely its own.

Not everyone has the temperament to cope with the complexities of this industry. For those who do, the restaurant business can be an exciting challenge and a ladder to success.

There has never been a more opportune time to start a food service venture. First, the potential market is very large, and all indications are that the population—and the potential market—will continue to grow. Second, food service equipment, systems, controls, and other physical aids that have been developed over the years make the business of running a restaurant not only easier but more profitable. Third, increased travel, more leisure time, and the tendency to eat out more often have enlarged the market for food service of all kinds. Fourth, menu prices are higher, which means there is a better chance to make money.

On the other hand, one must be realistic. Just as there is danger in going skating without first testing the ice, there is also danger in opening a restaurant without knowing the difficulties, planning wisely, and seeking professional help.

SOME MISTAKEN NOTIONS

To begin with, what intrigues people about a restaurant and impels them to open one? Most of the inspiration comes from mistaken notions about this business.

Low Investment

People look around a restaurant while dining and get the idea that it doesn't cost much to open a place like this. Actually, the cost is very high today, running into hundreds of thousands of dollars for even a moderate-size operation.

The confusion comes when the novice's estimate of the cost of the equipment is based upon the cost of household equipment. For example, a large domestic combination refrigerator-freezer can be purchased for $300 or $400, whereas the restaurant reach-in refrigerator, which does not even have automatic defrost, will cost several thousand dollars. The reason for this is that household refrigerators are mass-produced in standard models while commercial refrigerators are produced in very small quantities and have more options than some automobiles.

The next everyday error is in estimating the cost of the restaurant building. Again the diner looks around a restaurant that isn't much bigger than his house and estimates that the cost will be comparable. Yet the fact is that, with all the building codes and regulations, the cost of a building for a food service operation would be six to eight times as much per square foot as a dwelling.

The first thing to realize, then, is that the investment is substantial.

High Profits

Everyone who ever dines out has at one time or another been convinced that restaurant profits are enormous. Forgetting the elegant dining spots, it is common today to pay $3 to $5 for a dinner. A quick estimate of supermarket prices for the pork chop, baked potato, and so on, leads the average person to conclude that the profit on the food served in restaurants must be staggering. Ask people outside the industry what they estimate restaurant net profits to be and their figures will run as high as 50 percent. Yet anyone who knows the food business is aware that a well-run restaurant with a good volume of sales will be satisfied with a 10 percent net. And when we think of all the poorly run places with low sales, the high profit picture becomes blurred.

Everyone Is an Expert

The assumption that expertise at home can be carried over into the operation of a restaurant is another large factor in the launching of so many eating establishments. We all eat three meals a day and almost everyone has tried his hand at cooking, even if only on the backyard barbecue unit. Many of us even give a dinner party for 20 guests now and again, and there are few difficulties in serving all these people.

Commercial cooking and service of food is an entirely different operation, and it is much more difficult for many reasons, as we shall see.

I Can Do It Better

There is a little bit of the conviction in all of us that we can do things better. When we get poor food and service, our first reaction is, If I were running this place, such things would never happen! You may be right. Inexperienced people have set themselves up as restaurateurs and become famous and prosperous, but the odds are against you.

Encouragement

A bit of encouragement can spur one on to opening a food service operation. It comes about usually in either of two ways.

This town needs a good restaurant is probably number one on the list. Actually, most towns could use a good restaurant, but this doesn't mean that one would be successful. Usually there are reasons why no good eating place does exist, and it would be wise to study the situation carefully before taking the leap. Strangely enough, even many large chain operations have fallen for this reasoning and as a result are saddled with some operations that are not too successful.

6   RESTAURANT PLANNING

Second, many people have been *talked into* this business by salesmen of equipment or land. Any good salesman will paint a rosy picture (otherwise he is not a good salesman) and soon someone with money in the bank makes a withdrawal and opens a restaurant. The 1960s saw much of this, with franchise chains selling thousands of operations that later proved to be failures.

REASONS FOR STARTING

Food service operations are conceived and launched for many reasons, but generally we can define five basic approaches to starting a restaurant.

Individual Project

The greatest number of food places get their start as individual projects. Even some of the largest chains began this way, with no thought of expanding as they have. It is common knowledge that the risk and the percentage of failures in the food service industry are the highest in the retail service industry. Yet thousands of restaurants open each year, and many fail after a very short time in business. Nineteen seventy-one was a year notable for failures, because added to the poor individual efforts were the many collapses of the so-called franchise chains.

Expansion and Growth

Many of the new eating operations we see all over the country are the result of expansion and growth. These places can come from two sources: (1) The individual operator who has a successful operation and decides to open more restaurants in the hope of increasing profits and building a large chain, and (2) the successful chain which is constantly on the lookout for new locations.

Necessary Supplement Operation

Necessary supplement operations are by far the most stable and longest lasting in the food service industry. These are the restaurants on toll roads and in transportation centers (airports, railroad stations, and bus terminals), hotels, motels, amusement centers, industrial plants, and many other locations that have what might be considered a captive audience. Many of these food operations are actually subsidized by the main activity because food and refreshment are a necessary convenience. This field has fewer problems of survival than the freestanding place, but does have the problem of selecting the right kind of food service for the people it is to feed.

Franchises

At the present time, franchises are a subject few people want to discuss or even think about in our business, but they must be considered as a prime factor in the launching of many new food service operations. One unusual aspect that will be considered later in this chapter is that even though everyone thinks the *franchisee* is the only one who can be hurt, many *franchisors* have suffered in the franchising process.

Reopening a Restaurant that Has Failed

Many new ventures in our field consist of eating places that have failed. They may be reopened by an individual or a chain. Such a place is most easily recognized by the window sign *under new management*, though it is difficult to see why such a sign should be expected to serve as a drawing card. Later in the chapter there will be more on this endeavor.

Does all this make it sound as though no one should open a new food service operation? If we consider only the preceding points, the picture is indeed black. But there is much more to the picture. We will need many new and remodeled eating places if we are to feed our growing population. However, it is time we have a realistic view of what is involved today in opening and running a restaurant, and that is what this book is all about. The bad eating place not only does damage to itself but hurts the entire industry. Think of how any individual feels after several bad experiences in restaurants, and it is not hard to understand why he becomes reluctant to eat out. In contrast, consider New Orleans, San Francisco, and other cities that are well known for their good restaurants. The percentages of people eating out regularly in these cities are much higher than in other locations. Frankly, it would be better to have a good restaurant for a competitor than a poor one. When your competition is good, it spurs you on to do a better job, and both create satisfied customers who eat out often. This has been demonstrated time and again in the past and can make the future better for our industry.

IMPORTANT CONSIDERATIONS FOR THE INDIVIDUAL

To paint a factual picture, let's point out some important things to consider before undertaking a food service operation. Again, this is meant to encourage the right approach so that more people will be successful and we will have many more fine eating places. For the individual there are two possible roads to take. The first is the small, inexpensive, badly equipped restaurant that can, with very hard work and great effort, be built into a successful operation. This has been done many times in the past and it can be done again, but one must realize that it is more difficult to do today and requires years of hard physical labor. The second choice is a well-planned, attractive place properly equipped at the beginning to do a good job and, what is more important, to do volume business.

Because the odds for succeeding are much higher with a well-planned operation, let's look at the things to consider down this road.

Competition and High Standards

The competition for diners-out is keener today for many reasons. The American public has traveled more, for one thing, and is accustomed to higher food service standards now than in the past. In your early thinking about opening a restaurant it would be wise to consider this seriously and to decide on an operation that will meet these higher standards. Trying to operate a facility that is inadequate would be comparable to trying to box with one hand tied behind your back.

The Initial Investment

Well planned does not mean expensive. For the most part, operations planned by experienced people in our business cost less than some poorly planned places. However, the basic items must be included from the start. The initial investment may not be as low as you think, but if it is geared to what you intend to accomplish, it will help you make a success of your business. For example, the cost of the property, whether it is to be leased or purchased, is an important factor in your thinking at the start. The less expensive location may seem most attractive as far as investing is concerned, but the more expensive location may generate much more business and therefore higher profits. It would be wise for anyone contemplating a new food service operation to put in time and effort to find out what the investment will be, because this is where most people get into serious trouble before the restaurant opens its doors. Go to a reliable consultant or to someone in the business and find out the actual amount of money needed to start the kind of restaurant you are contemplating.

Once the initial investment has been established, think in terms of what you will need for the opening when the physical plant is ready. Beyond the cost of the land, building, and fixed equipment, there is a considerable outlay for other items such as china, silver, glassware, pots, pans, and inventory of food. New people in this business are often overwhelmed at the amount of money needed at this point —money that was not discussed in the beginning—and it is difficult to get much credit in a new venture like this. So this cost must not be overlooked.

The Breaking-in Period

Another area in the opening of a new food service facility that is too often forgotten or passed over quickly is the task of opening and getting the business on its feet; that is, the breaking-in period.

Few restaurants attract huge crowds at the beginning or make a profit for the first month or two. With the shortage of skilled help today, you will probably have to hire employees in advance of opening and institute training programs. *The customer may know that you have just opened, but he does not forgive poor service and food.* Because the arrangement and employees are new, productivity per employee will be low, and until systems and methods have been taught, it is difficult to make a profit. All this means that after financial arrangements have been made for land, leases, and fixed and expendable equipment, a supply of cash will be needed for opening expenses and for deficits during the initial breaking-in period.

Future Cost Increases

In the conception stage, think positive about future success and there will be a better likelihood of making a profit and staying in business. With today's costs of doing business, each type of food service operation has a certain breakeven sales level. Take the time to find out what this level is for your particular facility and plan accordingly. One highly successful chain has learned from years of experience that it cannot succeed with a restaurant of its type that does less than $500,000/year in sales, and it therefore does not even consider anything below this figure.

Knowledge like this is important not only to a large chain but to the individual. For example, if you build a restaurant planned and equipped to do a maximum of $100,000/year in sales, with no possible way to expand the building or parking or equipment, the chances for increased profits in the future are very slim. In fact, as costs rise each year, the profit on this hemmed-in restaurant will drop. Every business should grow year by year if it is to be successful for a long period. Even if the original place is not fully built or completely equipped, allow for the possibility of expanding at a later date.

The Employee Problem

Earlier in the chapter, "I can do it better" was mentioned as an incentive for the start of a new operation. This is the right attitude, but it takes more than mere words to make it come true. Good foods, recipes, methods, systems, and controls are not hard to find now and these factors should offer little trouble for the newcomer, but the employee problem is another matter. For example, consider the following recent figures.

An average restaurant with 35 employees will lose $12,600 a year because of turnover. Several years ago the national average of sales/year/employee was approximately $13,000. Assuming we have become more efficient and the average is now $15,000 per year, the average restaurant with 35 employees will produce a volume of approximately $525,000 per year and will spend 2 percent of these sales for turnover.

Loss of an unskilled employee can cost $100, a skilled worker $1,000, with a $300 average for all employees.

Restaurant turnover averages well over 100 percent annually, reaching rates of 300 percent to 500 percent (as compared with 4.6 percent for manufacturers and 6.1 percent for food manufacturers).[1]

This explains why restaurants so often provide bad food and bad service. The president of one very large chain recently said that unless we learn to reduce the difficult work and drudgery, it will become even more difficult to find employees.

Because the figures just cited are so bad, the food service industry is beginning to do many things to reduce its high turnover, not by choice but because this situation must be corrected if the fourth largest industry in America—the food service industry—is to have continued natural growth and hold its position.

All this means that the conception period is the right time to prevent

[1] The turnover statistics in this section are from *Nation's Restaurant News,* January 17, 1972, p. 2.

trouble. If one is inexperienced, it might pay to work in the industry or at least talk with as many experienced persons as possible about the help problem. There is no doubt that the problem can be solved, and it will be just as soon as the industry decides to act and not just talk. After World War II, there was a period called by one writer the "ten wasted years" when all the effort of the industry was focused on Washington to keep the minimum wage law at $1 to $1.25 per hour or, if it was raised, to make sure the food service industry would be exempt. This was fuzzy thinking. Even if the industry were granted the exemption, how are you going to get or keep good employees for less money than everyone else is paying? If the effort had instead been focused on working out ways to increase productivity and wages, our industry would be in much better shape today.

In the early 1960s one large and successful chain of fine restaurants in Italy undertook to make its operations more efficient so that fewer employees could be used, not to increase profits but so as to pay the same hourly wage that a large manufacturer was paying. This is the type of positive thinking needed.

As your plans develop, give a lot of thought to your employees, with particular attention to their wages, hours, and working conditions. Many food service operations are still being designed without facilities such as lockers, dressing rooms, toilets, and places for employees to rest and eat. What is more, automatic equipment and simple devices such as hand trucks, dollies, and other labor-saving tools are eliminated by planners in their effort to reduce investment costs. This is poor thinking. Put the matter of hiring, training, and keeping good employees high on your list when you are conceiving that restaurant where the food and service will always be just right, and you will go a long way toward realizing your dream.

IMPORTANT CONSIDERATIONS IN EXPANSION PLANNING

The best thing that can be said for expansion and growth is that they are healthy for the chain as well as for the individual operation and the public could use many more good places to eat. There are a number of considerations for both the individual and the chain to think about in opening new operations and in expanding.

Individual Expansion

Generally it is the successful company that expands (discounting the recent franchise explosion when both successful and losing businesses were building more and more places). The successful individual should think about a number of points.

Before going into another geographical area, make sure your type of operation will have appeal there. Often a single restaurant has grown slowly over the years in a certain locality and built up a large clientele because it gives customers what they want. But people in the new area may not want the same things, and there could be trouble.

Be sure your staff is ready and large enough for expansion, because an inadequate staff could hurt not only the new place but the existing successful one as well. Most individual places have grown because of the efforts of one or more dedicated people, and often a new manager who is hired to operate a second facility will not put forth the same effort.

Expansion will provide the opportunity to advance and reward good employees who have been with a company for years. Any worthwhile employee wants to advance and do better, and expansion is an excellent way to move up those deserving individuals.

Realize that the new place will cost a lot more than the existing one, which means higher amortization and expense.

Profits will not be doubled with two restaurants or tripled with three, as most people think, because the overhead and other expenses of running multiple units rise rapidly and cut into this increase. One growing chain that years ago had an overhead cost of 4 percent on $4 million in annual volume was taken by surprise when its overhead cost reached 8 percent at the time its sales reached $10 million a year.

Chain Expansion

A chain operation's financial statement will reveal total income and expenses and total profit; it will not be itemized to show which individual units are most or least profitable. Yet chains do have operations that show little profit or in fact are losing money. However, when a successful and profitable operation consists of a hundred units, the few losers do not show up in the total; the mistake is hidden and perhaps not serious. Certainly it can be carried for a time while efforts are made to improve the situation. Furthermore, a chain's greater financial flexibility allows it greater freedom. Most large chains have been able to branch out into other activities—motels, grocery sales, in-flite feeding, industrial feeding. If one or two restaurants in so large an operation have a bad year, other elements of the business can make up for the loss. However, there are certain things for the chain to think about.

Before opening a new operation make sure it will have appeal in the new area. It is by no means unheard-of for an operation that has been highly successful in one city to build an identical unit in another city at a fine location and not succeed.

Be sure the staff is capable and large enough to handle the growth. The staff should be expanded *before* the new facilities are built; otherwise the chain will have difficulty in opening the new operation or will have to neglect the existing locations.

Finances must be in order when the program begins; otherwise the older places will suffer when management tries to stretch the available funds to cover the cost of building and running the new place.

When a chain expands too fast, mistakes are made in choosing locations and areas with the result that the new units are not successful. Often the chain will not admit such an error and will use its money and its most talented employees in an effort to change a poor unit into a good one. This hurts the existing successful places by taking away good supervisors and by drawing off money needed for remodelings and improvements at the proven locations.

Trying to counteract such mistakes also does one other serious injury to a chain that is not evident until later. When an outstanding employee or manager is put into the failing operation and asked to revive it, he may be unable to do so no matter what his skill. Eventually this valuable employee will resign because he has become discouraged or the parent company will dismiss him because he could not succeed.

IMPORTANT CONSIDERATIONS FOR THE NECESSARY SUPPLEMENT

The necessary supplement type of company (the one with the captive audience) does not have the usual expansion problems. As a rule, both parties in this type of service will wait until the last minute before expanding or adding to the operation because customer dissatisfaction is not considered serious when he has no other choice.

The biggest problem in this field is in selecting the right food service to do a certain job for a given number of people. It is not uncommon for the wrong type of food service to be selected for these captive customers. For example, the authorities on many toll roads have chosen to establish fine table service restaurants which do not meet the needs of most people using the roads. Many complaints have been voiced for these reasons: (1) The restaurants are usually quite a distance from the nearest town, and help is hard to get. This makes it difficult for operators to provide table service. (2) The people using these roads pay a fee to save time, and they do not want to lose time waiting for food service. (3) As cars become faster and the total time spent on the road diminishes, the food needs of the driving public change. (4) Alcoholic beverages cannot be served, and this discourages those who do want to have a big meal, but want a drink with it.

For the toll roads and other express highways of the future, these factors will have to be studied and a more suitable food service offered. A good variety of fast foods or even self-service in attractive surroundings at moderate prices would much better serve the needs of travelers on toll roads.

Airports have problems with their feeding facilities, because needs have changed here too over the past few years. Not only is the average traveler in a great hurry but in most cases he will get a substantial meal on the plane. Furthermore flights are shorter now, which means the traveler may be arriving at his destination in time for his evening meal. The elaborate service restaurant here needs to be studied for yet another reason. When there are flight difficulties, food service operations at the airport are swamped with business that they cannot handle.

A little more flexibility is needed here, and perhaps some added self-service would be useful. There must be a level of service between the plush restaurants at these captive audience operations and the old-style snack bars which are seldom appealing. Perhaps it is time to offer something new that would be attractive to the traveler and give him the type of food and service that would tempt him to eat at the airport. It would also be more flexible and easier to operate during the feast and famine periods of business.

Motels, particularly those out on highways away from the center of town, have difficulties today providing satisfactory food service to their patrons. It is no easy matter to run a restaurant for the long hours required and make it pay. The average motel should not even consider room service today. It is hard enough to find staff to serve in the dining areas without trying to set up trays and deliver them to rooms.

Here again a new approach is needed. Perhaps an attractive fast self-service buffet breakfast service requiring only a few employees would satisfy most of the guests and get them on their way in a hurry. For the motel that is out of town, it might be practical to stop serving lunch, and concentrate on a good dinner well suited to the motel guests.

By cutting down on the number of employees needed and on the long hours of unprofitable operation, it would be possible to offer food service that the guests would enjoy. And this in turn would bring people back to the motel. For example, one successful motel sets out a free continental breakfast for all its guests—juice, toast, and coffee—and lets the guests serve themselves. This can be most enjoyable for the guests and can solve the problem of trying to serve a large meal with no help.

Not only must toll roads, airports, and motels study existing conditions and adapt to changing circumstances but other captive places also must reevaluate their food service and make changes as needed. For example, a number of fine resort hotels are specializing in elaborate buffet nights with a variety of themes, and the guests enjoy the novelty. Here again, fine table service is coupled with a buffet so each guest can select what he wants.

In all necessary supplement feeding, the first consideration must be the needs and desires of the people using the primary function (the motel, the highway, the shopping, the plane) and the best food service must be devised to satisfy the most people. We go to the airport to take a quick flight or meet one; we pay a toll on a road to get to some other place fast; we stop at a motel to rest up for the next day's drive. In all these situations meals are secondary.

Perhaps a change in food service is in order at these facilities. The first and foremost consideration should be the customers and what they want. The days when we established restaurants patronized by a select few are long gone. For example, the railroads used to ignore the majority of passengers and provide only expensive dining cars that drew fewer and fewer customers. Now train travelers can get a bite at a snack bar. We must realize that times have changed, and we need to change too.

IMPORTANT CONSIDERATIONS FOR FRANCHISES

Our last method of growth, the franchise, has been the subject of much publicity and unfavorable comment in recent years. Yet this is an important phase of the industry, and the method of developing new operations will improve. Now that the speculative fever has subsided, this system can again be used by experienced firms and people to provide good food service operations that are badly needed.

The Franchisee

For the inexperienced, becoming a franchisee is still an excellent way to enter the food service business if three conditions are met.

First, a thorough investigation must be made of the company. There are numerous publications that will provide information about the steps to take and even advise on certain companies. If the prospective franchisee is not sure of a company's financial condition, it would pay him to go to someone with experience who can understand financial statements.

Second, for anyone about to invest a large sum of money, it would also be wise to travel and personally investigate existing operations of the company. Observe the business they are doing and the condition of the places; and above all, talk with present holders of franchises. If there are problems and difficulties, they will quickly be brought to the surface.

Third, there are excellent companies selling franchises that are particularly suited to the novice. In many cases, they will help select a location (backed by years of experience in selecting locations and areas) and will make available a complete package with every detail of the operation spelled out. In addition, they can provide valuable advertising and promotion that are beyond the reach of the individual operator.

The inexperienced newcomer to the food service franchise operation must realize that he will face problems. One is *restrictions.* Most successful chains have worked out their plans and operations in exact detail and insist that no changes be made. To some aggressive franchisees this can become a source of increasing friction when they feel ready to make changes or do things differently. A second problem is *competition.* If you find a good location and have a good business going, it won't be long before some other franchise will open near you. This means more work to meet the threat and perhaps some loss in sales.

The Franchisor

On the other side of the franchise coin not much has been said about the companies and their difficulties. For example, many well-intentioned people buy a franchise and have a successful opening, but soon tire of the long hours or of working on Saturdays, Sundays, and holidays. So they turn the operation over to a young grill man, and as usually happens when owner-management steps out, the quality of the operation slips. Or the parent company manages to get a new setup well launched and on its way to success, whereupon the franchisee begins to complain about buying products from the parent company or about paying a certain fee. He is now an expert and wants no part of the parent company any more.

Sometimes the franchisee decides he can buy supplies for less than the franchisor charges, and of course he can, especially if he does not worry about quality. This will eventually hurt the entire franchise operation because the public is as much aware of changes in quality as it is of portion cutting.

By far the most difficult thing for the parent company to combat is the franchisee's desire to change the menu and the items handled. The man with a hamburger franchise sees other people selling fried chicken and decides that he should get a piece of that business for himself. The factor he overlooks is that the chain became successful with a fixed menu, and the physical plant was designed to handle this well. Each item he adds to his menu complicates the operation and slows the service, and all the added waste and added problems in training and help will soon leave him making less money.

All this hurts the parent company because it has a total image to maintain, and a few poor operations can hurt very much indeed. This explains why many large chains now are buying back franchises as fast as they can in an effort to preserve their total image.

REOPENING AN EXISTING FAILURE

For many of us it would be best not to consider reopening a restaurant that has failed unless we are very brave, very rich, or very foolish. This is a popular road because the investment is low, the present owner has hundreds of reasons why he did not succeed, from ill health to lack of time, and the new owner is led to believe that all he must do is put forth a little effort to build a fine successful business.

One who is experienced and has money to invest in wiping out a bad image is best equipped to start this way. Americans who eat out have a funny habit of not returning to locations where they have had bad experiences, and if you reopen one of these places you must have patience and skill as well as money to rebuild the business.

True, chains have taken over failures in certain locations and made a success of them. However, the first thing they do is to completely remodel each place and give it a new look. Then, they pour in money and personnel enough to get the operation running smoothly so that business can be built back. Along with this, they can concentrate on an advertising and promotion program to rebuild in a hurry.

Lest it be thought that reopening a failure is always doomed from the outset, let it be said that there *are* instances where this can be done successfully. For example, there are attractive restaurants that do a good business but do not make money because of a lack of control. It would be possible to take over such an operation, institute modern controls, and succeed where the previous owner had failed. Other places could be improved by shortening the hours of operation or changing the food service and menus. Still other operations have been run successfully for many years and come on the market because the owner actually wants to retire and get a well-deserved rest.

The biggest factor in favor of reopening a failure is that the investment is low as compared to the new venture, with its new building and new equipment. When the investment is lower, the fixed charges are less, and there is a chance to make some money. In considering this kind of venture, be sure to study the situation carefully, and always get advice—from a professional if possible. A little extra time spent in careful and thorough investigation will pay off in the long run. Many operations that had been failing have been brought back to life over the years—some by just changing the physical setup for greater efficiency and better service. What makes this road an attractive one today is the high cost of starting from scratch. But spend at least as much time investigating and planning as you would for a new operation.

Chapter 2

CHOOSING A LOCATION: 33 CONSIDERATIONS

Location is a most important factor in any food service operation's success or failure. Finding the right location is such a complicated task that many large companies are using computers to help, often with great success.

No one who is an old hand at selecting locations would pretend to be infallible or suggest that there is an exact formula for picking the ideal spot. Some restaurants in what seem to be excellent locations are doing very little business, and others in spots that no expert would pick are doing an excellent volume.

BASIC FACTORS

Assuming that you want to find a site for a food service operation, how do you go about it? What aspects make one location more suitable than another? For a start, here are four points that are basic.

First, good location alone will not ensure success if your food service facility does not do a good job or is not appropriate to the area.

Second, there are two approaches to selecting a location. One is to look for a location suitable for a specific type of food operation. The other is to adapt or design the food operation to fit a specific location.

Third, the selection of a site will vary for a chain, for an individual operator, and for the first in a projected group of restaurants.

Fourth, it is possible to do a good business in an out of the way place, but it takes a good operation and time! In other words, the bad effects of a poor location can be offset by doing a fine job, as many flourishing restaurants have amply demonstrated. But it must be remembered that they have succeeded despite the location, not because of it.

Whether or not you will be using a computer to help in site selection, here is a list of 33 points to consider.

1. State
2. City
3. Suburban
4. Rural
5. Population density
6. Potential for growth
7. Income level
8. Type of operation
9. Market potential
10. Local support
11. Meals to be served
12. Seasonal or year-round business
13. Highway
14. Intersection
15. Direction of street traffic
16. Location on the block
17. Visibility
18. Traffic counts
19. Who travels?
20. Future roads
21. Foot or car traffic
22. Speed limit
23. Traffic lights
24. Access
25. Parking
26. Investment cost
27. Fill or excavation
28. Piling and sewage
29. Fire and police protection
30. Local codes
31. Neighbors
32. Supplies and deliveries
33. Competition

Though this is a healthy list of things to check, its purpose is not to frighten or confuse but rather to stress the importance of spending enough time in selecting the site. If you can avoid one small error in choosing a location, the time will be well spent. Considering the price of land, building, and equipment, investing a little money in cautious investigation here will help you avoid costly errors. Let's look at the list of 33 considerations in more detail.

THE POPULATION CENTERS

1. *State.* It has been proved again and again that the volume of sales per food service operation is much higher in some states than in others. This has been confirmed by chains that have identical facilities in many states and can compare volume business. For example, Ohio, Indiana, and California have many high-volume food operations of all kinds. Even if you have identical operations in similar locations in some other states, the three states just mentioned would produce higher volume.

Not all the reasons for this are known, but these states do have many good restaurants, and people are inclined to eat out more often when they can look forward to good meals in good restaurants. Compare the noteworthy fact that Philadelphia's per capita consumption of ice cream is one of the highest in the country, and that the Philadelphia ice cream companies have been turning out top quality ice cream for years.

2. *City.* In-city locations are faced with many problems, some of them of recent origin. Such things as pollution, crime, transportation difficulties, lack of parking space, size of the investment, and high operating costs are adding to the many other problems facing operators here. Of course, the subsidized captive food services are doing well, as are most city locations during coffee breaks and lunch hours. But dinner is another thing. Snack, fast-service, and self-service operations that can draw enough trade during the business part of the day will continue to do well, but the service restaurant will have a difficult time.

Recently it was revealed in New York City that a rather sizable number of fine restaurants were having difficulty, mainly because of price. Contrary to what some food service experts are saying—that price means little if the surroundings and food are excellent—there is resistance to high prices. For years the *expense account* carried these restaurants because companies were liberal, but today even large companies are looking with disfavor at the cost of these meals.

It is difficult to predict exactly what type of food operation will be best for the big city of tomorrow unless people move back in large numbers. Although lunch business and snack bars are doing well in all cities, the dinner business has been hurt because so many people have moved away. If a city attracts many tourists and conventions, restaurants will be needed even for dinner. The night club type of place that dispenses liquor and provides entertainment is doing well in some cities.

A venture into a full-scale restaurant in a big city today would require special study and research, because all cities are different and the particular conditions must be carefully analyzed. At the present time, a city restaurant would be better for someone with a well-known name, a good reputation, and substantial resources, not for the beginner.

3. *Suburban.* The service restaurant seems to have found a new home in the suburbs, as have shopping centers and many fine stores that had only downtown locations a few years ago. Here one has a chance to get the regular family business that is so beneficial to a restaurant. Even though breakfast and lunch business may not be as great as it is in the city, more money can be made by serving dinner only than by staying open for breakfast and lunch.

It should be noted that suburban restaurants generally have not been too successful in shopping centers. They can be situated in any one of a variety of spots in or near the suburbs as long as there is ample parking space and the surroundings are pleasant. Unlike big city residents, the people in the suburbs have cars and use them.

4. *Rural.* This may seem an odd classification, but there are some very successful operations located out in the country. However, the important thing to consider here is that many of them have been in business for years and have built an image that attracts people from miles around. This could mean a long, hard road to success at a rural location.

5. *Population density.* Figures on population density are easy to obtain and tell you how many people live or work within certain distances of the site you are interested in.[1] If there are very few people within five miles of the site, for example, you are faced with the problem of attracting customers from more distant points. If you plan an operation where people stop for a bite on impulse, density will be very important to you because customers generally do not decide in advance to eat at an impulse place but rather stop when they see the place and decide then and there to have a bite to eat. In addition, if you are planning a specialty operation such as a pancake house, it is best to pick an area with heavy population saturation, because a specialty operation does not as a rule have regular customers who come in several times per week.

---

[1] For pertinent information on the distribution of population, see demographic statistics published by the Bureau of Labor Statistics, Government Printing Office, Washington, D.C. Information on the distribution of food service facilities is available from the National Restaurant Association, from state restaurant associations, and in trade magazines of the restaurant industry.

6. *Potential for growth.* Many surveys have been made on growth, decline, and shifts in population, and this information is available locally from the chamber of commerce, city hall, or a good realtor. Often just a few dollars will get you the facts you need as to whether you are choosing a growing area. Naturally, you want growth so your business will increase each year.

7. *Income level.* Income in the surrounding area is a significant gauge if you pick a site where local business will be a factor in total volume. This can be done by carefully noting the surrounding territory in person and seeing the general level of the houses, the other businesses, and so on. It is very important today to merchandise within the price range of your local market. More and more operations are learning the value of attracting a large number of people and having them come back often. This is the best way to produce profits as opposed to the old theory that you should have a 30 percent food cost. It is better to net 10 percent on $500,000 than 20 percent on $100,000.

When you check into a neighborhood's income level, don't overlook a significant aspect of this figure: *disposable* income. In other words you need to know not only the general level of income of the residents in your immediate area but whether they have any left to spend after paying their monthly bills. For example, in a new development where young married couples with families have just purchased and furnished new homes, even though their income is good, they may have little excess cash to spend on eating out.

TYPE OF OPERATION VS. LOCATION

8. *Type of operation.* Whether you want to open a pizza parlor, a bar and grill, or a seafood house, be sure the kind of food operation you are contemplating will be right for the area. If you own a chain, the job will be to find the right spot for your particular type of operation. An individual can look for a location first and then design and adapt the food service to fit.

As an example, it has been said that one large national chain counts the number of church steeples within a certain radius of each location being considered, then weighs this factor heavily in deciding whether its kind of place is likely to succeed.

9. *Market potential.* Will the people who live in the area be interested in the particular operation that is being planned? Is the site you are considering in a good area for a service restaurant or is it better for

a snack place? If you want to open a steak house you are not likely to do well in an area full of retirement homes. Some riding around and on-the-spot observations can help you make a logical choice.

10. *Local support.* Will the operation you are planning have the backing and support of people in the area? A plush restaurant in a low-income area or a Coney Island hot dog stand in a high-income area cannot expect to get much support from the local citizens, and a noisy drive-in may stir up opposition in a quiet neighborhood.

11. *Meals to be served.* You should have some advance estimate of what meals you will serve or what will be the best meal in the location you are considering. Then the operation should be planned around this. For example, one large chain does most of its business at breakfast, and its plan is necessarily different from that of a suburban restaurant that draws neighboring families for dinner. It is possible in certain areas to serve dinner only and make money, if your operation is planned for this. Unless the location is most unusual, few restaurants can attract peak business for all meals including late night diners. The place that is open 24 hours a day is becoming increasingly difficult to plan and operate at a profit.

12. *Seasonal or year-round business.* In tourist areas, at some highway locations, and in certain weather areas, the location will produce what is known as seasonal business, sometimes referred to as feast or famine business. This kind of place can be difficult to run because when you are busiest, everyone else in the area is also busy and getting help can become a problem. In addition, during the slack time you may lose all the money you made during the height of the season.

ADDRESS

13. *Highway.* Most of the activity at highway locations has centered on the toll roads and interstate highways. Toll roads have a captive audience and are of course closed to anyone but the operator selected by the authority. Interstate highways usually prohibit eating places on the road itself, and there has been quite a flurry of site buying at the intersections or exits. Most of these sites have been taken by service stations, motels, and self-service food chains, and are not too advisable for the individual operator or the service restaurant. On other highways the best choice of a site would be at a busy intersection with large motels and a town nearby. And, because of the high speed of automobile travel, it takes excellent billboard signs in advance to get motorists to stop.

14. *Intersection.* Although intersections and corner locations have the greatest exposure, a problem has developed lately that should be considered. If the corner has a traffic light and marked lanes and the intersection is a very busy one, your customers may have great difficulty in leaving your parking area and getting back into the flow of traffic.

15. *Direction of street traffic.* In most cases locations on one-way streets do not do as well as those on two-way streets. If the street picked now carries two-way traffic, it would pay to check with the city planning department to find out whether there are any plans to make changes in the traffic flow.

16. *Location on the block.* Because of the problem of getting in and out of a corner location, many operations are now locating in the middle of a block or between highway intersections. Property here is ordinarily not as expensive and your customers will be able to get in and out much more easily.

17. *Visibility.* This is most important in a site, particularly if you plan an impulse type of operation. If your building, sign, or entrance is not clearly visible from the approach, you will lose many customers who might have stopped. This is increasingly true as cars travel at greater speeds and the possibility of turning around to come back is more and more difficult.

18. *Traffic counts.* The number of cars going by a potential site is another important consideration. The figures on traffic density can be obtained from local government agencies, or people can be hired to use counters and actually check traffic at various times of day. Years ago an average of 15,000 cars per day was considered high, but with four-lane highways and more cars on the road, this would be low today. Exposure is desirable to a restaurant because even the person who does not stop at first will come to remember you and he is more likely to stop at another time.

19. *Who travels?* Along with the traffic count, you must know what people are driving by and why. In addition to the average total daily count, it is important to have counts at various times of the day. For example, a location could have a very high average daily count made up of two rush hours: people hurrying to work in the morning and home again in the evening. If this makes up most of the total, you will draw few diners into a restaurant no matter how heavy the traffic. Actual observation of the passing cars and occupants will reveal much about who travels.

20. *Future roads.* Many eating places have failed in the past ten years because of new roads and highways which bypassed their formerly good locations. Before signing a lease or buying a property, check

with local authorities and planners to see what roads are being contemplated for the future. Don't take a salesman's word that nothing will happen to affect a particular location. Investigate for yourself. Check with the city planners, the state highway department, the local chamber of commerce, the businesses in the area.

ACCESSIBILITY

21. *Foot or car traffic.* Will your customers arrive on foot or by car? This is easy to determine and will help you decide whether the type of operation you are planning will fit the location.

22. *Speed limit.* Naturally the lower the speed limit at the location, the better for your customer and for you. Drivers can pull in and out with more safety when the speed limit is low and you do not need as much visibility as you would on a road with high speed limits.

23. *Traffic lights.* It is important not only to study the effect of existing traffic lights on a proposed location but to investigate the likelihood of future installation of lights. In busy areas, lights at advantageous locations can help your customers move in and out freely and safely. In addition, lights bring the traffic to a halt and give prospective customers a chance to see your operation and decide whether they want to stop for a bite.

24. *Access.* Unless most of your customers will arrive on foot, the site you pick must have easy access for cars, with wide cuts and preferably two separate driveways for entrance and exit. If the cuts are too narrow, people driving in or out may bump over the curb and be badly shaken. Be sure to check with the proper authorities in advance to find out whether good access in and out is possible.

25. *Parking.* If your proposed operation is for automobile traffic, you must have ample parking space to do business. Many areas now have strict codes and regulations that specify the number of spaces you must have for businesses of certain types and sizes. A figure that often works well is one parking space for each two seats, but this does not always apply.

Before making the big investment, study the site; don't just assume that the area will be large enough for parking. Draw up a rough site plan, with the building and parking indicated, or have someone do it for you. And don't forget these three other items: local easements by code, which will have much to do with locating the building and parking area; employee parking, which could take as many as ten to fifteen spaces on a busy night; and one or two car widths of space for a trash area or dumpster.

Remember, too, to have at least one area blocked off for deliveries and to make the spaces and driveways large enough; otherwise you will have many minor accidents that will hurt your business. Many drivers are not expert at parking a car, and it is wise to make it as easy as possible for them. Finally, you will want to light the lot at night, and there must be space for protective barriers around the light poles; otherwise they won't remain standing for long.

PROPERTY CHARACTERISTICS

26. *Investment cost.* The importance of projecting costs on a contemplated venture is stressed from time to time in these pages because you must have some financial goal or plan. If a site is too expensive, the leasing cost, ground rent, or purchase price will be more than the proposed operation can carry and stay in business. The cost must fit the plan, or the whole project will be headed for trouble. For example, one self-service fast food chain rented a busy but not well-suited location for better than $42,000/year in ground rent plus taxes, a grand total in excess of $50,000/year. A simple cost projection would show that this could not work. For example, assuming the place did $300,000/year sales, it cannot pay 16 to 17 percent for ground rent and make money.

The way to calculate site costs is to figure a normal 3 or 4 percent for ground rent or write-off and then project a reasonable total yearly volume. Many people justify a too-expensive site by pinning their hopes on a very high figure for potential sales that will never be reached. If one site is too expensive for you, look for another site. Don't try to justify an unrealistic price with unrealistic projections.

27. *Fill or excavation.* Having to use an excess of excavation or fill to prepare a location for building could prove so expensive that it will distort the costs out of all reason. A good architect or builder can advise you in advance about this.

28. *Piling and sewage.* These two items are often overlooked in negotiating for property. Test borings can reveal whether the costs for piling and shoring will be excessive. Because sewage, septic tanks, or drainage fields can be so expensive, investigate in advance by checking the local regulations. Failure to do so may put you in the position of one chain that subleased a prominent location and building from

another chain. Because the new operation was different from the old one, the local authorities forced the new company to install new septic tanks and drain fields at an added and unanticipated cost of $15,000.

29. *Fire and police protection.* Recent figures on the increase in crime as reported by the press and other media make it plain that you must know what kind and amount of police protection you will have. This will determine the kind and amount of protective measures you must take.

Most food service operations deal in cash and are of course attractive to the holdup man. The less protection you will have from the police, the more you must provide yourself: daily trips to the bank, large, heavy, built-in safes, barred windows, and so on. In some cases the amount of police protection has affected the closing time at night. You may also have to consider extra steps to ensure the safety of your guests and employees. You may need to consider parking lot and street lighting, having someone at the entrance to check people coming in and going out, and perhaps even having escorts for female employees leaving late at night.

If you have weak fire protection, you will have to install an automatic sprinkler system or other devices to control any fire before it gets out of hand. Insurance companies will pay for fire losses, but if the amounts they must pay are excessive, the rate they charge will also be excessive. A careful investigation here could save you a lot of money and spare you a lot of problems.

30. *Local codes.* The most important code to check first is the zoning code; this will spell out the types of places permitted in a given area. Then, too, there are new ordinances to consider, on noise, pollution, traffic hazards. Be sure the operation you are considering will have full approval at city hall before signing for the property. The fact that a location is zoned for business does not give you blanket approval. For example, some localities now have a ban on new drive-ins.

There are other regulations that could cause trouble in dealing with local governments, and these must be considered before purchasing or leasing. For instance, most areas today have restrictive regulations about *signs,* and on some new highways they are not permitted at all. If your operation will depend on erecting a large billboard down the road to attract the motorist, make sure such a sign is permitted. If signs are forbidden beside a main highway you may need a larger and more expensive sign on the site than you had originally anticipated. Otherwise you will not be able to draw customers to your operation. Investigate this carefully at the start.

Local ordinances sometimes make getting a *liquor license* very difficult. If a bar will be a main part of your business, check on whether you can get a license and how long you will have to wait for it. Don't be content with a salesman's assurance that a license can be had. Make application and find out for sure that a license is available and when it will be issued.

Now that more and more communities are placing emphasis on *environmental problems,* make sure you know of any unusual regulations at your site regarding air and water pollution, noise, exhaust emissions, and so on. Normally, these and other regulations, such as the number of wash basins and toilets you must install, are the responsibility of the architect. You as owner must check into licenses and permits, but the architect must assume the responsibility for exhausts, ventilation, sewage, and the rest. In fact, he should advise you in advance on many of these items that could be a source of trouble. If he is a local architect, he knows what is required; if he is not he must check the local codes.

ENVIRONMENT

31. *Neighbors.* This is usually a small matter, but it doesn't hurt to at least check this point. What do the nearby businesses look like and what are they? Are there houses close by? A residence near a public eating place with a parking lot and much activity can become the source of complaints about noise.

32. *Supplies and deliveries.* Some locations are remote from good food and equipment supply sources and it is important to be aware of this when selecting a site because the longer the distance, the more costly the deliveries. If the designer or planner knows there is a problem, he can take this into consideration and provide larger storage areas to reduce the number of deliveries.

33. *Competition.* This is probably the first thing everyone checks when considering a location. Many prefer a site with no competition, but the fact is that good competition can actually help. But it pays to note the nature of the competition and be prepared to meet it if you are to succeed.

There is one other point that merits consideration before picking a location or signing a lease. Some businesses must provide food service for employees at locations where there is not enough volume to make a restaurant profitable. In cases like these, the companies will subsidize a food operator and actually pay a fee to have the food service. In this case a bad location would be good for the food service operator since he would be assured of a management fee plus expenses each month. For example, a publishing house might build a new plant and office building out of town away from other restaurants and be forced to provide an employee cafeteria. Since there would probably be only one meal served daily five days a week, this facility would run at a loss if the publisher did not pay a supplementary fee.

There are other considerations to take into account—future development, changes in population age groups, and changes in eating habits, to name a few—but the list in this chapter covers the principal items to check when selecting a location. The main thing is to investigate thoroughly before purchasing or signing a long-term lease for land, a new building, or an existing failure. Although computers and expensive investigation (aerial photographs, for example) can help, you can do a lot of checking yourself. A little walking, riding, and talking can uncover many things of interest. Then, with a clear picture of the location's positive and negative aspects, seek the advice of a professional consultant or planner. He will help identify and analyze those specific aspects of the site that will have the greatest impact on the investment costs and the ultimate success or failure of the operation you are planning.

Chapter 3

PLANNING THE FOOD SERVICE AND LAYOUT: FOR PRODUCTIVITY, VOLUME, AND PROFIT

Good planning and physical layout are important keys to success in the food service industry. All too many food service operations are having serious operating difficulties today because these points have been ignored. There is one very obvious reason why good planning is so very important now: we do not have and cannot afford the extra employees needed to compensate for a bad plan and layout. Recently it was revealed that one board of education serves 28,000 meals per employee per year and a prominent university serves 27,000 meals per employee per year, whereas operations that have to show a profit are serving only a few thousand meals per year per employee.

In 1936 a poorly designed dishroom was no problem. We hired more people to make up for the inefficiency and paid them $1 per day for ten hours of drudgery. Recently J. Willard Marriott, Jr., president of The Marriott Corporation, stated: "By 1980 it will be almost impossible to hire employees to perform menial and unpleasant tasks.

Companies in our industry that don't change their jobs will have impossibly severe manpower shortages."[1]

These changes should have been made ten years ago. They are within the reach of all operators and can be put off no longer; we must make them now. Our concern in this chapter is therefore not only with planning for profit but with planning to eliminate some of the menial and unpleasant jobs. Much of this information will be spelled out in more detail in other chapters on warehandling, food service, food preparation, and so on. Instead of the usual vague generalities, specific systems and many new ideas will be set forth. Unless our industry takes action now we will still be averaging only $12,300 per employee per year in sales ten years from now.

A recent article explained in great detail one method used to ascertain the correct location of equipment for the various functions in a food service operation: time, motion, steps, number of trips. Yet the kitchen described differed little from restaurant kitchens of fifty years ago.

Why do we go on having our pots washed by hand? Why do we go on having the staff make endless trips to walk-in coolers and storerooms instead of bringing large quantities of supplies to work spaces in one trip? Why do we go on having the pot sinks located away from the cooks' table so each cook can take soiled pans to the sink one at a time? It's time we adopted some of the new systems and methods that have come on the market in recent years.

The increased efficiency and productivity we need so badly will not come from some one change such as the introduction of frozen foods or the installation of an automatic broiler; they will come from the combination of hundreds of relatively small improvements that together make up a more efficient system and plan. The old system was to plan everything else first and wait until the last minute to lay out a kitchen and related facilities in whatever space was left over. Add to this the reluctance of operators to try anything new or different, and it is easy to see why we have so many places giving bad service, serving poor food, and probably going broke. Some years ago an operator expressed the idea that if he could wait it out until we have another depression or another war it would be unnecessary for him to update. With this kind of thinking it is little wonder that our progress has been slow.

So much for the unpleasantries. Now let's get down to specifics that

[1]"The Eighth Decade: There's a Chair Reserved for You at the Bargaining Table," *Institutions/Volume Feeding*, January 1970, p. 112.

will help in the running of your operation. Every effort has been made to include inexpensive improvements that the majority of operators can afford. Total automation has been tried in our industry and has not worked well because of the high cost. However, many separate components are now being marketed to help with the problems of service.

STEP 1. DECIDING ON THE TYPE OF OPERATION

To develop a good food service plan, there are a number of steps to take. Although what follows may seem to require an excess of preliminary effort, this procedure will save time and money and reduce errors to a minimum.

Set down in as complete detail as possible the type of operation desired and what is to be accomplished, considering the type of food to be served, the hours and days you plan to be open, menus, projected sales, type of service, features, cooking methods, serving utensils, what food will be prepared on the premises, and what kinds and quantities of supplies you expect to purchase regularly.

Type of Food

Many operations today feature special types of food—American, country, seafood, Chinese, western, Polynesian, open hearth, barbecue—and build the entire operation around this theme. It is even possible to combine several themes. In any case, before making any specific plans or having sketches drawn, decide on the food you wish to serve. If a theme is to be developed, let all planners know in advance. For example, if you are going to feature Polynesian or Chinese foods, a special range and other special equipment will be needed.

Hours and Days of Operation

Make every effort to decide on hours of service in advance. Even though you may change the hours after being in business for a while, it will help at all the planning stages to know how long you expect to be open each day and how many days of the week. If you are going to serve breakfast, lunch, and dinner each day, this will call for one kind of layout and equipment; just serving lunch and dinner will call for another; and if you are going to serve dinner only, this will again change the requirements.

Menus

When the location has been selected, the potential audience measured, and the types of meals decided on, it is time to write the actual menus, listing most of the items that will be served at the various meals. (Chapter 15 on merchandising offers guidelines for preparing your menus.) This also means pricing and establishing a price level. Granted that you cannot set each price to the penny at this point of the planning, but you can at least decide on a range of prices to help with the planning. If your dinner price range is between $2 and $3, for example, the planning will be entirely different from that of a restaurant whose prices are in the $7 to $10 range.

Projected Sales

Once you have decided on the type of operation and the price range, you will have to set a projected sales figure. In addition to a yearly sales goal—let's say $300,000—you will also have to project a pattern or flow of business during the week and during the day. A $6,000 average weekly sale doesn't necessarily come in at a steady rate of approximately $900 a day. You could have a couple of slow $200 days and a couple of busy $2,000 days. The planners will need all the information possible on this, because a good design and layout should allow you to adapt for both the slow and the busy periods. For example, if you think there will be days with $2,000 in sales, your average check is forecast to be $2, and you plan to serve dinner only, you must be able to feed approximately 1,000 people in the course of an evening. Knowing this, the planners can determine vital details such as parking space, seating space, and kitchen equipment.

Type of Service

Service can vary greatly, even from meal to meal in the same establishment: table, counter, table and counter, self-service, buffet, buffet at certain times, tray, arm, cart, take-out, and so on. It is precisely because the variety of choices is so great that the planners must have some advance knowledge of your intentions.

Many restaurant operators have tried to combine all kinds of service in one facility but this is not advisable. Careful study and research will indicate the best type for you, and it will pay to design for a particular type rather than try the jack-of-all-trades route. The multiservices operation can be designed but it will be expensive and difficult to operate. Not only is there a problem of increased investment, but the operating costs, particularly in labor, will be heavy.

Features

Sometimes features are dismissed as a gimmick, but they are being used more and more today in food service operations. Open hearth cooking, display service kitchen, oyster bar, lobster tanks, pastry carts, cooking at the table, wine barrels, fresh-baked bread, espresso coffee, and hundreds of other good promotional schemes can be used to attract customers. But be sure the planners know in advance so proper facilities can be included at the start and you can avoid expensive last-minute changes to plans and buildings.

To cite one example, self-service salad bars are popular today, but space and equipment must be well located in the dining area for this—or if you decide to serve from a cart, there must be room for the carts to move around in and convenient facilities for replenishing them. A last-minute decision might entail expensive utility changes and even revision of the seating layout. Planning for the features in the beginning so that adequate facilities can be included may mean the difference between success and failure of your features.

Cooking Methods

The printed menu does not always explain cooking methods: ready to order, 20 minute preparation time, salads ready to pick up or tossed at the table.

Go through the menu carefully after it has been drawn up and let the planners know what cooking methods you expect to use. Do you intend to cook ahead and hold food in thermotainers for fast service, or is it your wish to cook to order? Will the lobster tails be oven-broiled or broiled under an open flame?

If you wish to serve freshly squeezed orange juice, you need counter space and equipment as well as refrigeration space where the fresh oranges can be kept chilled, to say nothing of a trash can for the peels. Only by having all this planned in advance can you carry out your idea and serve the juice quickly and efficiently.

Serving Utensils

In most restaurants the china, flatware, glasses, and so on are more or less standard, but you may wish to have such variations as sizzling platters to make the service of food attractive and just a little bit different. List these items for your planners so that proper provision can be made. For example, there's no point in having sizzling platters unless you can heat them quickly and have a place to clean them well. These are details, but it is the sum of many such small details that can make your operation a success.

Food Preparation on the Premises

You will have to decide in advance what items on the menu will be prepared on the premises and what items will be convenience foods, frozen foods, or pre-packaged foods (prime ribs of beef can be purchased oven-ready or you can cut off the short ribs and trim). This information is essential to the design of an efficient food service operation.

If you don't supply this information in detail, the equipment layout man has one of two choices. He can assume that almost everything will be prepared on the premises and provide one or more of every piece of equipment that could be needed—at enormous cost to you. Or he can assume that you will use mostly convenience and frozen foods and fail to include items that you do need. For instance, you may want to bread all your own seafood instead of buying it breaded. This is fine, but the planner will have to provide space and equipment for breading. Similarly, if you intend to cut your own meat or do your own baking, the designer will have to allow for this in the plans.

Purchasing

Give some thought to your purchasing requirements and keep the layout people advised. For example, if you intend to use a lot of frozen food, there will have to be ample freezer space. If you will not be able to get frequent deliveries and intend to buy in large quantities, there must be adequate storage space.

In sum, plan your menus, merchandising, food handling, service, and so on as far ahead as possible and in detail so that you will be ready when you reach the drawing stage. An experienced food service consultant can be of great help in these decisions. And don't bite off more than you can chew. Curb that tendency to do everything at one time in one place. Instead, keep everything simple. Your future success will be based on how *well* you do something, not on how many things you try to do.

STEP 2. SEEKING OUTSIDE HELP

When you have gathered all the information, you are ready to turn it over to an experienced food service consultant or designer. Together you can then discuss what you want and what your ideas are, so that he will have a good basis on which to start work.

STEP 3. ALLOCATING THE SPACE

The designer's first step will be to make a preliminary space allocation plan (see Figure III-1). It does not take an experienced designer long to make a scaled drawing showing space allocation if he has the basic

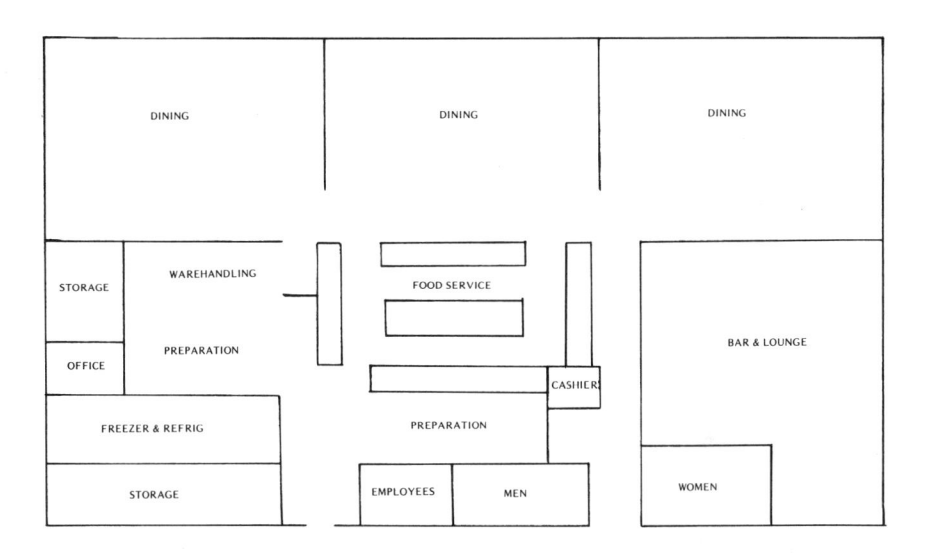

Figure III-1. *Preliminary space allocation plan*

38 RESTAURANT PLANNING

information, and this simple drawing can help to determine a number of facts that you need before you go any further.

1. The space allocation plan will give you the total square feet of building needed. From this you can estimate building cost and quickly ascertain how much property is needed or whether the site you have or are considering will fit.

2. It will give the exact number of seats (the plan in Figure III-1 specifies 176 seats in the dining area, 20 seats at the bar, and 28 seats in the lounge). With your menu and seating information, you can produce a reasonable figure on gross sales.

3. The rough plan will provide a basis for discussion of all main functions: size, location, control, traffic and product flow, food preparation and service areas.

4. By computing various areas it is possible to tell whether the plan is efficient or wasteful. The plan in Figure III-1 allows for over 200 seats in a building 96' × 56' or a little over 5,000 square feet. A quick glance at the sketch will show that most of the area is for sales.

5. If the space allocation plan meets all the requirements, the consultant or designer can proceed with the next step of establishing the work and product flow, detailing the equipment needed, and pinning down the exact area requirements.

This step-by-step procedure for planning works well and saves time and money in the end because changes and improvements can be made before the expensive detailed equipment plans and architectural plans are drawn. What has happened often when detailed, finished plans have been drawn without preliminary plans and preliminary sketches is this: Before construction began, serious errors were found in the plans. But the cost of an entire new set of detailed, finished drawings was so very high that the place had to be built according to the old plans, errors and all.

Ten chapters that follow include specific suggestions to help with planning:

Chapter 4. Food Service Equipment
Chapter 5. Food Preparation Equipment
Chapter 6. Warehandling
Chapter 7. Miscellaneous Equipment
Chapter 8. Purchasing and Storage

Chapter 9. Food Preparation
Chapter 10. Food Service
Chapter 12. Moving Toward Automation
Chapter 13. Equipment for the Future
Chapter 14. Remodeling and Expansion

Refer to each of these chapters when the time comes to plan or design these particular areas; even Chapter 18 on control and profit will present ideas that should be considered in the early planning and design stages.

Planning and design will normally fall into one of four areas: (1) Totally new operation with no set limits; (2) new operation in a fixed space; (3) remodeling an existing operation; or (4) updating or changing a chain type of operation. In each of these types, no matter what kind of food service is being considered, the same general planning procedure should be followed so that there will be fewer mistakes. If we rush to open a food service establishment, but wait until the last minute to design kitchens and service areas, we will skip over things we know we should do, or do things we know are wrong, because there is no longer time, money, or space to do the job right. Don't say you will worry about the details later. Once the facility is open, needed changes are not made and the cost of the error continues over the years.

Above all, don't act in haste. As the opening draws near, for example, if you rush to get the money coming in regardless of cost, you may spend more money on last-minute overtime than you take in during the first month. Places that open before they are ready may do business for the first few days, but then the sales will drop because of poor food and service. In some instances of premature openings, the operator has been able to maintain service only by using an excessive number of employees and paying excessive overtime, which means a loss even with good sales. An extra two weeks or more of planning, building time, and proper training would enable you to keep those opening day sales and even increase them because you are *ready* to do business.

These are the points to remember: Take time to plan correctly; wait until the facility is complete; allow time for training new employees; allow time for experienced employees to accustom themselves to the new routines; then open, preferably without great fanfare on opening day, and you will complete the first month with more sales and perhaps even a profit!

STEP 4. PLANNING THE PUBLIC AREAS

The first consideration in any plan should be for the public areas such as dining space, aisles, waiting space, and rest rooms. Remember that the customer is the one who pays the bills, so his comfort should come first. The list of steps that follows will help you plan your public areas well.

1. Assign the best and most convenient area to the seating. The criteria for "best" will vary with the restaurant: closest to the parking, with the best view, with the least noise, or whatever.

2. To make sure you have enough square feet of space to do the job, determine the number of seats necessary to produce the sales you will need to carry your investment and make money. This can be done with some accuracy. For example, assuming that your dining area has only enough room for 100 booth seats, you will seat 55 on an average even at busy periods. Your menu will produce a certain check average; assume that to be $2. At dinner a good turnover of the dining area is 3. If we multiply 55 × $2 × 3 (seating average times check average times turnover) we find there is a possibility of taking in $330 for dinner on a busy night. This same calculation can be applied to the other meals, giving you an idea of total sales possible.

3. People usually eat at meal times, so the average food service facility is busy only about 20 percent of the total time open. Despite all the promotions tried over the years, it is still difficult to get anyone to eat dinner at 3 P.M.

4. Determine in advance the number of square feet per seat, using the following criteria: *Crowded seating,* 10 square feet per seat, is used for schools and industrial dining facilities. *Average seating,* 12 square feet per seat, is normal for an average food service facility. *Deluxe seating,* 15 square feet per seat, is for the more posh places with higher check averages.

5. Detailed surveys have been made on the average number of people eating together in restaurants and the efficiency of various seating arrangements. Here are some of the findings.

In an average location about 50 percent of the customers will come in pairs, with another 30 percent consisting of singles and parties of three. The remaining 20 percent will be made up of larger parties.

Booths are generally most popular, particularly for two people sitting in a booth designed for four. This provides them with ample room, a sense of privacy, and little chance of being bumped by servers or other customers passing by.

Four-seater booths and tables are the least efficient. If you have only four-seaters, your seating will be about 55 percent efficient, which means that only about 55 seats out of 100 will be occupied at any one time even when you are busiest.

Deuce tables, arranged so they can be moved apart to accommodate two diners or together to accommodate larger parties, are the most efficient, giving almost 90 percent efficiency. In other words, 100 seats all in deuces would allow you to seat as many as 90 people during the busy time.

Booths designed to seat four are popular for family business. The children can be seated on the inside near the wall, thus allowing the parents to keep the children from running all over the dining room.

Provision must be made for larger parties. This is best done by installing wall banquettes (benches) and arranging deuce tables in front of them so they can be grouped or separated. Or the deuce tables can be arranged in the center of the space so that they can be grouped or separated. A combination of booths, deuces, four-seaters, and perhaps round tables seating six and eight, attractively arranged, will produce good results.

If land or building space permits, thought should be given to future expansion in the number of seats. This can even be indicated on the preliminary space allocation sketch.

6. Dining areas should be attractive and comfortable. The *decor* should be pleasing and should appeal to most customers. Design so the noise level will be low. Use acoustical materials, carpeting, and drapes to produce a quiet room. Pay particular attention to the *lighting*. Avoid glare or lights that shine directly on diners. Check the exposure so glare from the sun can be eliminated. Be sure that outside doors and air conditioning grills are designed and placed in such a way as to prevent *drafts,* which are very annoying to guests.

Provide ample *aisles* to ensure a good flow of traffic and cut the bumping and moving of guests to a minimum. Provide space where *hats* and *coats* can be put away as needed. Where there is family business, have *baby seats* and *high chairs* stored in a place where they can be easily and quickly brought to the tables.

7. Make some provision for a rush-hour *waiting line* just off the entrance where it will not interfere with the normal serving traffic or with customers who are paying their checks and leaving the restaurant. The maître d' or hostess must be able to control this area easily, taking names for each party and notifying them when a table is ready. If the space is well designed, customers will not mind a normal wait for tables. Situate the waiting line so that customers cannot wander

around the dining area looking for seats or, what is worse, sit down at a table piled with dirty dishes.

8. Rest rooms must be adequate. Each locality has codes specifying the proper size of rest rooms, but it is always wise to plan rooms that have ample space and are clean, attractive, and properly ventilated. Your architect or local building department can tell you about the applicable codes.

STEP 5. CHOOSING THE EQUIPMENT

Once the space plan has been approved for feasibility from both a practical and a financial standpoint, it is time to detail the equipment in other areas. Kitchens with identical space, facilities, equipment, and productive capacity can cost $50,000 or $100,000. To avoid excessive cost, ask your consultant or designer to do the following.

Use all the *standard equipment* possible and avoid custom designing. Today it is possible to lay out any type of operation with 90 percent or more of standard equipment. This is less expensive than custom-designed equipment and in most cases is superior because it has been field-tested and is better constructed. Unless a custom-designed refrigerator is created by someone well qualified in this field and is fabricated by an excellent, experienced shop, it will not be as good as a standard unit. In addition, standard units save the cost of design time and the bidders can save time and give you a better and more accurate price when they do not have to estimate the cost of building. Furthermore, the specifications for custom-designed equipment are usually more rigid and more elaborate than necessary.

The equipment layout should allow space for standard equipment. For example, standard work tables come in certain specified lengths. If your planner calls for a table 7'3" by 33½", only a custom-built table will fit. Instead of getting a standard, well-built work table 6' by 30" for about $200, you could end up paying $800 for a table that will do the same job.

Use *self-contained equipment* wherever possible, to cut down on installation cost. Avoid having to run long refrigeration lines from remote compressors or to install a drain in a refrigerator that does not have its own condensate evaporator. If the designer has to draw up a set of mechanicals showing the details of the electrical work, plumbing, and refrigeration, for example, the mechanicals themselves may cost more than the equipment.

Avoid the *oversizing and overequipping* that are common in food service operations. If you have first decided on the menus and what and how you are going to serve, this information will enable the planner to avoid specifying too much equipment that is bigger than you need.

Everything should be geared to your projected volume. If you have a service kitchen setup for one person, a six-foot grill is not needed because one person will not be able to use the entire surface and will work at one end. If you serve 100 customers an hour, a dish machine built to wash 5,000 pieces an hour is not needed.

The other thing to avoid in equipment planning is filling space. Should you be lucky enough to have a little more space than is needed at the start, leave it empty until later. You will save money and have less to clean and maintain.

Give careful consideration to the *choice of material*. For many years everything had to be stainless steel or white because these symbolized cleanliness. Yet the fact is that white and stainless steel surfaces show dirt most and are the most difficult to clean. Because they streak, they appear to be soiled even when they have just been cleaned. Now, however, other materials and colors are providing the same sanitation and a better appearance.

Modern plastics and fiberglass are being incorporated into food service equipment with good results. In some cases these materials take wear and abuse better than metals. In a test made in January 1972 a fiberglass material outperformed the leading metals in an impact test as well as providing color and easier cleaning. Plastic laminates on wood or pressboard also lend color, warmth, and texture and are less expensive and easier to modify or change. If there have been errors or omissions in design or errors in the dimensions of fabricated pieces, or if wall and floor dimensions are changed, a carpenter can make corrections on the spot with little difficulty, or changes can easily be made as needs change.

Consider all the so-called *package units* such as complete warewashing units that include machine, tables, and shelves. Many of these have been designed with great attention to detail and with an awareness of what is needed to do a good job. In addition, these have been installed in many places where they have been tested for efficiency and effectiveness.

Use *mobile or portable units* wherever you can for a variety of reasons. They can be cleaned easily because they can be moved. The units can be taken from the line and repaired in another area without disrupting the working areas. Separate items can be replaced without any cutting or rewelding. And the equipment can be rearranged from meal to meal, if need be, to improve the efficiency of the operation. Other than units with water and drain lines, practically all equipment can be made mobile with casters. One new line of reach-in refrigerators and freezers comes equipped with casters, which have been difficult to obtain in the past. Now that connected drains are no longer needed on refrigerators, they should be mobile to simplify the task of cleaning under and around them.

Select brands and manufacturers that can provide *repair service* in your area. Even new equipment may not work without repair or adjustment. Your equipment designer should make sure there are repair facilities for the units selected in your general vicinity.

When the equipment has been detailed and the layout is completely satisfactory, it is time to call in the architect. The architect should be experienced in food service or have a department to do this specialized planning. Otherwise it is best to have the food service facilities designed by someone who is expert at this. Once the architect has the food service plan, he is ready to go ahead with designing the structure and working out all the other details needed for a complete plan. Most architects use outside firms to do the engineering work such as ventilation, and they will not object to having someone work out the details of the food service facilities because it is so highly specialized a field.

As a rule the sequence of steps just mentioned will work better than having the architect design the building first and assign an area for the food service facilities. The food service designer will then be forced to work with this space even though it is not the right size or shape because making changes in all the architectural drawings would be too costly.

It will take an architect only a short time to make certain that the facilities plan presented to him can be worked into a building plan, considering such factors as the location of supports and columns, and then the food service consultant can proceed with the balance of his task. For anything more than a very small remodeling job you will want to get bids on the equipment, which means the consultant will have to furnish you with enough copies of the following:

1. Equipment layout plans to scale.
2. Complete list of all equipment, models, and so on.
3. Brochure of specification sheets on all standard pieces of equipment that are to be purchased.

4. Detail drawings of all custom pieces, with specifications.
5. Sets of written general specifications which give all the terms in detail for delivery, setup, and warranties on the equipment.

With this information, you will be able to get good comparative bids on your job from two or more equipment companies. And in turn, the information on the equipment will also help the architect when the time comes to get bids on the building. Part of this bid will be the cost of the mechanicals again (plumbing, electrical work, refrigeration, ventilation, and so on), and if the equipment layout is complete and clear, the contractors will be able to make more accurate bids.

There is a mistaken idea in our industry that using professionals and experienced planners will increase the cost. Yet the contrary is true. The professional know-how can save you money in both investment costs and operating costs. For example, it is the inexperienced operator who chooses the wrong colors and materials and creates an unattractive dining room, whereas a good decorator with the same amount of money—or even less—could create a much more pleasant effect in the same room. The professional food service planner will specify only the size and amount of equipment you need; it is the inexperienced planner who overspecifies because he does not know what is needed to make the operation work. And a good architect will be realistic in his estimates and will do everything possible to stay within your budget.

Part II

EQUIPMENT PLANNING

Chapter 4

FOOD SERVICE EQUIPMENT: FOR NOW AND FOR THE FUTURE

Years ago all food service operations prepared and cooked all food from scratch, and most of the equipment, talent, and labor was concentrated in this back-of-the-house operation. Most entrees were cooked to order. Help was plentiful, inexpensive, and easily trained because the employees specialized: range man, fry cook, broiler man, sauce cook, roast cook, vegetable cook.

Over the years there have been changes. As the cost of equipment and space rose, and as employees became less plentiful and expected to be paid more, adjustments were made. Convenience foods and frozen foods did away with the need for cumbersome equipment—peelers, grinders, meat saws, huge mixers, dough sheeters, roll dividers. The specialist who operated at one station was replaced by the more versatile generalist who could do a number of jobs more or less simultaneously.

As fewer employees were expected to do more in less time, and as the nature of their tasks changed with the advent of convenience foods, not only the equipment but the physical layout of kitchens had to change. At the back of the house was the main kitchen, where food was cut, portioned, cooked. Closer to the dining rooms was the front kitchen or service area, where the all-but-finished food could be brought in quantities, ready for the last-minute heating or frying or broiling or mixing that had to be done immediately before serving.

In the back kitchen the chef ruled the roost, and here the most skilled employees were to be found. After all, on them depended the reputation and the success of the house. The front kitchen was where the less skilled employees were assigned because the last-minute preparation was thought to require little more than a measure of speed and dexterity.

So the chef and his helpers went on preparing food with all the skill at their command. But nobody told the novice in the service area how long to fry the chilled breaded shrimp and the frozen french fries, or at what temperature. And the fact that fried shrimp was no longer one of the more popular items on the menu was attributed to changing tastes or rising prices, not to improper staffing of the service kitchen. Surely, with so good a chef, there couldn't be anything wrong with the food. . . .

STAFFING THE SERVICE KITCHEN: THE DREAM AND THE REALITY

Obviously, what our mythical service area needed was a tall (so he could reach everything), thin (so he could move fast and not take up much room), athletic (so he could work all day without tiring), young (so he wouldn't collapse of exhaustion or heat prostration) short-order cook with years of experience (so he would know how to do everything required of him) and a private income (so he wouldn't keep asking for a raise) and with no inclination to quit. . . .

That's the dream. But what is the reality? Today's short-order cook not only has a more difficult job to learn but has a lot more to do than just frying. Often, he has so much to do and at so great a speed that it is all but impossible for him to do his job well. He is discouraged by the pressure, and he is further discouraged when his boss goes off with other restaurant owners to plead for an exemption from the minimum wage law. So he watches the want ads every Sunday, and first chance he gets, he takes a job in industry where he can work shorter hours, make more money, and have weekends and holidays to himself.

Now a replacement has to be found, which takes more and more time because our short-order cook is not the only one discouraged by salaries and working conditions in our industry. So finding a replacement will probably mean hiring someone with little or no skill, investing a lot of time and effort in training him, and wondering how long it will take him to get discouraged and quit in turn.

But all is not lost. Employees with little skill can be trained relatively quickly to do a good job if they have a well-designed service area to work in and if they are provided with the proper equipment. It must be remembered, however, that a new layout filled with new equipment will accomplish nothing if employees are trained to do the same old job in the same old way.

WHO NEEDS A SERVICE KITCHEN?

As new refinements are developed in methods of preparing food, our need for a food preparation area—a back kitchen—is likely to diminish. But even if we should choose to use only ready foods and dispense with the traditional back kitchen, we must have a food service area and the equipment to go with it. Precisely which pieces of equipment are appropriate depends on the menu. For example, a salamander would be appropriate if lobster is a specialty of the house, but it would clutter up the kitchen in a corner coffee shop.

Small restaurants with low sales volume can combine food preparation and food service to save on equipment and employees. But restaurants with medium to high sales volume would be better advised to separate food preparation and food service for two important reasons.

First, two relatively small, well laid out kitchens can be operated more efficiently with less walking and less wasted motion than a single vast, sprawling kitchen.

Second, employee training is simpler and more effective when there is a separation and each job is less complicated. Also, the employee is likely to stay longer if the job is less demanding.

For most restaurants, the steadily increasing use of frozen, convenience, and ready foods will make the preparation area less important and smaller (as it should), and the service area will be more important and receive more of the attention it has lacked for many years. The more we go in this direction, the better our food, productivity, and service will be.

With exhibition kitchens and cookery becoming increasingly popular, it is essential that we know what equipment to use and, what is more, how to use it. Many of these show kitchens are well designed and attractive, using new easy-to-clean materials, bright colors, and good lighting. Such kitchens are most efficient when used to prepare limited menus.

Operators who insist on serving hundreds of items at one time will find their problems growing instead of diminishing. This is because small, compact kitchens that can be operated by fewer employees are difficult to design when a great many items must be accommodated. Just providing convenient storage at the point of use is impossible when there are too many items, with the result that someone must constantly run back to storage areas for supplies. Further, the more items there are, the harder it is to train employees to deal with all of them. And, with an extended menu, not only the cooks but the servers have problems in taking orders and getting all the items up at the same time.

THE EXCEPTION: CAFETERIA FOOD PREPARATION AND SERVICE

Only in cafeterias should the preparation and serving of food be combined rather than separated wherever possible. In fact, most cafeterias have separated these functions so much that the quality of the food has suffered. It is ironic that the one part of our business where they should have been combined has separated them more than any other. We all know how difficult it is to hold food that has been cooked and maintain both quality and temperature. If food is held at the proper temperature for serving hot, it will go on cooking and be ruined; if it is held at a temperature low enough not to cook, it will be cold at the table. Cafeterias could serve much better food if the cooking equipment—fryers, grills, broilers, vegetable cookers —were directly behind the service hot tables and food were prepared fresh in small quantities rather than being held for long periods.

A specific method of supplying the line must also be worked out. For example, in most cafeterias the fryers are placed in the back kitchen, usually far back against the wall, to save a few hundred dollars for duct work. This means that all fried foods must be prepared ahead in large quantities. But the best fried food results from preparing small batches frequently, not dumping 15 pounds of cold food into a fryer at once and hoping that the temperature will come back to normal before the food is cooked.

Now, when this huge load of fried food is brought out to the line, the runner has one of two choices. He can dump it on top of the few orders left in the serving pan, which will not help the few orders left on the bottom. Or he can remove the existing pan, put in the new one and dump the old orders on top. If customers are watching, they will of course insist on having the fresh food, so you may lose a few orders.

This explains one of the reasons why cafeterias and self-service restaurants have not been as successful as they should be and why they have not attracted a bigger share of the restaurant business. The customer has learned that the self-service operation has few of the popular cooked-to-order items and too many entrees of the stew type that are excessively soupy and lukewarm.

PLANNING THE SERVICE AREA

Planning the food service area and selecting the equipment are not difficult for someone with experience and a familiarity with all the new equipment that is now available. There are a number of basic considerations in planning this area.

1. The menu, the meals to be served, the way they are to be served, and the projected sales must be known before a top efficient kitchen can be planned and designed.

2. Wherever possible, the equipment in this area should be standard and mobile, as explained in Chapter 3.

3. Installing self-cleaning and easily cleaned equipment would significantly reduce what has long been one of the more disagreeable tasks in our business. If the equipment is difficult to clean, your cooks must tackle the job at the end of their shift when they are already tired, or you must hire a special crew to come in at night or during off-hours to do this. Using a cleanup crew has never worked well unless there is adequate supervision, and this makes it expensive. Self-cleaning and easily cleaned equipment is not used more because many operators balk at the added cost. What they overlook when they reason this way is the number of hours their employees will devote to cleaning the old-style equipment over the years, especially with hourly rates what they are now and what they will be in the future.

4. The equipment selected must have the capacity to do the job. If your service kitchen cannot produce the food fast and in the quantities needed, you will be forced to cook food ahead and put it in holding units. This means inferior food. It is always best to cook to order.

5. Consider several identical small units rather than one large unit.

54 RESTAURANT PLANNING

With a setup of more than one unit, you can turn equipment on and off to suit your needs during peak and slack hours. And remember that two smaller fryers will do a much better job than one large fryer, as is explained later.

Custom-designed vs. Standard Equipment

6. The food service area must be compact as well as have adequate capacity. The time you and your designer or consultant give to the design of this area will have much to do with your success and profits. Know that you have planned for everything. For example, the detailed drawing in Figure IV-1 illustrates how carefully the equipment must be planned so that there is a place for everything. This investment of time in the initial planning will save money in several ways. With a preliminary drawing that shows the equipment in detail, you can

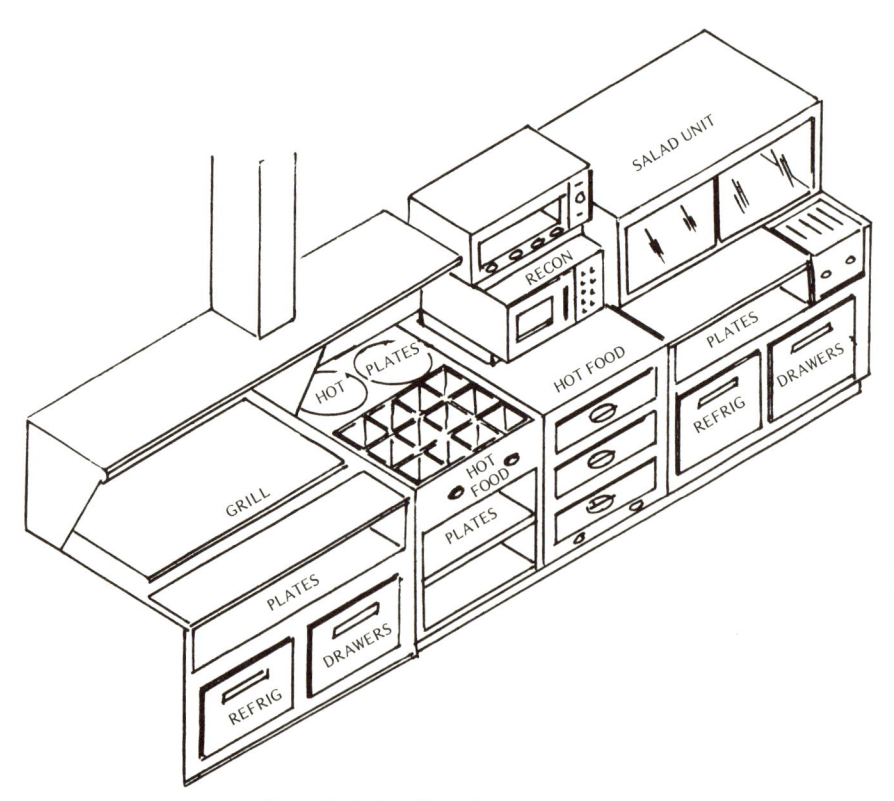

Figure IV-1. *Detail, food service equipment*

make sure nothing has been forgotten and there is a place for each item. Especially if you choose the kind of expensive custom-designed equipment shown in Figure IV-1, detailed preliminary drawings should be made to avoid errors and to assist both the architect's engineer and the fabricator-supplier in their planning.

The same arrangement of equipment shown in the figure can be made with standard pieces of equipment at lower cost. And there is a further reason to stay away from equipment that is custom-designed and welded together: not only is the initial cost high but any change is likely to be excessively costly. Yet we all know that new and better service equipment is coming, and changes will be advisable.

In contrast to Figure IV-1, the sketch in Figure IV-2 clearly shows the right approach. All the equipment is standard; it can be selected from catalogues and can be priced readily. Each piece is on casters and is mobile. This can be done today whether the equipment runs on gas or electricity. And should a more effective unit appear on the market, a substitution can be made in a matter of minutes without costly cutting and rewelding.

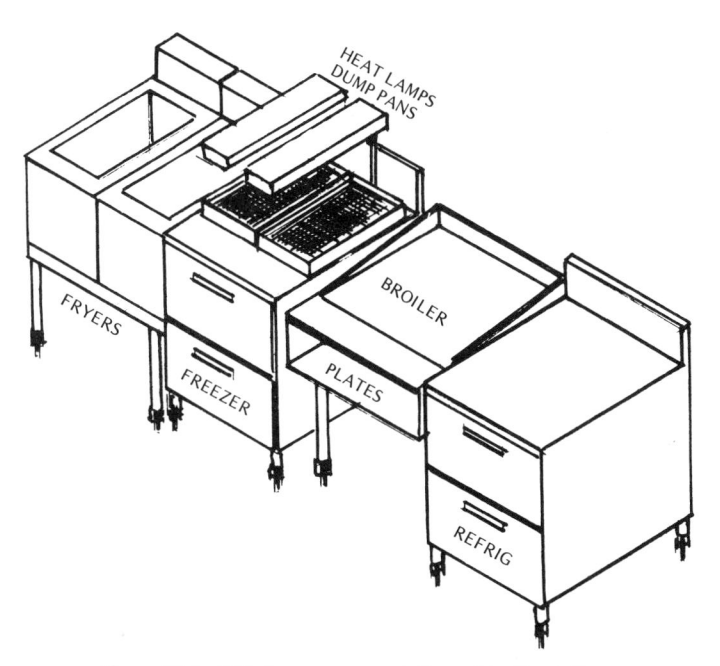

Figure IV-2. *Effective arrangement, fry and broiler station*

Note, too, how the many details for a good food service station have been provided for even with standard units. There are freezer drawers and work-top space next to the fryers. The drawers have been selected because it is difficult to open the door of a work-top freezer fully, bend down, and reach in each time something is needed.

The freezer work-top is an ideal place for one or two fry dump pans with heat lamps and drain screens. This makes it possible to fry in small quantities, dump into these pans, salt the food (never salt over the fryers), and serve seasoned, hot, drained fried food from the pans rather than dumping directly from fryers onto plates, which so many places do.

The broiler is also on casters, as it should be, because this unit must be pulled out and cleaned frequently. More fires are started by broilers and the grease they deposit than by any other piece of equipment. Also note that this broiler has a work board in front for setting down a plate or seasoning the meat, and it has a shelf below where plates can be kept handy. And the heat from the broiler will heat these plates and keep them hot.

Under the broiler is open space for a small refuse container. Most meats are protected by pieces of patty paper, and some provision must be made for disposing of these. And a work-top refrigerator with drawers is placed next to the broiler for easy and convenient storage of items to be broiled.

Many kitchens are designed with the cooking units one next to the other—range, then fryers, then broilers, then grills, with no spaces in between for dumping the food or assembling and arranging plates. In such a kitchen the cook has to walk across aisles carrying dripping cooked foods. This is not only unsanitary but dangerous.

The work-top freezer and refrigerator are both self-contained, which will save the cost of running refrigerated lines under the floor and locating the compressors out back somewhere.

Thus the two simple sketches in Figures IV-1 and IV-2 show the proper way to design a food service area. Some designers or consultants always specify beautiful custom-designed equipment that is symmetrical and is more likely to win an award for design than a group of standard pieces that may not be exactly the same height and depth. Yet the customer has little interest in the esthetics of the back of the house, and it would be more advisable to create an award-winning dining room where the customer *does* notice what you have created. He is more concerned with the service, prices, and quality of the food than with the look of the place where it was prepared. If you have created a beautiful, expensive kitchen you can bring guests back for tours. But you would make more points by doing a better job out front. And remember that you will probably still be using this custom kitchen long after it is out of date because you will already have invested so much money and because the changes cost so much more than they would with standard mobile equipment.

Gas vs. Electricity

Before going on to a specific list of recommendations for food service equipment, the question of gas versus electricity must be considered. This question has been argued back and forth for many years and will of course be argued for years to come.

The electric company will tell you that electricity is better and the gas company will tell you that gas is better, but you should weigh several facts before deciding one way or the other. Chefs and cooks, like most people, base their preferences on what they have been accustomed to using. For that reason, most of the decisions bear little relation to facts. But there are reasons for favoring each or a combination, and they should be considered in the course of planning.

1. Space requirements may have a bearing on your choice. To get the compact high-performance kitchens required today it is often necessary to choose the unit that is smallest but has the greatest capacity. Three or four inches saved here and there can make the difference between including and omitting some necessary item. Since a gas burner can produce more BTUs per square inch than an electric burner can, it may be the better choice where space is at a premium.

2. The availability of only one kind of power will dictate the choice in some cases; the cost of running lines from excessive distances will be the deciding factor in others.

3. If an all-electric kitchen is chosen, be sure to have extra capacity in panel boards so additional equipment can be added in the future.

4. Monthly operating costs should be compared for like pieces using gas and electricity. In some areas one or the other is less expensive, and this should have some bearing on your choice. Check with your utility company about unit costs of power, and ask your architect which is more economical in your area.

5. In an area plagued by severe storms, an all-electric kitchen will at times be cut out of service, and at those times you will be out of business.

6. Given normal conditions and use, gas equipment will require less maintenance and repair, so the availability of service and repair must be a factor in your choice.

7. In the area of the country supplied by the Tennessee Valley Authority electric power is very inexpensive; if you are in this area, you should certainly consider using electrical equipment. In Oklahoma the low price of gas should affect your equipment choice.

Before you decide either way, consult with your architect, his engineer, your food service designer, and the power companies. In addition, ask a few restaurant operators in the area what they pay monthly for gas or electricity. They can tell you in a hurry if one or the other is high.

What you cook as well as the quantities and methods will have some bearing on whether to use gas or electrical appliances. For example, if you operate a steak house, gas broilers would be advisable, according to the hundreds of operators the author has talked to. Large ovens are normally gas-powered and this opinion will come from the oven manufacturers. Here again, you can consult with equipment manufacturers because most of them make both gas and electric lines and will give you an unbiased opinion. Tell them your requirements and methods; they can advise from experience which would be best.

Most food service facilities use both gas and electricity. Naturally, one cannot use gas with no electricity, but it is possible to use electricity with no gas. Keep an open mind and make your selection piece by piece to get the results you want. And keep in mind the costs not only of the original equipment but of the charges you must pay each month in your area.

CHOOSING THE EQUIPMENT

Now let's consider some specific suggestions and recommendations on food service equipment. What is recommended here has been gleaned from years of experience and should enable you to do a good job at a profit. The listing is not arbitrary; if in any case you believe something else will work better, by all means use it. Nor is the listing absolute or complete. A giant industrial facility, a modest pizza parlor, and a tiny Chinese restaurant obviously have different needs. Whatever your needs, however, it would be well to keep in mind that a fast, experienced cook can turn out good food even with poor equipment, but it is best to plan a kitchen where you can produce good food with less experienced employees, because this is what is available today.

Another consideration that must be kept in the forefront is that your selection of equipment today should reflect the trends of the future. The industry has to find ways to achieve lower prices, more volume, and greater productivity. Much of this can be accomplished with better food, faster service, and of course, higher sales per manhour. And the place to accomplish it is not in the back preparation kitchen but in the front service kitchen.

Now, let's assume that the features of preliminary planning such as menu, hours of operation, actual or anticipated volume, how items are to be served, price range, and types of employees are established. Given all this, the next step is to consider the following specific suggestions in the selection of equipment for the service kitchen.

General Features

1. From now on, any food service equipment that is automatic, semi-automatic, timed, or with timers must be given first consideration if we are to serve good food and have high productivity. And make sure the choice is financially feasible (a $5,000 automatic broiler is a good idea only if it will fit your budget).

Fryers with automatic lifts will improve your output. Breaded shrimp cooked 15 seconds too long will be dry and unappetizing. And no cook doing a multitude of chores can time several items at once.

An automatic broiler or grill-broiler is most advisable. Again, not only can the cook not get to everything in a matter of seconds but meat should be cooked on both sides at one time.

Other pieces of equipment with automatic features should be used: pop-up toasters, automatic roll grills, automatic sandwich grills that release the product when finished, egg boilers, and the rest. These pieces will speed service and make your guests happier.

2. Emphasis has already been placed on buying self-cleaning or easily cleaned equipment. Fortunately, manufacturers have begun to make some equipment available: continuous self-cleaning ovens, self-cleaning broilers, grills that can be cleaned with a rag and water instead of scouring for hours with a grill brick. There will be more and more, and this equipment should be installed when building a new operation or remodeling.

The Major Items

3. *Reach-in refrigerators and freezers* are a must for the efficient food service kitchen, and they should be installed beside or under a cooking

unit such as a fryer or broiler, not across the aisle where they are out of reach. As explained earlier, even these units can be on casters for easy cleaning. Below the work surface (usually 36″ above the floor) refrigerators and freezers should be equipped with drawers rather than doors. It is very difficult to open a door fully in a congested aisle, bend down, and get something out. But it's easy to pull a drawer out part way and reach in for whatever you need.

Above the work surface level these units should have slides and trays instead of the usual wire racks. Trays, especially those made of plastic, are light and easy to wash, and they have edges that hold dishes in place. In contrast, wire shelves must be scrubbed with a brush or a pressure cleaner to get the dirt out of the many crevices. Also, it would be difficult to carry a wire shelf loaded with salads, whereas a tray similarly loaded could be carried with ease.

Slides will double your capacity (six or eight trays instead of three wire shelves), and if you use 13″ × 18″ plastic trays for food handling, the soiled trays are small enough to fit in the dish machine, which will save a lot of work.

4. *Sinks* may seem too mundane to be worthy of mention in this so-called age of automation, but so few service kitchens have sinks in a spot where they can be used for a great many chores and can eliminate much running back and forth and hand pot washing. The best way to keep a kitchen clean is to clean as you go. If there is no sink on the spot, the task soon gets out of hand.

5. *Reconstitution equipment* is almost a book in itself, but all service kitchens will one day have to use this equipment if they are not already doing so. The author spent two years researching the equipment and methods for properly reconstituting food, and the foremost thing this research made plain is that a great many units can be used for reconstituting.

    (a) *Fryers.* Even though these are seldom considered in this category, a large amount of frozen food is heated in this manner.
    (b) *Range top.* Orders of food can be heated in a small pan on top of the range.

At this point it might be helpful to mention the difference between the solid top and open burner range because this is not explained in the catalogues. The solid top is better for large volume operations, especially those doing a lot of preparation work. It produces more heat for cooking, but in the process it also heats up the surrounding areas. The open burner range is better for short-order work or for a kitchen where heat is a factor, because burners can be turned on and off quickly. Not only does this cut down on heat but it also saves on fuel.

- (c) *Boiling water.* Many frozen foods come in pouches that are immersed in boiling water to heat the food.
- (d) *Steamers.* Small steamers can be placed in the service areas for heating frozen foods.
- (e) *Convection ovens.* These are proving very efficient, especially for heating large quantities of frozen foods. They do the job faster and at lower temperature than regular ovens.
- (f) *Microwave ovens.* These ovens use electromagnetic waves that heat the water in food—and in the process heat the food itself. Most people think of these ovens first with regard to reconstituting frozen foods because of their speed. But there are many other methods, as can be seen from this list.
- (g) *Combination microwave and convection oven.* This is a new unit that can be effectively used for this task.
- (h) *Quartz ovens.* These ovens are lined with the hard, glassy, silicone mineral that gives them their name. When the oven is turned on, the quartz generates heat waves that penetrate the food.

This listing of equipment for reconstituting emphasizes that there are many ways to do this job. Each method has good and bad features, and your choice must be based on the menu you are using, the volume of business anticipated, the types of food served, and so on. It is always better to have more than one way to heat foods so that, in case of equipment failure, there will be an alternate and so that you can adjust to changes in volume of business easily and with little waste.

There is still much research needed on the handling and reconstituting of frozen foods. These and other convenience foods are here to stay and will be used much more in the future. To avoid problems we need careful planning and selection of equipment. See Chapter 10 on food service for more details on the proper handling of these foods.

6. You may need a *range with an oven* in the service kitchen. Burners are better than a hot top, because the hot top gives off too much heat. If an oven is required, it should be the self-cleaning type. There is a new small unit on the market for egg cookery in pans, consisting

of burners on top and a space below for top heat. If eggs over are required, they are started in the pan on the top; then the pan is placed under the top heat for finishing, which eliminates all turning.

7. If you need a large oven, select a self-cleaning *convection oven*, which has a sealed chamber and a fan that circulates the air. These ovens are very efficient and good for large-volume production and food service such as reconstituting and oven broiling, not to mention baking fresh rolls and breads.

8. *Grills and griddles* deserve much more attention than they are currently receiving. There is a hard-surface grill that not only is easier to clean but cuts down on the transfer of food flavors so common with old porous-surface grills. Two smaller griddles are usually better than a single large one. In the first place, one can be shut down and cleaned when business is slow. In the second place, you will serve better food and have happier customers if you can vary the cooking temperature. Hotcakes cook at a much lower temperature than meats, for example. A grill should have fast heat recovery and maintain its temperature so that the product will be consistent.

For several years now, manufacturers have been emphasizing large grills, six to eight feet in length. Unless you have the world's fastest grill man, he would not be able to work a grill of this size efficiently. Most grills are oversized, but you can avoid this mistake if you plan carefully.

9. There are almost as many makes of *broilers* as refrigerators on the market. For the standard service kitchen I would again recommend two small units instead of a single large broiler so that one can be turned off during the slow periods (this is another piece of equipment that produces much heat). These too can now be self-cleaning as well as mobile.

Unless your volume is so heavy that you need a broiler man, an open broiler is most practical even though it does not cook on both sides at once. The large upright broilers have their place, but they are hard to operate. Each time another order is placed on the fire, the heavy grate must be pulled out and then pushed back in. Unless you have ample room in the work aisle, constantly manipulating the grate keeps the aisle blocked. What is more, the meat is not visible as it cooks, and unless someone is operating this type of broiler with care, a lot of meat may be overcooked.

10. *Hot food servers* (formerly called steam tables) are gradually losing favor, and this is a good thing for the quality of the food. Keep the number of hot food wells to a minimum and you will do much to

eliminate excessive cooking ahead. Each well should have its own control and thermostat so you can set correct temperatures for a variety of foods. In addition, the standard 12" × 20" or 12" × 18" well can accommodate a variety of pan shapes and sizes. Round wells do not give the flexibility needed from day to day. And it is just as easy to ladle gravy from a one-third size rectangular pan (no. 2000 or no. 1800) as it is from a round insert.

The Secondary Items

11. *Hot food drawer units* are being used more and more because they keep certain foods better (particularly baked items), and they utilize space under work counters to better advantage. In addition, the food stored in them is not subject to drying and is protected from the cold drafts of any nearby air conditioning grill. Specify the type with the removable standard no. 2000 or no. 1800 pans for flexibility and ease of cleaning.

12. *Fryers* are important in any food service operation. Even though fried food should be the best food served because it is cooked to order, it is in fact among the poorest served in restaurants. Much of this is the fault of the fryer as well as the cook. Fryers should be equipped with automatic lifts. They should be compact in size. They should have high heat input for fast recovery and fast heat-up time.

It is best to have more than one fryer so that some units can be shut down when not needed, and so that each unit can be cleaned often. Also, shutting down some fryers during the slow periods will reduce not only utility cost but the cost of oil or shortening used. The life of oil or shortening is greatly affected by the length of time it is heated. One hour of down time is worth three hours of operating time.

Where there is a deep fryer there must be at least one dump pan with a drain screen and overhead heat so that fried foods can be removed from the fryer, drained, seasoned, and kept ready for service.

Fry baskets should be small; it is better to have two small baskets than one large one. Repeated tests have proved that more food can be fried in a given time if small quantities are submerged each time because the fat has a chance to maintain its temperature. Furthermore, food fried at too low a temperature absorbs grease, and a plateful of food saturated with fat will not bring your customers back for more.

13. *Plate heaters* are a must for good food service, yet it is doubtful whether one restaurant in a hundred is adequately equipped to serve

food on hot plates. (For some strange reason, only butter and ice cream are served on hot plates in many places.) The usual installation is one heated leveler or a single shelf under the hot food table. At best, most places are set up to serve about a third of the meal on hot plates. If you prefer heated levelers, install two so you can work from one while the other is heating. The important thing to remember about levelers is that the last plate in is the first out. This means that if you have only one leveler, you keep taking cold plates off the top and the hot plates stay on the bottom all through the meal. A sound idea is to supplement your service area hot plate storage with a reserve cabinet where enough plates can be kept hot to last through an entire meal.

14. Unless you have efficient servers or a coordinator of guest checks in the aisle, provide an adequate number of *infrared lamps* on the service shelf or table to keep plates of food hot until served. Where menus are long and complicated, it is difficult for the cook to get all the items up at the same time, and usually it is the hot food that comes up first and has to wait the longest. This is why you should provide enough heat to keep plates of food hot for a reasonable length of time.

15. One consideration often overlooked is the *temperature* of the food when it is served. If hot rolls and chilled fruit juice are being served to your customers at the same temperature, perhaps your equipment is at fault. Or perhaps the right equipment is being used in the wrong way.

Hot food serving units are meant to hold foods at serving temperatures of approximately 130° to 150° Fahrenheit. They are not designed or meant to *heat* food. When food is placed in these serving units it must be already heated. The classic example of misuse of these units is the thermotainer drawers from which hot rolls are served. Generally, there is one small thermotainer with two small drawers. Replenishing is accomplished by dumping cold rolls into a drawer on top of the warm rolls that are left from the previous batch. And, as is the case with a leveler, last in is first out, so you serve cold rolls and write off the thermotainer as a failure.

Remember that a server will always reach into the top drawer of a low unit to avoid bending. You can take advantage of this fact to make better use of your thermotainer in this way. Serve from the top drawer, replenish the top drawer from the supply of rolls in the bottom drawer, and, when that drawer is empty, refill it with a fresh batch of *hot* rolls.

Cold food serving units pose the same problem, but fortunately there are not as many complaints about this as there are about hot foods that are served cold. The failure to serve cold foods and beverages well chilled stems from a misunderstanding about serving units and capacities. Two examples will suffice to illustrate.

Reach-in food service refrigerators with sliding or swinging doors are usually small and have low-capacity condensers. The temperature averages an excessively high 55° in them during serving times when business is brisk and the doors are opened continually. Furthermore, many of these units are not equipped with self-closing doors. As a result, the doors are often not shut tight, cold air escapes, and the interior temperature rises even higher. Now, if the food placed into these serving units is not cold and in cold dishes, it will not be cold or even chilled when it is served.

The function of ice pans and snow pans is also misunderstood. If you pour warm tomato juice into a warm glass and set it into a bed of ice, it will take at least half an hour for the juice to chill. If the juice and other foods are not cold when placed in these units, they probably will not be cold when served.

Most service kitchens are set up to serve food properly for the first 20 minutes, but from then on there is not capacity or backup to do a good job. When you promise chilled tomato juice or chilled fruit cup, make sure you are equipped to serve it chilled to the last guest as well as the first during a given meal period.

With a *thermometer* it is a simple matter to check the temperature of foods that are to be placed into hot food serving tables or service refrigerators. An inexpensive probe thermometer with a dial (the kind used for checking the internal temperature of roasting meats) can be inserted into the pan of food, or a much more sophisticated electric probe thermometer can be used in the same way.

We must begin to pay much more attention to service equipment and facilities and less to preparation if we are to improve our service and productivity. And we must make sure that the employees serving the food have sufficient space and equipment to do a good job, because they are your direct contact with the paying guest. Many plans allow 20 to 30 lineal feet for a service kitchen where two employees will be working, but provide a service and pickup aisle of 10 lineal feet where perhaps 20 servers will be working at the same time. We have to take the guesswork out of our planning if we are ever to avoid the chaos that such an arrangement creates.

Chapter 5

FOOD PREPARATION EQUIPMENT: HOW MUCH DO YOU REALLY NEED?

In the design of today's food service operation, selecting the kind and quantity of food preparation equipment needed gets more complex as there are more and more variables to deal with. The old kitchens all had more or less the same pieces of equipment because everything had to be prepared from the start. If you served french fried potatoes, there was no question that you needed a potato peeler, a soak sink, and a french fry cutter. You also knew that you were going to cut, cube, grind, and chop all your own meats, so the customary maple chopping block, the hooks for hanging quarters or sides of meat, and the band saw were a must. Most of the fish was brought in fresh and had to be kept on ice, and of course areas were needed for cleaning and fileting the fish.

Today french fried potatoes can be bought cut, blanched, and frozen ready for the service kitchen fryer. This eliminates the need for the peeler and the cutter as well as the deep fat kettle that was installed in the preparation kitchen to blanch the potatoes. Meats can be bought cut, ground, portioned, and oven-ready so that no additional work is needed in the preparation kitchen. If they are bought frozen, all that is necessary is to thaw them and take them to the service kitchen without the stop in the preparation area.

To carry our comparison a bit further, not only do we not have to cube the beef, but we can buy beef burgundy and beef stew already prepared and ready for thawing, heating, and serving. We can bread our own seafood in the rear kitchen, or we can buy it breaded and ready for the deep fat fryer in the service kitchen.

What all this means is that in deciding on the preparation area and equipment needed, you can choose the work you wish to perform today as against the old-fashioned operation where everything had to be made on the premises. Not only can you buy frozen pies and rolls ready for baking in the oven but you also have the choice of a regular or convection oven to do the job.

One sound method for determining what is needed in the preparation area is to hire a qualified equipment and layout specialist who knows not only the equipment but the new foods and the methods of preparation and handling. If he is qualified, he can save on the initial investment and also on your operating costs for many years to come. The next step is to make up your menu or list of items that you want to serve, with particular emphasis on the entrees or main dishes. (Ice, coffee, orange juice, cereal, and the rest do not affect the plan at this stage of design.) Your list should include all the items that will need preparation: steaks, seafood, fowl, vegetables, salads, desserts. Then you have to consider each item, one at a time, with your designer or food consultant and decide whether you are going to prepare it or buy it ready. This is not a difficult task, nor will it take a lot of time, because you will not be writing the complete menu or deciding on pricing.

If you choose to bread the seafood yourself, the designer must know this so he can provide sinks, breading tables, and racks for the finished product. If you are going to buy most of the food frozen, he will need to provide ample freezer and refrigeration space for storing and thawing these products. The important point is that you decide first on the items and then on how you wish to handle each one.

WHAT FOOD PREPARATION ENTAILS

When a restaurant is planned to do a substantial amount of food manufacturing and preparation, more than just labor and food requirements increase. Consider also the increased needs for equipment, facilities, and servicing.

1. More storage space.
2. More walk-in refrigeration.
3. More purchasing, deliveries, receiving, and accounting.
4. Larger heating, hot water, and exhaust systems.
5. More equipment and more building space to house it.
6. Higher monthly operating costs for utilities and maintenance.

As these needs and costs are increasing, sales may be slowing if the need for people to be involved out back with the increased manufacturing takes talent and effort away from servicing the customers out front.

It is also important to realize that food preparation equipment is much more expensive than food service equipment. This can be quickly proved if you price just one piece of apparatus—say, for example, a combination tilting kettle and compartment steamer. And, for reasons that Chapter 6 on warehandling makes clear, if you do a lot of food preparation you will need a large machine pot washer—at great expense. So it is important to remember as you plan that food preparation equipment has a high cost. Most restaurant operators are shocked at the cost of equipment and make cuts—most of them in the service kitchen. You can't buy half an expensive preparation kettle, but you can decide to make do with one fryer instead of three. This is a serious mistake because both the service and the quality of the food will be hurt right from the start. It would be better to cut out the preparation kettle altogether.

However, a certain amount of food preparation equipment will be needed. And so this chapter includes recommendations on how to determine what is needed as well as suggestions on types of equipment to fill basic needs. And throughout the emphasis is on reducing both investment costs and operating costs.

GUIDELINES IN SELECTING THE EQUIPMENT

Before a good plan can be made for a preparation kitchen the following must be established:

1. Menu and merchandising program.
2. Type of food service.

3. Price range and volume.
4. Methods of purchasing, storage, and so on.
5. Employee availability and degree of skill.
6. Exact food items to be prepared.
7. Whether you will prepare and freeze any foods yourself.

Avoid the customary method of including one or two of everything just to be on the safe side, because this can cost you a lot of money unnecessarily. If you establish menus and procedures in advance, keeping in mind that the trend is to limited menus and fewer items to handle, your planner can design a much more efficient operation for you. Doing a limited number of things better than your competition will bring more success than serving hundreds of items poorly. In most restaurants nowadays, if business starts to decline, the menu is expanded and the number of items served becomes larger and larger. The usual result is that business gets worse and worse. If the operator were instead to examine his operation, ascertain what he was doing wrong, and correct the existing problem, he would be more likely to get his business back on the right road.

Because you do have such a wide choice in the design of a preparation area and the selection of equipment, the listing that follows does not suggest specific pieces of equipment, but offers guidelines to help you decide what equipment you need. Most of what follows will help you get more for your money and avoid the waste so common in this area.

Choose Standard Equipment

Buy all the standard equipment possible, for the reasons explained in Chapter 3. In buying very expensive equipment like this, it is best to stay with well-known brands whenever you can, even though the cost may be more, because replacement parts will be more readily available. And make sure the equipment can be repaired quickly, for preparation equipment can be complex, with many moving parts and adjustments.

Choose Mobile Equipment

The advice on mobility that applies to service equipment applies equally to preparation equipment. Not only will mobility make your cleaning job easier but it will enable you to change the arrangement of production lines and work areas readily to suit changing needs. The concrete tiled base design appears frequently but should be avoided for very good reasons. First, these raised bases are expensive and hard to plan. Second, raised bases usually mean custom-designed equipment and higher cost. For example, a custom work table on a raised concrete tiled base can cost four to five times as much as a good standard table on casters, and the standard mobile table will do a better job. Third, once a concrete base is installed, you are locked into a set arrangement so expensive to change that you will be forced to suffer with it for years after the system becomes obsolete.

Buy the Minimum

Once again, don't fill space with useless equipment. One of the bitter facts about food equipment is that it is always easy to buy equipment, but it is a difficult task to sell used equipment. Unlike the automobile business, there isn't even any trade-in. When reviewing your list of preparation equipment, if you have the slightest doubt about whether a piece is needed, delete it from the list and wait until later. For a good example of overbuying of preparation equipment, carefully examine the next restaurant plan you see and note the work tables in the preparation area. A work table is the item added to fill an open space whether or not it is needed. Most preparation kitchens in restaurants have one, two, or three workers, yet they may have six to eight work tables.

Choose Self-cleaning Equipment

Specify this, by all means, because the cleaning job is a big one. For example, there are several self-cleaning range ovens available now and your new kitchen should utilize all the labor saving possible.

Design for Easy Cleaning

This has to do with floors, materials, utilities, and so on in addition to the mobility of the equipment. For example, all utility connections except floor drains can be suspended from overhead in this area so that scrubbing and hosing will be easy. In food manufacturing and processing, sanitation is a must—as recent cases of food spoilage point up—and you should insist on a design that makes thorough cleaning easy. Many food processing plants have electric cords that drop from the ceiling and can be moved on an overhead track to simplify changing lines and areas. Tile walls and quarry tile floors are very good but expensive, and this is why many processing plants are using epoxy-based paints on concrete blocks for easy cleaning.

FOOD PREPARATION EQUIPMENT: HOW MUCH DO YOU REALLY NEED? 71

The more preparation you do, the more you will need disposers, compactors, and the rest to handle waste. Make sure the disposers are the proper size for the job; otherwise you will be in for a lot of repair calls and expense.

Buy Flexible Equipment

A good back kitchen design will provide flexibility for maximum equipment use. A slicer on a mobile table can be shifted from place to place in the back and perhaps even moved out front at serving time to slice meats for those popular hot meat sandwiches. The open utility rack illustrated in Figure V-1 is an ideal slicer stand because one or two pans can be added to the sides, and when the pans are removed you have a mobile unit that will go through doors and can be used in the service area. Another good example of flexibility at low cost is the mobile rack with cold plate and heater unit shown in Figure V-2. This can have a multitude of uses.

Figure V-1. *Open utility rack*

Figure V-2. *Mobile enclosed rack with heater unit in place*

1. It can increase the storage capacity in walk-in storage areas.
2. It can provide additional locked storage if needed within a given area.
3. With the prefrozen cold plates (Figure V-3) inserted, the rack can be used as a hold unit for salads and desserts.
4. When the heater unit is inserted, the rack will keep foods hot for parties and banquets.

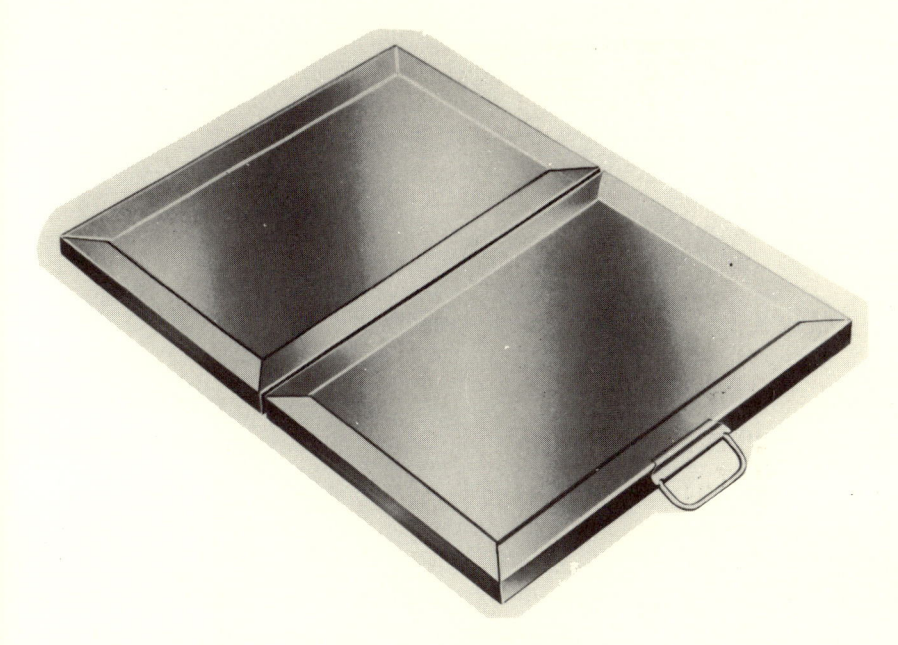

Figure V-3. *Cold plate for mobile enclosed rack*

The high cost of equipment makes it important that you get full use from every piece. Both flexibility and mobility will help you achieve this.

Make a Minimum Investment

As has been said with regard to several other items, the investment in the back of the house should be as light as possible. Extra touches here raise the cost but do little to improve sales or productivity. For years the emphasis has been on the back, and more design awards have been made for expensive preparation areas than for service areas. But the time has come to reverse this and concentrate on the selling part of our business. Reductions in cost and investment must be made somewhere, and many things can be done back here to save money without hurting workability.

1. Leaving concrete floors bare instead of adding a finishing surface.
2. Painting concrete block walls instead of covering them with another finish.

3. Using the prefab walls of the walk-in refrigerator and freezer as a wall for the dry storage area.
4. Using floor-to-ceiling wood studs covered with open-mesh wire for well-ventilated locked storage areas.
5. Putting walk-in refrigerators and freezers outside the building, with access through a connecting door in the building wall.
6. Using standard equipment with standard finishes. Good acrylic and enamel finishes are less expensive than stainless steel, which is always an extra.

Choose Labor-saving Equipment

If the cost of labor-saving equipment of any kind is within reason, it should be specified. Sometimes simple items such as a three-shelf utility cart (Figure V-4) will save countless trips between storage areas and work areas. The mobile rack shown in Figure V-2 can be used to store salad ingredients in a walk-in refrigerator. Then, with the cold plate inserted, it can be wheeled out to the salad work area in the morning and function as a cold work box. Thus one piece of equipment that can be moved from job to job can save time and energy as well as the cost of added equipment. With thought and investigation it is possible to cut down on work and effort with versatile but inexpensive pieces of apparatus.

Choose Multipurpose Equipment

This will give you the most for your money in the least space. For example, a tilting braising pan (Figure V-5) can do a number of different jobs from braising meats and preparing sauces to cooking stews, and it has the further advantage of being easy to handle and to clean. Mixers and choppers can be mounted on portable stands and can be equipped with many attachments to perform a variety of jobs in more than one area. A firm in Europe is making what it calls a Universal Kitchen Motor Unit which has excellent possibilities. It is a large motor mounted on a mobile stand, and it operates various units such as a mixer, a slicer, and a grinder. Thus one piece of equipment will provide maximum utility and save money and space. Another multipurpose unit is the combination range, broiler, and oven shown in Figure V-6, a very useful piece of equipment in any kitchen.

FOOD PREPARATION EQUIPMENT: HOW MUCH DO YOU REALLY NEED? 75

Figure V-4. *Three-shelf utility cart*

Choose Equipment in the Right Size

It is important to select the correct size as well as number of items for each job, because a kitchen that is either underequipped or overequipped cannot operate at peak efficiency. The best way to do this

Figure V-5. *Tilting braising pan*

is to seek the aid of someone with experience, give him all the facts about what you want to do, and ask his advice about how much equipment of what size will give you the best results. If you have not worked out a menu or merchandising plan and do not know what you are going to prepare for how many, the planner will have to play it safe and overequip, which is expensive and wasteful. The more menu items to be prepared, the more difficult the job of selecting the correct equipment in the right sizes. Remodeling existing operations is easier because there is information available on just what is prepared and in what quantities, but planning a new operation with nothing to go on but

FOOD PREPARATION EQUIPMENT: HOW MUCH DO YOU REALLY NEED?

Figure V-6. *Combination range, broiler, and oven*

guesswork is a formidable task because no one knows what items will sell or what items will have to be dropped at a future date.

Look for Automatic Timing Features

When selecting pieces of equipment for the preparation area, it would be well worth your while to order models that have automatic timing features. As in the food service area, the employees in the back will be doing a combination of jobs at once, and automatic timers will help them considerably. Mixers are equipped with this feature so the exact time can be handled by the machine; ovens have signals that indicate when the time has elapsed. These features help your employees make sure that your products are made correctly.

Investigate Automatic Equipment

Automatic equipment is available for food processing, but most of it is too costly and requires too much skilled maintenance to be used by the average food service operation. If your operation has high volume, it is worth investigating semi-automatic equipment to help with the production. However, consider your needs carefully before making an investment. For example, cutting machines are available that can cut up 40 or more quarts of salad in a matter of seconds. But they may not be practical for two reasons. First, it is unwise to cut a whole day's supply of green salad at once; a wiser policy is to cut and prepare salad often during the day so it will be fresh and crisp. Second, it will take far longer to clean such machines than to use them, so they will not save as much time as you may expect. In a word, be sure the machines you buy fit your production and can be used enough to warrant spending your money on them.

Many people in our industry may disagree on the wisdom of deemphasizing food preparation and manufacturing, but to anyone who has had experience with both systems, it is clear that this is the right direction for the future. It's time that we take a lesson from so many other industries and let retailing and manufacturing develop as separate businesses within the same industry, instead of clinging to the old way of having every business perform both operations.

One last point that bears thinking about is that when you manufacture a product and make mistakes, the loss is yours, whereas when you buy a poor product from someone else, you can return it for credit.

Chapter 6

WAREHANDLING: DO IT BY MACHINE

We use the term warehandling instead of the usual dishwashing or pot washing because the actual washing is a small part of this task. The handling of dishes, flatware, glasses, cups, pots, and pans is the biggest single job in any food service operation, requiring the most effort, motion, and time. Unfortunately, little or no intelligent planning has been put into this because most people know little of the department and its problems. Manufacturers sell dish machines, and that is as far as they will go. Yet a dishwashing machine is only one component of the many that together make up the warehandling operation. Having to buy all the warehandling pieces separately and assemble them yourself is in fact roughly comparable to having to buy the various components of your car separately and assemble them yourself.

THE WAREHANDLING PROCEDURE

Regardless of the size of the operation or the amount of items to be washed, the following is a logical and practical warehandling procedure.

1. Have the warewashing area centrally located to reduce the distances traveled.
2. Bring the soiled ware from the dining areas to the warewashing area in a minimum of trips; pre-sort the various items as much as possible.
3. Deposit trash in a proper receptacle, whether it be a lined can or a compactor; place large pieces and heavy food particles in a disposer or lined can.
4. Place silver or stainless ware in soak tanks or pans; sort glasses and cups directly into proper racks located overhead.
5. Insert plates, dishes, and bowls into the racks. In a small operation with a single-door machine, the remaining food and gravy is washed off by a hand-operated spray; larger machines have a pre-scrap unit that automatically washes this material off as soon as the rack enters the machine.
6. Put the racks of dishes into the machine, where the ware goes through a timed wash cycle in hot water (between 150° and 160°) with detergent, then is rinsed twice, the final rinse at 180° for sterilizing.
7. Put the silver and the racks of cups and glasses through in the same fashion when enough have been collected to fill the racks.
8. When the ware comes from the machine there should be ample clean dish table space where the racks can be set for draining and drying.
9. Place the racks of dry glasses and cups directly into mobile carts for transport back to the area of use without any handling of the cups or glasses. Place dishes and plates directly into clean dish carts and return to their points of use. Sort the silver into proper containers and return to points of use.

Proper warehandling has many advantages. One is reduction of breakage and chipping, which can amount to 3 to 5 percent of sales in operations with poor facilities. Another is reduced turnover of help. Once the drudgery and hard labor are reduced, you will need fewer employees, and those you hire will stay longer. The costs of turnover are high, though they do not appear on the profit and loss statement: overtime when you are short-staffed, agency fees, training time, low productivity while the new employee is learning his job, and loss of customers if the service suffers and diners become disgruntled, to name just a few. Still other advantages are that dishes, glasses, and other equipment are cleaner and more sanitary and that there is less noise because unnecessary handling of the equipment is eliminated.

One way to figure whether you can afford proper warehandling is to consider the cost of broken plates. A good plate costs approximately $1.50. Suppose someone drops a whole stack (doesn't this seem to happen every time you go into a restaurant?), and $30 worth of plates are broken. Doesn't sound too bad until you remember that you must do $300 in sales to make up this one loss.

WAREHANDLING CONSIDERATIONS

Following are the points to consider in planning and operating warehandling more successfully.

At the planning stage, the allocation and placement of space for warehandling are second in importance only to the dining area, yet the usual procedure is to leave these functions till everything else has been considered, and then to use whatever space is left over.

The size of machine, tables, and space needed will depend on whether the operation is small to medium ($100,000 to $500,000 in annual sales), medium to large ($500,000 to $1.5 million in annual sales), or large, feeding thousands of people in very short periods of time (cafeterias, in-flite operations, large industrial facilities).

Hand pot washing as we now know it should be eliminated from *all* food service operations.

Manufacturers should design and sell not just machines but complete packages. All the miscellaneous equipment should be included in the package, such as racks, dollies, carts, pans, and trays, to make a complete, efficient system.

Manufacturers or representatives will have to provide instructors and supervisors for a short time to show employees how to operate the system, or they will at least have to furnish a set of clear instructions.

How you are going to handle trash and garbage should be determined in advance. This is an important part of the total system that is often neglected.

Now let's retrace our steps and consider these points in detail.

After working out the general considerations including the size of the building and the placement of the dining area, select an area for warehandling that is as close as possible to the dining rooms and service stations, so it will be readily accessible. The reason for this becomes apparent when you remember that for each person served you use six to eight pieces of china and other tableware to say nothing of pots and pans. This means moving and handling many items and much weight. If warehandling is far from the points of service, the work load is heavier than it need be, not just at the start but for years afterward.

At the same time that warehandling space is being selected, it should be correctly sized. Every new or remodeled operation can project volume or numbers to be fed, and this should decide the choice of a total package system that will handle this amount or more. Dish machine manufacturers have said they are obliged to make so many different lengths and models of machines because their equipment must fit into spaces that are not planned, but are adapted from whatever is left after everything else has been worked out.

THE SMALL TO MEDIUM WAREWASHING OPERATION

Small to medium operations can very well use a package unit that I have designed (see Figure VI-1).

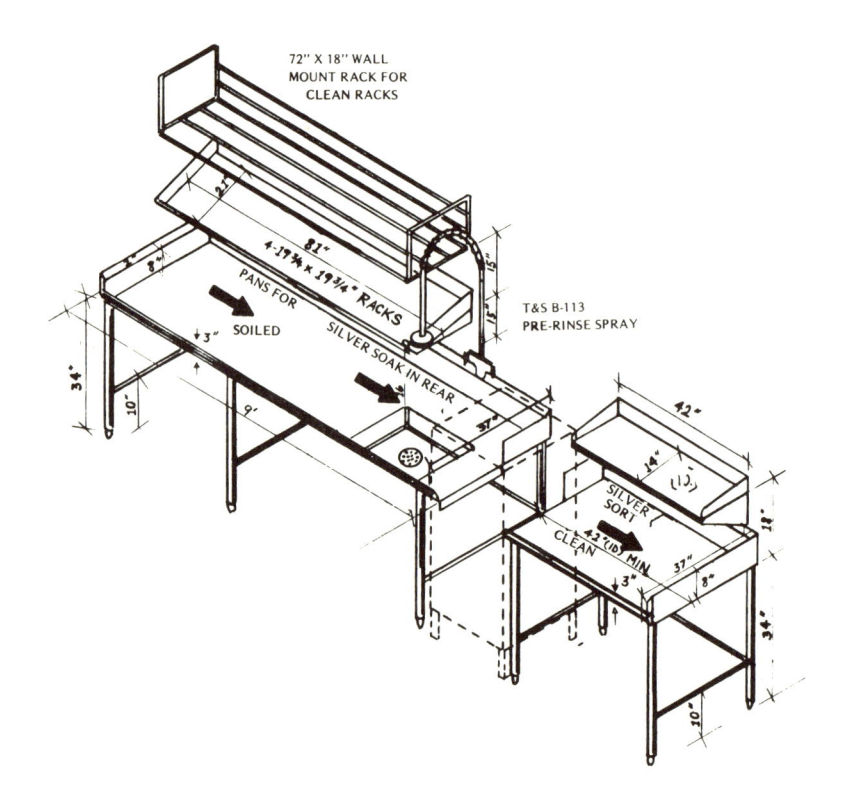

Figure VI-1. *Package warewashing unit*

Manufacturing this as a complete unit would lower the total cost of the equipment. And it will of course do a much better job because the supporting tables and equipment needed with the machine have been designed to save motion and steps and to get maximum efficiency from the machine.

All dish machines are rated at a specific number of dishes or racks per hour. These ratings are perfectly sound on condition that the supporting tables and miscellaneous equipment are adequate to the job. Otherwise the ratings mean nothing. In tests made for a leading chain, the dish machines were found to be operating at only 25 percent of their capacity because the loading and unloading were inefficient. This chain had been advised to buy larger machines to handle its increased business, but a careful survey revealed that it was not the machines but the auxiliary equipment that had to be changed. Many restaurants whose business tops the $500,000 per year level use a single-tank machine and have little trouble with warehandling because they have carefully worked out the support.

THE MEDIUM TO LARGE WAREWASHING OPERATION

Medium to large operations should use a two-tank conveyor machine with pre-scrap. Most of these are rated at approximately 6,000 pieces per hour, which is enough for quite a large business in this day of high check averages. The large business with quantities of dishes and glasses to wash and no time to pre-scrap by hand should have a wash and pre-scrap tank. Again, the supporting tables should be of correct design to allow operating this machine near its capacity.

There are two basic layouts for a large table warewashing operation. The round table operation has the operator stand at the side and place ware directly into racks that are conveyed into and out of the machine. (See Figure VI-2.)

The U-shaped or rectangular design sketched in Figure VI-3 has the operator working inside the U to feed items into the machine and take them away. For those who prefer this type, the manufacturer should design the proper tables, as illustrated in the package unit shown in Figure VI-1. Otherwise a machine with a capacity to wash 6,000 pieces per hour will probably be functioning at about 1,500 pieces per hour.

Unless one has actually washed dishes it would be difficult to decide between a round and a U-shaped arrangement. The round unit is better than the rectangular for a number of reasons.

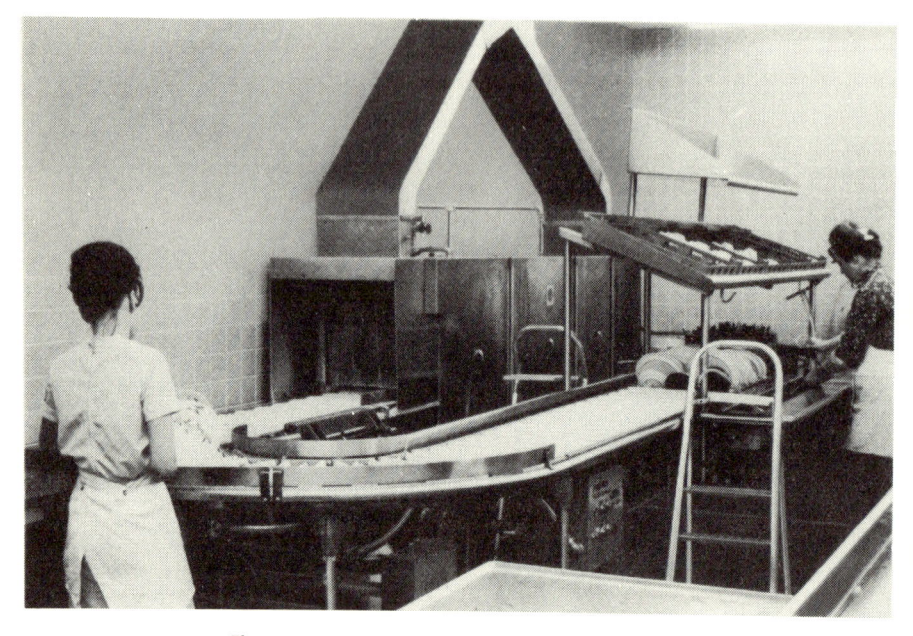

Figure VI-2. *A round table warewashing operation*

1. It has been carefully engineered and tested in many operations so that a complete package can be furnished with everything thought out, from silver soaking to rack storage.
2. In most cases, the round is no more expensive than the U because each U unit is custom-designed.
3. Usually the round unit takes up less space.
4. If some clean piece has not been taken off the round unit, it can go through again without harm and without stopping the loading process.
5. Less handling is required with the round unit because dishes are placed directly into the racks and then the racks are taken around and through the machine mechanically. In the U system, on the other hand, dishes are placed on the soiled table, stacked, and put into racks

which must then be pushed or lifted by hand, carried as much as ten to twelve feet, and put into the machine. To save time, the loaded racks are usually lifted and carried over instead of being pushed around on the approach table. Unless one has done this for hours, it is hard to imagine how exhausting the job can be.

The U-shaped design shown in Figure VI-3 improves on the usual arrangement by having the machine at the end of the tables so it will take the loaded racks around and out without all that manual labor. This machine also cuts some six to seven feet off the total length of the unit.

6. A new feature has been designed for the round unit which adds much to the total operation. This is a recirculating scrapping trough with 3 h.p. disposer which can be placed out front where the ware is sorted to go into the racks. Heavy garbage can be flushed down here immediately. In addition, a trough from the automatic pre-scrap section of the machine leads to the same disposer. This will flush away any remaining small pieces of food to keep them out of the wash tank.

If the planner designs the pot and pan washing correctly and places the salad and vegetable wash sinks near this area, the same disposer can be used to flush away trimmings from salad and vegetable preparation and the soaked-off particles from pots and pans before they are placed into the warewashing machine. This is another example of what detailed professional planning will do: not only save on the amount of equipment but get more use from the equipment on hand.

7. Most custom-designed U-shaped systems do not have enough space at the discharge end, so either table space is provided for only one or two racks of clean ware to come out of the machine and drain or a right turn is added. If the right turn is used, someone must be stationed here to pull the racks around the bend. Otherwise the loading must be stopped frequently, which cuts down on the efficiency of the machine.

Understand that large machines are not only costly to buy but costly to operate in terms of labor, utilities, and detergents, so make sure they are properly designed. With good supporting items, you can operate the machine fewer hours per day and save money. Or you can do what so many operators are doing today: wash ware between meals and utilize the warehandling operators out front to help speed service and turnover. (If we begin calling these employees warehandlers instead of dish and pot washers we may find it easier to remember that there are many ways to use their services more efficiently.)

86 RESTAURANT PLANNING

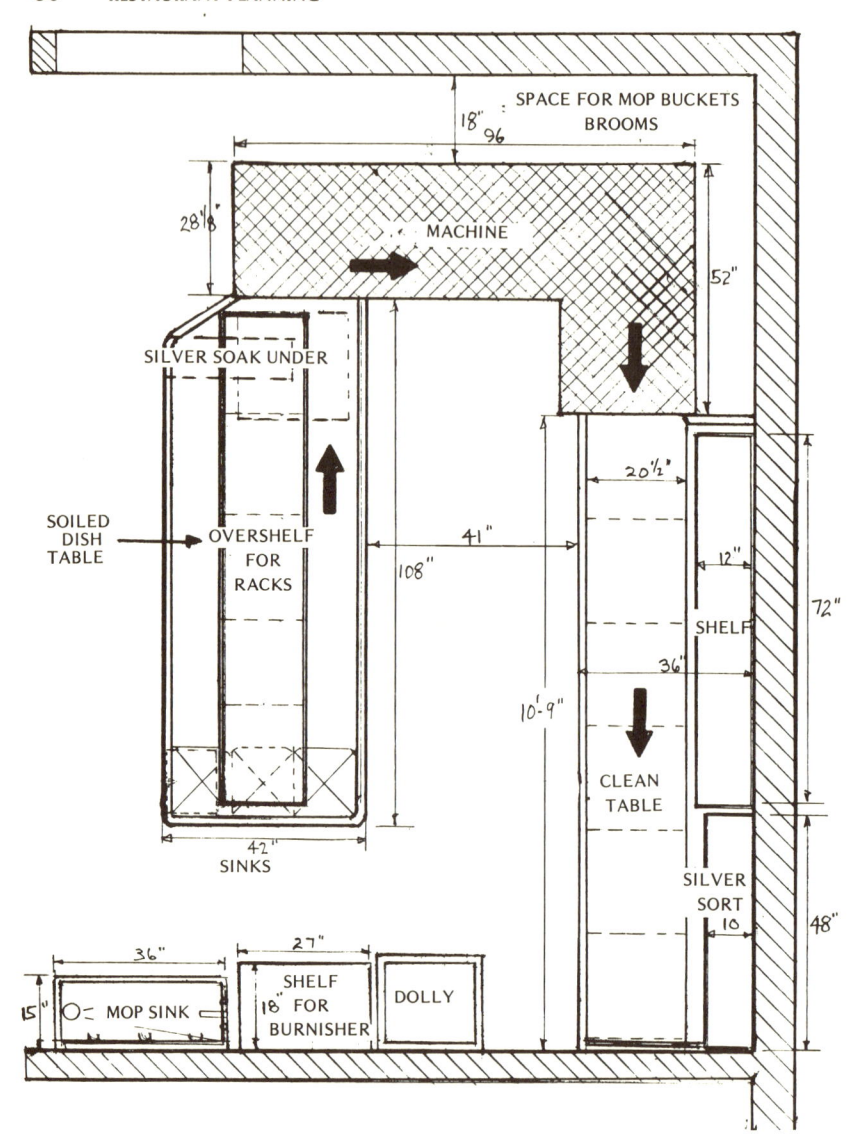

Figure VI-3. *A U-shaped warewashing operation*

This sketch shows an efficient layout for a U-shaped warewasher. Note the small amount of floor space needed for the tables and the large machine. Note also how the operator works between the tables and does not push racks around to the machine.

THE LARGE WAREWASHING OPERATION

The large operation that feeds thousands per hour and uses a great many trays should be equipped with a flite type of machine. Here again the support equipment—tables, conveyors, carts—should be designed by the machine manufacturer as part of a complete engineered package. These machines are 18' to 30' in length, have a belt as wide as 30", and can wash 9,000 to 12,000 pieces per hour. Dishes and trays are placed on the belt manually at one end and removed manually at the other end. Loading and unloading this many pieces requires many people and takes a great amount of space for breakdown as well as for all the carts and dollies needed to move this much ware.

To get an idea of the capacity of this machine, let's assume that you can feed in and remove 8,400 pieces per hour and that you average six pieces per customer. This means you can feed 1,400 customers per hour. Most restaurant dinner checks average $6, so if you are contemplating doing $8,000 to $9,000 per hour, then a flite type of machine is for you.

Before leaving the subject of package systems, whatever the size, a word about three things that manufacturers should do about the machines. First, all dishwashing machines should be made of stainless steel only. Because of the water and constant dampness, optional parts in galvanized iron or painted iron should be eliminated altogether. This would also eliminate many options in specs that confuse the buyer and vary the pricing. Second, the many sizes and lengths should be reduced by mass producing only two or three models, which would lower the prices and put an end to some of the confusion. Third, all machines should come complete with booster, exhaust system, and all other features essential to the installation and operation of the machines.

POT WASHING MADE EASIER

Now we come to the real problem child in all food service operations: pot washing. As a starter, this function should simply be considered part of warehandling, not treated as a separate problem. It is increasingly difficult to get anyone to stand over three sinks full of dirty, greasy water and scrub pans hour after hour, but this will soon be unnecessary for several reasons.

1. Manufacturers are working to develop economy model pot-

washing machines that will be low enough in price to be practical even for smaller operations.

2. One manufacturer of domestic dishwashers has introduced a new machine with more spray force that will wash egg dishes, pots, pans, and baked-on casseroles, and the manufacturers of small commercial dish machines are trying to do the same thing so that even the smallest food service operations will be able to have machine pot washing and do away with the hand methods.

3. Polyethylene soak sink carts (see Figure VI-4) and portable racks for clean pots and pans cost less than custom three-compartment sinks with drainboards and overshelves, and the savings can be applied toward machine washing.

4. Portable soak sink carts work better than the permanently installed sinks now in use. These mobile soak sinks can be placed near or under cooks' work tables, thus eliminating all those individual trips to the pot sinks. In the future, if you have a combination machine for washing dishes and pots, these mobile soak sinks can be filled with soiled pots that soak while the dishes are being washed, and then the pots and pans can be washed. As explained, given proper dishwashing layout and design, the machine would be needed for dishes only at certain times, so it would be advisable to wash pots in the same machine in order to get full value from your investment.

5. Chapter 7 on miscellaneous equipment explains in detail the proper selection of pots, pans, and trays so that manual dishwashing can be eliminated and all utensils can be machine-washed and sterilized.

6. Chapter 9 on food preparation emphasizes that food service operations of all kinds should do less manufacturing in the future—that is, use more prepared foods and do less cooking from scratch. This will reduce the number of pots and pans to wash. With low-temperature roasting and the automatic cooking equipment now available, there need be no tedious hand scraping and scrubbing.

7. Not only does machine washing lessen the work load but it makes pans and utensils more sanitary. The three-compartment pot sinks now in use have a booster heater in the third sink to bring the water temperature for the final rinse to 170°. Standing over water that is this hot is like taking a steam bath, and handling pans that have been rinsed in such hot water is very difficult. This is why many employees turn off the booster, and the utensils are not properly sterilized.

8. Medium to large food service operations cannot afford to be without pot washing. Because an operation of this size will have a large two-tank dish machine with automatic pre-scrap, many of the smaller items—stainless steel pans, trays, utensils—can be put through the dish machine to speed and simplify the entire warehandling operation. And

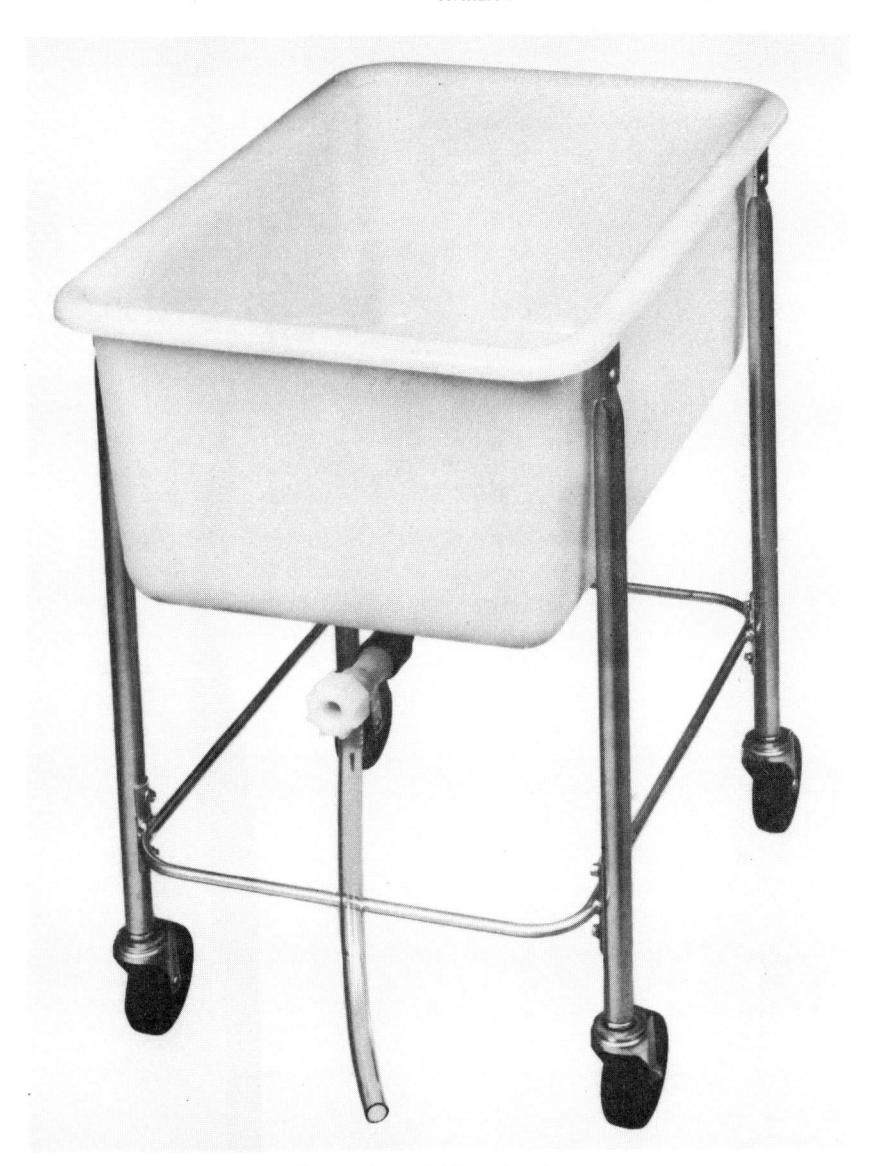

Figure VI-4. *Mobile soak sink cart*

who knows? Perhaps the manufacturers of this larger machine will one day make a combination washer to handle everything. This would be a real space-saving and money-saving piece of apparatus that should find a ready market.

9. A very large food service operation that needs the flite type of

dish machine or a hospital with many carts and racks should consider a rack pot washer. With the proper unit, an entire mobile rack can be placed into the rack washer, which washes pots, pans, and racks at the same time. These can then be moved to the point of use without all the rehandling now being done. Then the other racks, carts, shelving units, trash cans, and so on can all be washed and sterilized automatically without any washing and wiping by hand.

Regardless of the type or size of food service operation, machine pot washing is available or soon will be. Then we can forget our problems with pot washing and create one efficient warehandling department that will deal with all the troublesome jobs.

SELECTING THE PROPER CARTS

The correct small miscellaneous equipment is described in detail in the next chapter. But carts are discussed here because they are essential to the proper working of a complete warehandling system. Whatever the size of the operation, mobile carts should be used as much as possible. Why carry dishes a few at a time when they come out of the machine? A much better way is to put them directly into carts for moving back to the points of use. The mobile clean dish cart shown in Figure VI-5 provides space for the empty racks that accumulate as clean dishes are unloaded in the service areas.

The mobile silver sort cart shown in Figure VI-6 works well and does a lot of work in a small space.

The big advantage to mobile carts is that they reduce rehandling, and transport more ware per trip without physical strain. The cost of these mobile units can be offset by eliminating all the stainless steel wall shelves and undershelves that are seldom used or cleaned.

DISPOSING OF TRASH AND GARBAGE

The handling of trash and garbage has always been most difficult and unpleasant, especially for the one who must move, dump, and clean the cans. It is important to decide in advance how this will be done; much depends on local codes, location, septic tanks, and so on. There are three methods to consider: pulping in disposers, compaction, and incinerators.

Pulping in disposers. Once you have determined that a disposer can be used, make sure you get one large enough. Usually a small unit is specified to cut down the initial cost, then it later proves inadequate

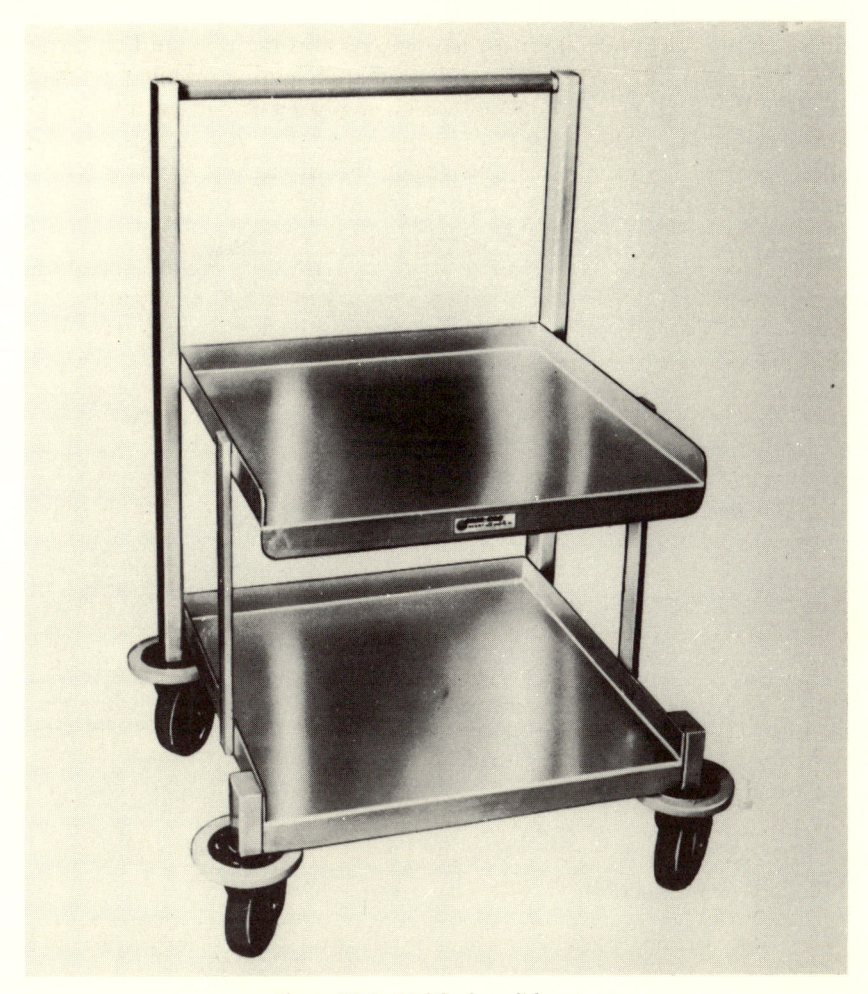

Figure VI-5. *Mobile clean dish cart*

to the job. The disposer that is kept near the warewasher should be at least 5 h.p. to do a good job.

Compaction. Becoming more popular each day, compactors such as the one shown in Figure VI-7a are on casters, which means they can be moved from one location to another. For example, the unit can be kept in the preparation or receiving area in the morning to take cans, boxes, and other discards. At warewashing time it can be moved to the head of the scrapping table. With a simple rubber guard, dishes can be scrapped directly into the compactor rather than into cans which must be emptied into the compactor later. This is another way of saving

Figure VI-6. *Mobile silver sort cart*

time and motion. The metal insert shown in Figure VI-7b has been designed to help prevent puncturing of the plastic bags so that even cans and bottles can be compacted.

Incinerators. Because of the current concern with reducing pollution,

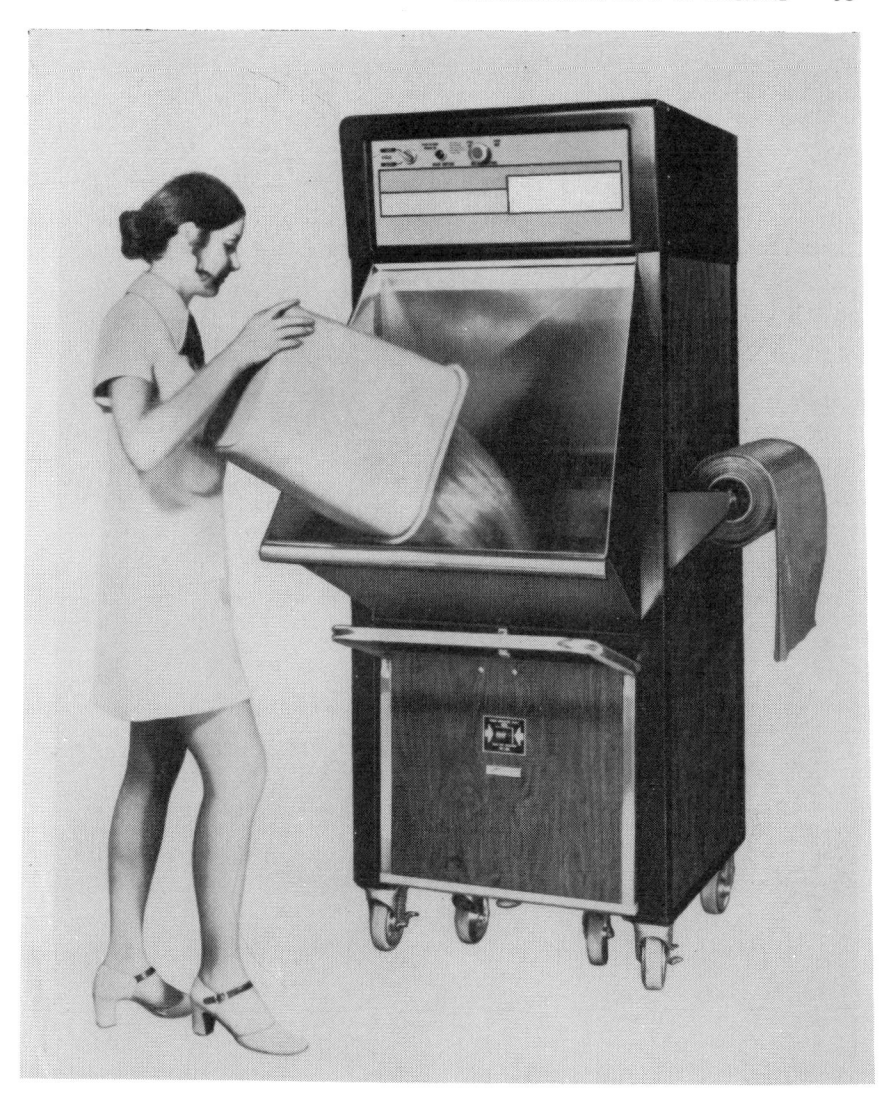

Figure VI-7a. *Mobile compactor*

be sure to check local ordinances carefully before buying an incinerator. As with disposers, if you decide on an incinerator, be sure to get one with sufficient capacity. Otherwise you may have to pay a man by the hour to stand at a small incinerator putting in trash bit by bit.

In this chapter the focus has been on the area where warehandling

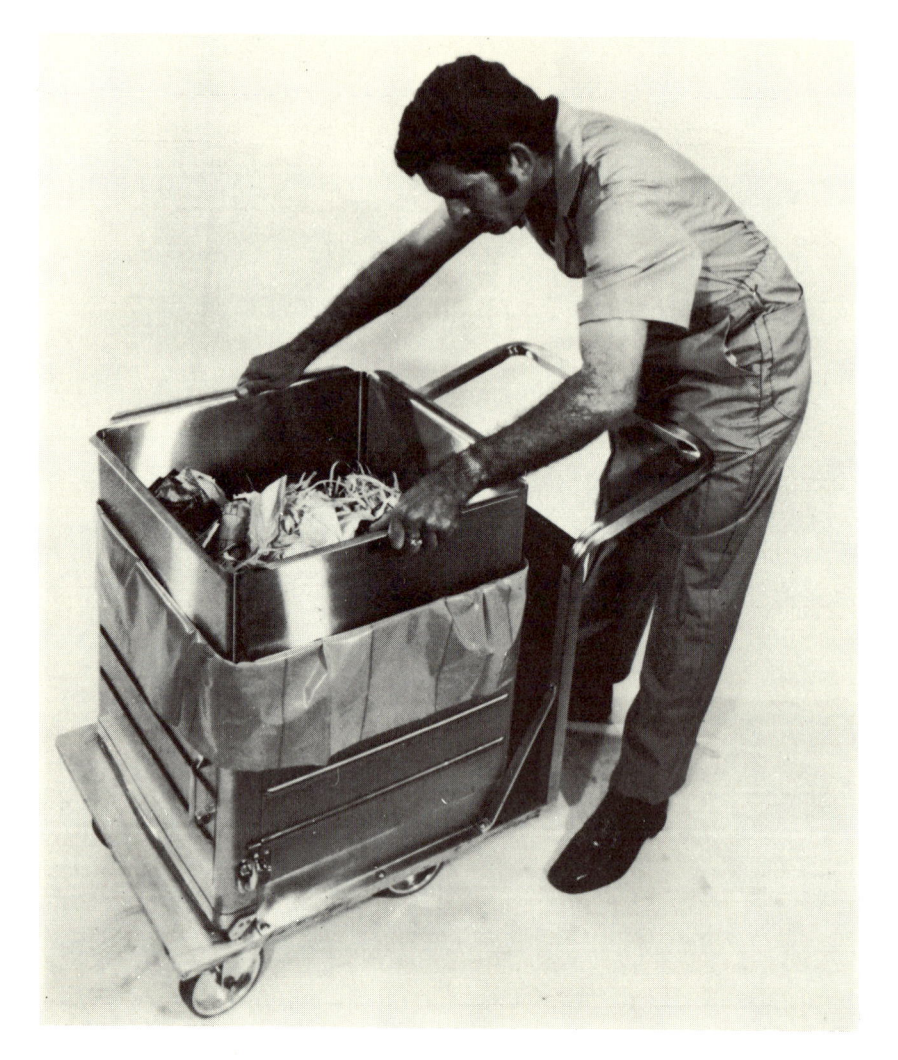

Figure VI-7b. *Metal insert for compactor*

is carried out and the equipment essential to an efficient operation. Now let's consider what ware we will be handling in this area with this equipment, as detailed in the chapter that follows.

Chapter 7

MISCELLANEOUS EQUIPMENT: EFFICIENCY MAKERS

Whether you are building a restaurant, remodeling one, or simply replacing existing equipment, it is just as important to study your needs for the so-called minor items as for the major. Briefly, miscellaneous equipment can be defined as all the equipment needed for a food service operation that does not usually appear on the floor plan or in the detailed equipment list that goes with the plan.

Normally miscellaneous equipment does not require specific utility connections for electricity, gas, water, or drains. With few exceptions, all equipment that does need utilities should be on the plan and in the list. But many designers do not consider the smaller equipment in the planning stage, and this can be a costly oversight. The plan should include all items like burnishers, toasters, roll grills, sandwich grills, slicers, and choppers, together with their utility requirements, so that there will be a place for them and proper electrical connections when the time comes. Instead of providing a single place to plug in a toaster, for example, it is wise to plan several places so that the toaster can be moved for maximum use. Even small toasters take 208/220 volts, and these lines are expensive to run later. The largest part of the extra charges incurred in opening a restaurant comes from the necessity to make provisions for these smaller pieces at the last minute.

Miscellaneous equipment includes expendables or expense items such as dishes, which can be very expensive for a food service operation if careful plans are not made for handling them. Some enterprises have excessive dish and glass breakage due to improper handling methods. More serious, small pieces of glass and china can get into the food served to guests and result in costly litigation and increased insurance rates.

In addition, miscellaneous equipment covers auxiliary pieces like carts, racks, and shelving units, which must be on the plan because they are large pieces that space must be provided for. For example, few plans ever allow space for baby seats and high chairs because the designer is trying to show all the seating he can to impress the owner. When the restaurant opens, the problem of storage for these seats is never solved.

COMMON MISTAKES IN ORDERING

In most cases the selection and ordering of miscellaneous equipment are left to the last minute—turned over to a manager who hasn't even seen the plan for major equipment, or to an equipment house that pulls an old order from the files and duplicates it. Not only are such procedures costly but they will saddle you with a lot of gadgets you will never use and leave you without some excellent equipment that would have helped the operation. In most food facilities that have been in business for years, unused pots, pans, and other items that were bought for the opening are still taking up valuable storage space. Often a new restaurant owner will object to buying something like an electric can opener that would be a great help to the employees, but does not hesitate to order two or three huge stock pots costing hundreds of dollars that are almost impossible to handle.

When miscellaneous equipment has been ordered correctly, none of it should be stored away out of use. Operations that are short on serving equipment out front often have supplies of it unopened in the back. The excuse given is that the more put into service, the more broken or lost—which is not true and never will be. In fact, the highest breakage comes from not having enough service equipment in use. To save money, space, and handling, do not buy glasses, dishes, flatware, and other equipment that you do not need in service. The equipment dealer will carry the inventory for you.

Not only must miscellaneous equipment match the planned equipment and fixtures, but it must fit the menu, merchandising, service, preparation, and all other functions of the operation. For example, if convenience potatoes are to be served, there is no need for a peeler or a french fry cutter, although these are still being specified and installed in places that will never use them.

Improper ordering of small ware that causes these items to exceed the budgeted figures can necessitate cuts elsewhere that will leave the operation short of useful equipment for years. Too much china or too many expensive pots may be ordered, and the compensating reduction may be made in an item like cup and glass racks, which always shows up as a large investment. As a result operating costs are increased because insufficient racks lead to high breakage.

Most modern advances in design and efficiency have been in miscellaneous equipment rather than in the larger fixed pieces such as ranges. If the designer is not aware of these new items and you do not specify them in the orders, suppliers will often provide the old-style equipment that has been used for years. Take advantage of improved models; in most cases they will cost no more.

In short, more labor can be saved by the right selection and use of miscellaneous equipment than by equally efficient exploitation of the heavy fixed equipment. If the small items are not in the right place and giving good service, there will be much wasted motion and money. No operation will be successful in the future unless all factors have been carefully planned and meshed to produce an efficient total.

CHINA, GLASSWARE, FLATWARE

Since the largest part of the miscellaneous equipment investment goes into china, glassware, and flatware, select these items on the basis of practicality, unless the restaurant is an exclusive, high-priced operation. Plan to use as few kinds of each as possible in order to reduce the costs and the work involved. Several sizes of dinner plate, three or four platters, and a great array of casseroles create a confusing service problem, require extra space, represent a large investment, and cause a real problem in heating them all for proper service. Likewise, why have 6-, 8-, 10-, 12-, and 14-ounce glasses when 6-, 8-, and 12-ounce sizes will do the job? The biggest difficulty with stocking

98   RESTAURANT PLANNING

many sizes and shapes of dishes is finding room for sufficient quantities of them in the service areas.

Attractive standard patterns and designs are available that are relatively inexpensive and easy to replace when loss and breakage deplete your stock. Special designs, shapes, colors, and monograms are not practical for the majority of operations. It is silly to spend a lot of extra money for a service plate in many colors with a gold name or emblem, knowing that it will be covered with meat, potatoes, vegetables, and gravy when placed before the guest. In the same way, odd colors in glasses and china may look good on display or hanging on walls, but remember you are selling food, not china! Select dishes that will merchandise the food.

Flatware should be chosen primarily for utility, since it is probably the fastest disappearing item in our business. Both guests and employees take it home, and some pieces find their way into the garbage and trash. Fancy crests, prestigious names, and unusual designs tempt souvenir hunters and increase costs. (Crests on ash trays, china, and other items produce the same unfortunate results.)

If the flatware you choose is too expensive, your tendency will be to buy sparingly and stint on putting it in use, which can be a major factor in slowing service. Today there is a choice between silver and stainless flatware. Even though the modern stainless ware is very attractive, many operators still insist on using silver. If you make this decision be sure you have the proper facilities for taking care of it. The most satisfactory way to keep it bright is to have a burnishing machine near the area where you sort the silver and, as you find dull pieces, put them into the machine.

Whether you prefer silver or stainless, there are metal and plastic boxes, compartmented boxes, and round containers for sorting flatware and taking it back to stations. The sorting should be done in the warewashing area; then the individual containers can be taken into service areas as needed. If noise is a problem, use plastic containers to reduce the clatter.

Of all the items of miscellaneous equipment, the initial order of china, flatware, and glasses should be a little heavy rather than a little light. If you have doubts about ordering one or two 20-gallon stock pots, by all means order one; later you can decide whether you need another. That extra pot will be with you for many years, but a few extra pieces of china will be used sooner or later depending on your system for handling. Normally the orders for these items are figured on so many times the total seating according to rules of thumb like those in the following tables. (Remember: even though your plan shows 200 seats, you will not be feeding that many at one time. If these seats are grouped in fours only, average occupancy will be about 110. If all 200 are in deuces that can be moved, on occasion you may seat as many as 180; but since an average is about 75 percent, figure on 150 seated and eating at one time.)

China Pieces Per Seat

Bread and butter plates	3 times
Salad dishes	3 times
Dinner plates	3 times
Cups	4 times
Saucers	3 times
Individual platters	½ time
Bouillon cups	2 times
Sugar bowls	½ time
Individual creamers	2 times
Table service creamers	½ time
Fruit dishes	3 times
Sauce boats	½ time
Cereal dishes	2 times
Grapefruit dishes	2 times

Glassware (dozens required)

	50 Seats	100 Seats	200 Seats
Juice	8	12	24
Iced tea	8	10	20
Water	16	24	32
Sherbet	8	12	18
Fruit cocktail	8	12	18
Parfait	6	10	12

Flatware

Teaspoons	4 times
Dessert or soup spoons	2 times
Tablespoons	¼ time
Iced tea spoons	1½ times
Bouillon spoons	2 times
Forks—utility	3 times
Cocktail forks	½ time
Utility knives (serrated)	2 times
Butter knives	1 time

These guidelines, of course, will have to be adjusted to your particular operation. For example, if you feature parfaits, increase the number of parfait glasses.

PREPARATION AND SERVICE KITCHENS

Because there are hundreds of miscellaneous items available, it would be impossible to cover them all. But descriptions of some particularly helpful items may serve to illustrate the importance of miscellaneous equipment as well as offer useful suggestions.

Cutting boards. Plastic cutting boards are excellent because they are easy to handle and clean. Order enough, and place them for convenient access. Remember that even the cutting boards on the fronts of larger equipment must be removable for cleaning.

Trash and garbage cans. Again, it is better to select from the many plastic models on the market because they are lighter weight, easier to clean, and less noisy than metal. Put them where they will save steps and prevent litter on the floor. By all means use plastic bag liners to reduce can cleaning and provide easier and more sanitary storage until trash or garbage is picked up.

Nonstick pans. These can be used to advantage, particularly in the smaller sizes, since they can be quickly rinsed and reused without being carried to the pot sinks to be done later. But note that if the cook doesn't have a utility sink nearby, rinsing is not possible without needless steps.

Filtering fat. Perhaps you will use a semi-automatic filter with pump, which will be shown on the plan. If not, provide filtering equipment

MISCELLANEOUS EQUIPMENT: EFFICIENCY MAKERS   101

Figure VII-1. *Portable bins for ingredients*

and keep it near the fryers, not only for easy access but as a reminder to filter the fat.

Portable bins for ingredients. Flour, breading, and many other ingredients can be conveniently stored in inexpensive, lightweight portable bins like those in Figure VII-1.

Can openers. Instead of the standard hand-operated openers, consider electric models; they aren't that much more expensive and do an excellent job. In large-quantity preparation they make it possible to open a case of cans at once without removing them from the case.

Small plastic trays. Compared with the large 18″ × 26″ metal tray, plastic trays 18″ × 13″ are much easier to handle. Also, they can be washed in the dish machine to reduce the load at the pot sink.

Small dispensers. As shown in Figure VII-2, small dispensers give portion control, speed cooking, and eliminate a lot of dripping and mess. They are excellent for depositing the right amount of beaten egg into a pan or on a griddle for scrambles and omelettes.

Figure VII-2. *Small dispenser*

Butter spreader. This provides a fast, easy method for putting butter on bread and rolls.

Small tomato and vegetable slicers. These units (Figure VII-3) give uniform cuts and fast service, not only saving time but eliminating the need to slice the vegetables so far in advance that they dry. Many operators are unwilling to use them because slicers will not cut soft tomatoes and because the knives become dull and must be replaced. This is faulty reasoning; it is just as difficult to cut a soft tomato with a knife, and hand knives too must be sharpened to do a good job.

Portion scales. It should be unnecessary to mention an item like this, yet there is not only no working scale in most kitchens but no place to put it while working. Many kinds are available; one or more would be an excellent investment.

Ladles, spoons, scoops, spreaders, knife sharpeners. These so-called minor items are of major importance in food service to control portions and speed service. If a portion of soup calls for a six-ounce ladle, see that one is there for the job; if the server has only a four-ounce size,

Figure VII-3. *Tomato and vegetable slicer*

104   RESTAURANT PLANNING

he must dip twice and spill quite a bit. Scooping a no. 20 scoop of sandwich salad mixture onto a sandwich gives portion control and saves time compared with dipping with a teaspoon. When these items cannot be found in a kitchen, management usually explains, "We had them, but they got lost." It is hard to understand why such equipment cannot be replaced as easily as teaspoons.

Check holders. Although they are overlooked in most operations, holders help the cooks keep checks in proper order and fill them correctly.

Thermometers. These inexpensive items will help maintain the quality of your food. Use them to measure food temperatures and to check the various thermostats from time to time.

SERVICE

Bus pans. One recent innovation in small equipment is bus pans, which are convenient not only for removing soiled ware but for other storage uses. Again, plastic is better because it is lighter and makes less noise. The example shown in Figure VII-4 with a separate place for flatware is a good design to save loss on this item.

Figure VII-4. *Bus pan*

MISCELLANEOUS EQUIPMENT: EFFICIENCY MAKERS 105

Tray stands. Service operations that do not have service carts will need tray stands. Make sure the aisles are large enough for them and use them for service only, not as a dumping place for dirty dishes.

Butter service. For some reason this very important item is usually overlooked in planning. As a result butter chips are left out in an open dish to go soft, melted butter is poorly handled, and the only time a customer gets hard chips is on top of cold hot cakes. Try scooping some whipped butter on top of hot hot cakes for a change.

Figure VII-5. *Hot syrup dispensers*

Plate and platter covers. Though they are seldom used, covers can be most helpful in your service. Their main convenience is not in keeping food hot but in stacking plates or platters of food to be carried neatly out into the dining area without ruining the appearance of the food. Try putting four 11½" platters of food on a 14" × 18" tray without covers; then order covers.

Hot syrup dispensers. If you serve hot cakes or waffles, use a dispenser (Figure VII-5) to make sure your guests are getting hot syrup. Pitchers of syrup do not stay hot.

Insulated pan holder. A new item that is available for 12" × 20" pans or smaller combinations is the insulated holder, which can keep foods hot or cold without utilities. It will be especially helpful in older operations.

Flatware dispensers. In choosing among the many dispensers (for example, Figure VII-6), here are some lessons of experience:

1. Use plastic to reduce noise.
2. Sort flatware in the warehandling area, not in the dining room.

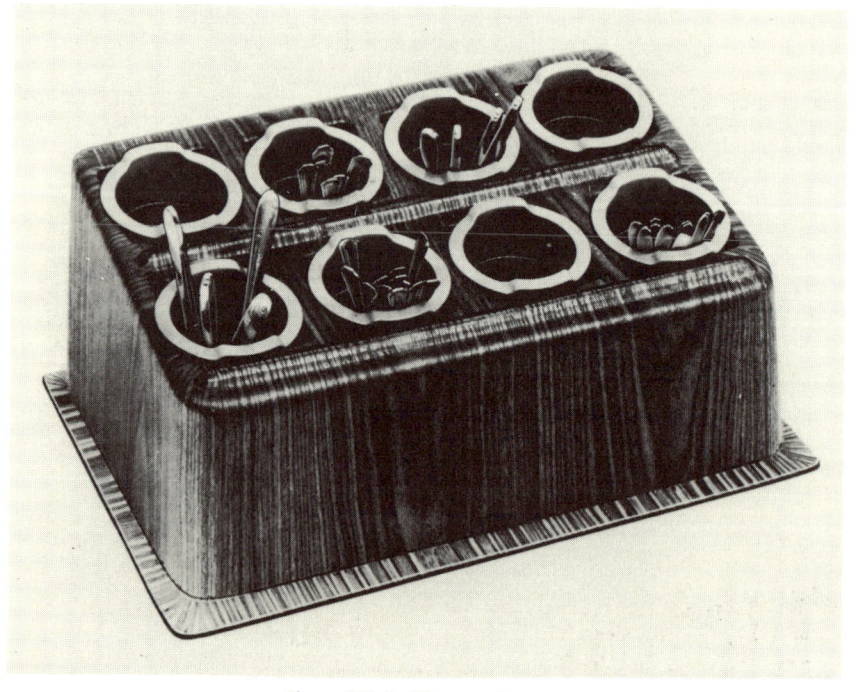

Figure VII-6. *Flatware dispenser*

3. Sort into individual containers, not into four or more compartmented containers. If forks are needed on a service stand, it is foolish to bring out knives and spoons too.
4. Avoid drawers. They are noisy, and it is difficult to balance a tray and open a drawer.
5. Regardless of how it is washed, flatware should be sorted and placed in the serving area so the server will grasp it by the handle.

Cup and glass racks. In many food service operations these are being used only to move the dishes into and out of the dish machine. Cups and glasses are then removed to trays or carried out by hand a few at a time. If you wish to cut breakage and speed service, order enough of these racks so that it will not be necessary to transfer. When the rack of cups or glasses comes from the dish machine, stack them on dollies and take them direct to service points. After you calculate how many cups and glasses to have in service, get enough racks to handle them. Note these recommendations:

1. Again, plastic racks (Figure VII-7) are lighter, quieter, and less likely to scratch ware and service stands.

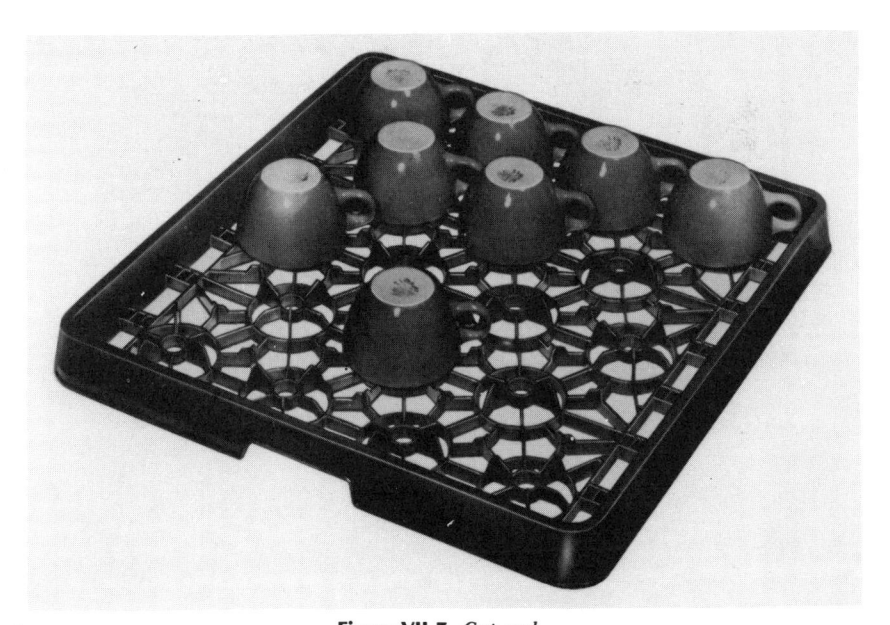

Figure VII-7. *Cup rack*

RESTAURANT PLANNING

2. Half racks can be considered for lighter weight and storage in small, tight places like areas under counters.
3. Make certain you order enough. Because this can be quite an investment, too many managers try and make do with half as many as they need. Heavy breakage for many years is the result—and cups and glasses are not cheap either.

Ladles, spoons, scoops. These are as important for the servers as for the cooks. Have the proper sizes to give good fast service.

Nonslip trays. An excellent investment for preventing accidents where they hurt the most.

Ash trays, salt and pepper shakers. A dirty ash tray on the table is unappetizing, so have enough to replace it with a clean one. Don't forget salt and pepper shakers, either; in too many places they are either empty, clogged, or lost.

These are the little details that make for success. Proper ordering and use of these "minor" items not only ensure better service and food for guests but help the employees work well and keep cheerful. Many exit interviews show that it was often the small annoyances that caused an employee to quit. The fact that the cook is hampered by inefficient tools affects his service to the waiter, and dissatisfaction spreads all the way to the guest. In other words, watch the little things, and the big will take care of themselves.

Part III

PLANNING FOR EFFICIENT OPERATIONS

Chapter 8

PURCHASING AND STORAGE: PLAN FOR CONTROL AND ACCESSIBILITY

More improvements can be made in purchasing and storage than most people realize, because these functions have not been researched as fully as some of the more obvious areas of the food business. The following recommendations for the physical management of purchasing, receiving, space layout, equipment, handling, and distribution will save you time, money, and effort. These suggestions are supplemented by the discussion in Chapter 18 on control and profit, which explains the accounting needed with food and materials.

FIVE PURCHASING RULES

Limit the Number of Items Bought

Not long ago a large chain of restaurants installed an expensive computer but soon learned, like many other managements, that computers cannot perform miracles. Before the machine was returned to the manufacturer, however, the company used it to get some information on inventories—the number of items handled in the restaurants in relation to sales. To everyone's amazement each restaurant was offering more than 740 food items (including salt and pepper), while 92 percent of the sales came from only *46* items. Added to all the work involved in counting, ordering, receiving, and handling these 740 items was the spoilage because so many of them did not turn over properly. Thus the first step in purchasing is to reduce the number of items you are buying and trying to sell.

Limit the Menu

The word "sell" is important because this is how you determine what to drop from the menu. Many years ago I had an enlightening experience in checking Roquefort cheese sales. Each morning when I inventoried the walk-in box, there was no Roquefort and I placed an order for more. Yet while watching the kitchen and service during meals, I never saw it being sold. At last I discovered that the night cleanup man was throwing out each day's cheese because he thought the green mold meant that it had spoiled. The other wrong approach to finding what is selling well is to ask the cooks or servers; they will always say that everything is selling well.

The proper method for determining sales is to use your guest checks or multicounters and get actual counts on what is being sold. It is not necessary to check all the items, because you know what the best sellers are. The listings to watch are entries like stewed prunes, pineapple juice, grapefruit juice, All Bran, squash, and hundreds of others the public does not buy frequently. These items get added to the menu because many operators think that the more foods they carry, the more customers they will have and the more business they will do. Facts prove otherwise; for example, a Florida restaurant with tremendous business has the same four entrees each night. It often happens that new foods creep into the menu when a few guests and servers request the items they prefer. Do not add these items; be polite but firm and serve the foods you know are selling by the checks and the cash register.

Use Frozen and Convenience Foods

A related point is that if you buy frozen beef stew (one item), you have eliminated the need to order, receive, store, and issue some twelve to fifteen items. Obviously this will save money in labor, space, time, and waste. Hundreds of companies manufacture quality frozen and convenience foods, and the odds are that you can find exactly what you want with a little investigation and testing.

Keep Inventories Low

Another chain management that was looking for ways to reduce food costs and increase profits (a never-ending task) realized that the food inventories in its restaurants were large because someone had decided they should carry enough food for a week or more in case of an emergency. It was decided to experiment in some of the restaurants with smaller inventories of food and supplies—amounts to last only one or two days. At the end of six months the restaurants with the smaller inventories had 1 to 2 percent lower food costs than the others. The reasons were that (1) managers ordered only what was needed, and this reduced waste and shrinkage, (2) with less crowded refrigerators and storerooms, it was possible to use the old food first and the inventory taking was easier, (3) there was far less pilferage.

This is the principle used in other retail industries; the faster you turn over your inventories, the bigger the profit. As Chapter 7 demonstrated, the same applies to stocks of china, flatware, and glasses. Don't put a thousand dollars' worth of this equipment in your storeroom—let the equipment house and the supplier carry the inventory. All the china, flatware, glasses, and similar items you have should be in service. If you cut your inventories and invest the money, your gain is twofold.

Stay Away from Bargains

The last basic rule on purchasing is the most difficult to learn. It is natural for everyone to want a bargain, and it takes some of us years to understand that in most cases there is no such thing. My advice to food service operators is to set standards, prices, and specifications and buy from reputable companies at going market prices. The large chains with their staffs of purchasing agents and their test kitchens do not buy bargains; why should you? (Naturally you should check with other suppliers from time to time to avoid costly marriages with suppliers.)

There are two types of bargains to avoid. One is the case where tomatoes are selling for 25 cents/lb. and someone calls or comes to the back door with tomatoes for 15 cents/lb. Bitter experience shows that you should refuse the offer. Remember one important thing about the cost of food: Your cost is the cost on the plate that is served to the customer, not the amount that you paid for the ingredients. The 15-cent tomatoes will be inferior, and each usable slice will cost you more than each usable slice from the 25-cent tomatoes.

The other bargain to stay away from is the large-quantity purchase where the salesman gives you 10 cents off on a case if you buy 100 cases. The only thing you can do on this sort of deal is lose! By the time you crowd the cases into your storeroom, move them three or four times, and suffer breakage, you will have spent much more than the 10 cents you saved. Besides, how do you know this item won't go down more than 10 cents after you buy it?

If you want to be a broker and gamble on whether food will go up or down, then be a broker. If you are serving food, then devote your time to seeing that the food you buy is being received, stored, issued, and served right and that you are getting your money's worth. In a short time you will gain much more than by wasting hours shopping for bargains.

RECEIVING

Once you have learned good purchasing habits, the next step is to receive what you bought correctly. Much money is lost each day in our business because management cannot see the value of checking in what has been bought—even though this practice is a simple one that most housewives meticulously follow. Here are a few simple rules:

If you do not receive the goods yourself, appoint one person with responsibility for the task.

Make sure he knows what has been ordered. A copy of the order must be available with the quantities and prices quoted. On major items, have the specifications on hand so they can be checked easily if there is any question about the merchandise being delivered.

Have a receiving area—a place where the order being received can be set down and checked before the invoice or delivery ticket is signed. Count and weigh merchandise; if you cannot do this for every item, then by all means spot-check. Once it is known that you never check incoming merchandise, you will be in for a lot of shortages. Even if you are a manager for a unit in a large chain, check the items you receive from your commissary or company warehouse; experience shows that many shortages can occur even in a situation like this.

Never have the driver or deliveryman put the merchandise away for you on shelves or in your storage areas. Once you have checked the order and signed the slip, you or someone in your employ should stow the supplies where they belong.

The very simple rule to remember is: Make sure you are getting what you order and pay for, and see that it does not walk away later. Here again, for every dollar lost you must do at least ten dollars in sales to recover the loss.

SPACE DESIGN AND LAYOUT

Any time you are designing a new operation or remodeling an existing one, it will pay to know a few easy rules about efficient use of space for storage, whether it be refrigerated, freezer, or dry storage. (In Chapter 3 on planning, the best location for storage space was considered in connection with the efficient utilization of total space.) Storage functions receive a minimum of thought in planning, yet when you are paying $35/square foot for a building, 200 square feet saved represents quite a bit of money.

The first principle to keep in mind is that you are interested in lineal feet of shelving, not square feet of space for storage. There is no set standard for the amount of lineal feet of shelving that will be needed; the decision must be made by someone with experience in the particular situation. The variables are the menu, the items served, the meals served, serving time and days, preparation, frozen foods used, convenience foods used, deliveries possible, the volume of business, and the number of people fed. Following, however, are some general guidelines:

The best length for the units is the longest possible, because you will save on uprights.

The best depth is 21": this will fit most cases and pans.

Four shelves to a unit are advisable, and the best height for normal use is 66" for posts. The shelves should be adjustable to fit your products. (Standard walk-in coolers and freezers are 7'6" or 8'6"; anything higher is getting into the realm of fork lifts.)

For general use and efficient storage in the case, allot about 60 percent to four-shelf units and 40 percent to low dunnage racks.

Leave space for some tall pan racks—both open and with doors —because they accommodate the largest number of pans in the smallest number of lineal feet. If you store 18" × 26" pans on the regular shelves, you can get only four in 18 lineal inches, whereas a tall rack can hold twenty.

116 RESTAURANT PLANNING

Excessive aisle space in storage areas does nothing for you. In the case of refrigerators and freezers, it wastes money in keeping aisles cold.

The layouts in the accompanying illustrations demonstrate the efficient use of space. As shown in Figure VIII-1, a narrow space can be fitted with two rows of shelving and one aisle (36" to 42" in width), or two aisles and four rows of shelving can be installed in

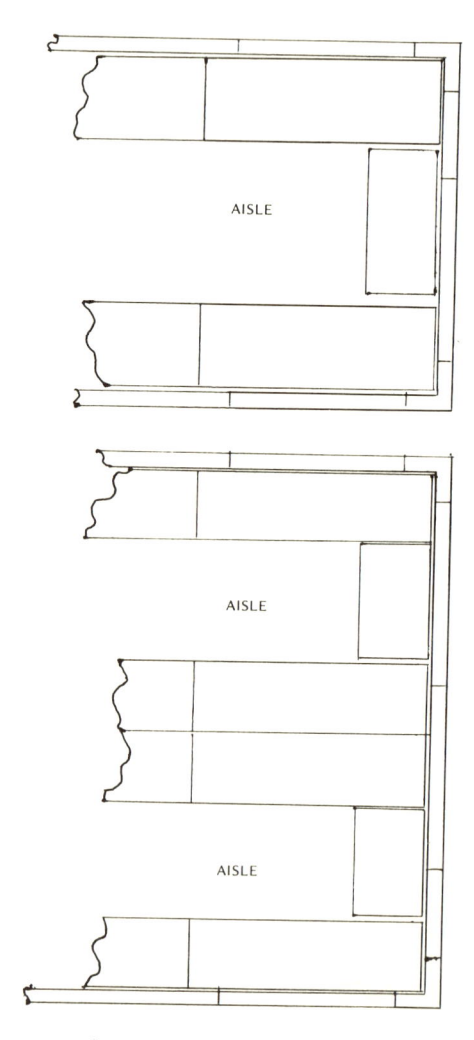

Figure VIII-1. *Layout of a storage area*

a wider area. In either situation you are getting the maximum lineal feet of shelving space in the minimum square foot area.

In Figure VIII-2 the cooler and freezer are placed next to the dry storage area, so that the wall of the cooler-freezer and the outside wall of the building become the walls for the dry storage area. With such an arrangement the cooler-freezer is less expensive not only to buy but to operate, because the freezer door does not open directly into the hot kitchen. In addition, since you will be handling more and more frozen foods as time goes on, and since the best procedure is to put them into the cooler for 24 hours or more before reconstituting, this cooler-freezer layout saves steps and time.

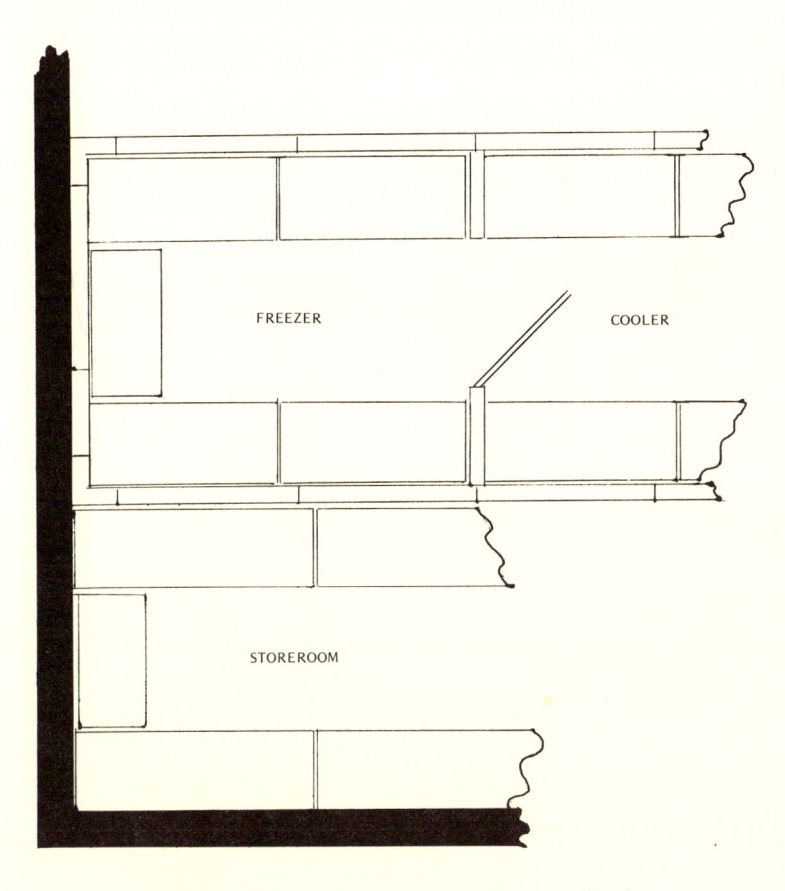

Figure VIII-2. *Layout of a storeroom, freezer, and cooler*

118 RESTAURANT PLANNING

In another arrangement shown in Figure VIII-3, a cooler or freezer is constructed outside the building on a concrete slab with a door leading into the building. In the case of a new building, this layout saves the square foot cost of the building. In the case of a remodeling, it enables you to pick up that needed extra cooler or freezer space at a low cost.

In all three of the sketches, note how the 4"-thick walls for the refrigerators and freezers are planned in standard modular lengths of sections. This will save you money when ordering.

Mention should also be made of an efficient storage system used mainly by libraries and firms that must keep files and papers in a very small space. Shelving units of varying lengths are made on casters and placed on tracks. For example, it is possible to have eight of these shelving units together with only one aisle space. On the end of each unit is a sign listing its contents. The user selects the section he wants and gets access to it by moving the others back and forth. However, these units are expensive and difficult to clean, which explains why they are not more widely used in the food business.

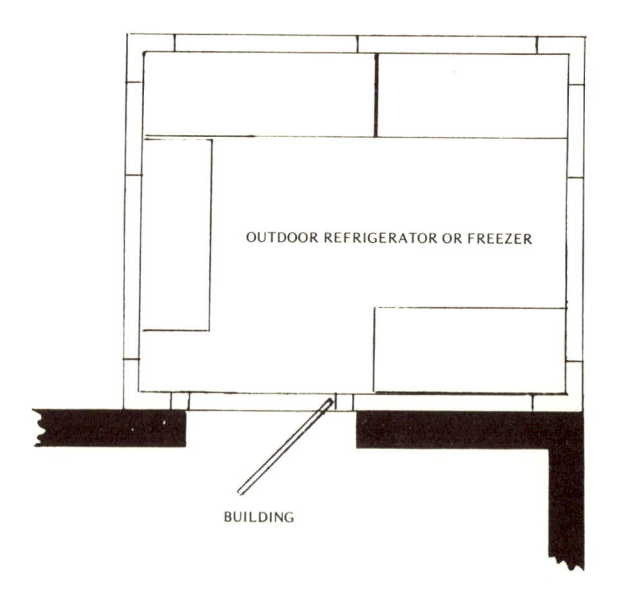

Figure VIII-3. *Layout of cooler or freezer constructed outside building*

EQUIPMENT

Among the equipment necessary for the storage handling function is a receiving scale, which can be a simple, inexpensive model like the one in Figure VIII-4 as long as it is placed in the receiving area where it can be seen and used. This area should also have a two-wheel handling truck that will save hand carrying and extra trips (Figure VIII-5). If space is available, a four-wheel platform truck will further ease the handling chore.

To increase productivity, utilize small mobile shelving carts (shown in Chapter 5, Figure V-4) to take items from the storage areas to the places of use.

Also plan to have mobile vertical storage racks (Figure VIII-6) that will provide maximum storage per lineal foot of space. Assume your cooler-freezer has only shelving units, which are normally four shelves high. Put one pan (12" × 20") on each shelf, one above the other,

Figure VIII-4. *Receiving scale*

120 RESTAURANT PLANNING

and you get only four pans of storage in the vertical space. In the same space, a vertical rack stores sixteen to twenty pans and trays of various sizes.

This type of vertical rack is also available in an enclosed version

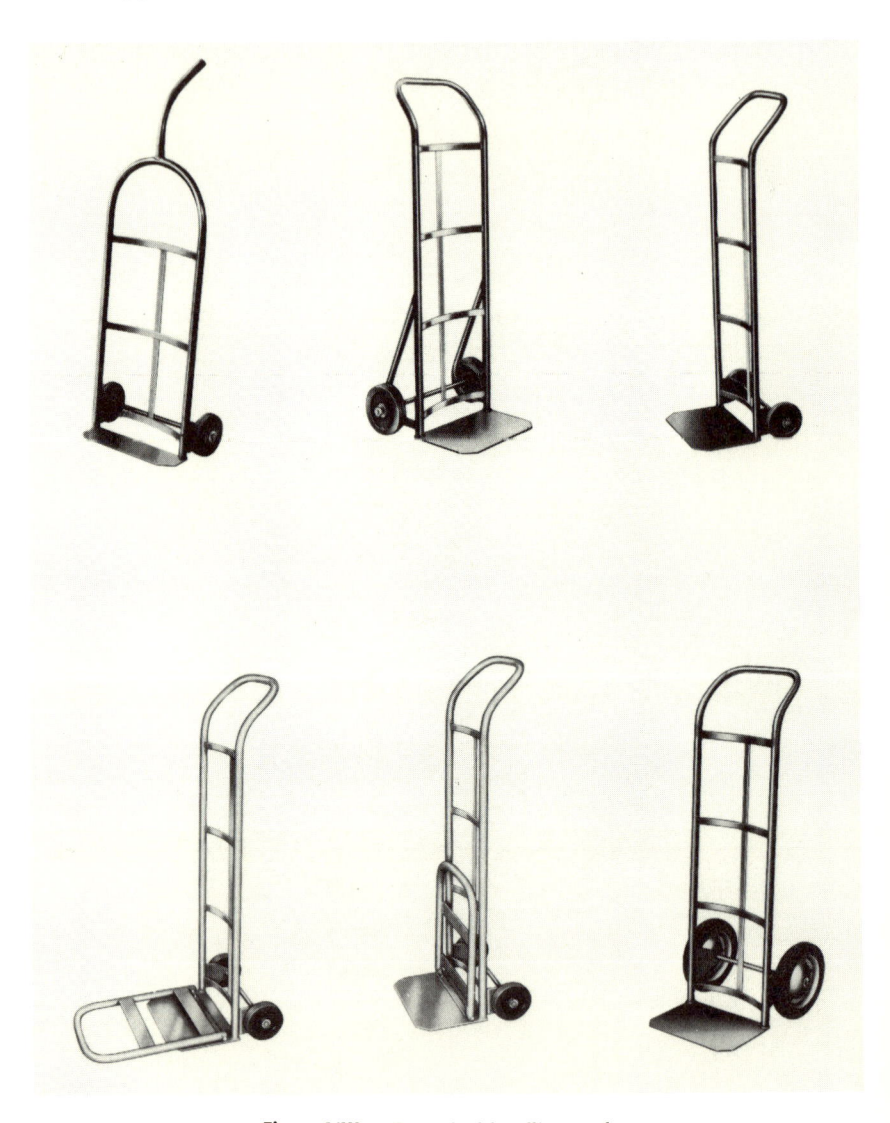

Figure VIII-5. *Two-wheel handling trucks*

Figure VIII-6. *Vertical storage racks*

122 RESTAURANT PLANNING

with a door. It has many uses: It can be placed in the walk-in cooler-freezer for locked storage of small valuable items such as steaks; it can transport food from one building to another; and it can be converted to a proofer, a heated food cabinet, or a cold cabinet (valuable for parties, banquets, and catering).

Figure VIII-7. *Refrigerator or freezer shelving*

Shelving for storerooms and walk-in freezers and refrigerators is a confusing subject that no two people in the restaurant business will agree on. For dry storage I feel it is best to use flat shelves. For refrigerated or freezer space, however, it is best to use louvered shelves (such as those in Figure VIII-7) or solid shelves with raised ridges, to provide circulation of cool or cold air around the product.

For dry storage a unit with flat, solid shelves is best because you do not need air circulation and the flat shelf is easiest to clean. The choice between stationary legs and casters is up to you. A stationary unit must be either carried out for cleaning or cleaned in place, whereas casters provide more flexibility. In addition to the four- or five-shelf units, at least one third of the total lineal feet of shelving must be allotted to dunnage racks (Figure VIII-8). These permit storage of full cases and greatly increase your storage capacity (more reasons for dunnage storage will be given in Chapter 18 on control and profit).

For refrigerated and freezer storage, again solid shelves seem to be the answer: they are easier to clean, and they prevent spillage from one shelf to another. Solid shelves are available with raised areas for better circulation. I recommend casters here, because it is very unpleasant to wash shelves by hand in cold areas. At least one third of the

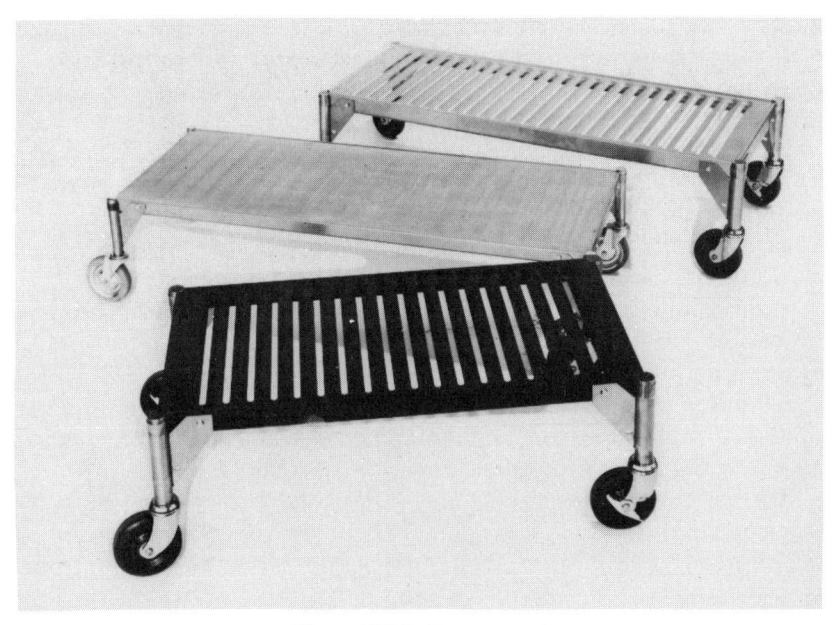

Figure VIII-8. *Dunnage racks*

total shelving footage in these two areas should also be dunnage racks, and they should be on casters.

In large-volume operations like schools, cafeterias, and hospitals, all the shelving should be metal on casters. These units, together with other racks, tray carts, and such equipment, can be cleaned quickly in an area with a steam or pressure hose. Even better is a rack washer that will not only wash all the items mentioned but machine-wash all the pots. In many hospitals today the pots and pans are still being scrubbed by hand in huge sinks, and shelving units and tray carts are being hand-washed in the cooler or freezer. It is unfortunate that the industry did not give closer study to this area of unpleasant high-turnover work, because it can be eliminated. Yet we persist in anachronisms like requiring employees to rinse out mops after each use—though we don't even provide a place or utensil to do the job.

HANDLING TECHNIQUES

As Chapter 6 on warehandling emphasized, the movement of material into, within, and out of your establishment is the biggest single job, and you or some responsible person in your organization should study the best way to handle all stores and supplies used. If you continue to do the job by hand and muscle power, ours will continue to be the number one industry for hernias. Strangely, it is simple to correct the situation without great cost.

First, buy a few simple pieces of equipment that have been illustrated in this chapter and Chapter 6. They will enable your employees to accomplish their tasks easier, faster, and at less cost. For example, instead of carrying ten cases to the storage area one at a time, a man can do the job in two trips with a two-wheel truck.

Second, show your employees how to do their jobs in the simplest and easiest manner. An old saying in our business is that if you want to know how to wash dishes, ask a dishwasher—yet in all my experience I have never seen a man in this position who had the time and the facilities to study time and motion and to research better ways to do the job. It is up to management to work out better methods.

Most restaurant operators today complain about the shortage of strong, young, aggressive people. Perhaps with the right equipment and improved methods, we could use people not so young or strong.

ISSUE AND DISTRIBUTION

After supplies have been received and stored correctly, the next step is to issue and transport them to the points of use. Here is another area where planning can save time, steps, labor, and money.

In most cases owners want to put the storeroom, cooler, and walk-in freezers near the kitchen or serving area, because employees make hundreds of trips to them daily. Storerooms and walk-ins, however, are not meant to work out of. Change systems; provide reach-in refrigeration and freezer space at each work point, whether it is in the preparation or service area. For dry storage utilize the mobile units that have been described in this chapter, and place them near points of use.

Teach employees to quickly inventory the storage areas near them once or twice a day. They can make a list of what is needed, go to the storeroom or walk-ins with a cart, and get all the supplies in one trip.

This controlled issuing also reduces waste, because under the old system when a service area ran out of an item like napkins, several people usually rushed to the storeroom and opened the first case in sight.

In the study of time and motion, the first lesson is that a person is not producing when walking; he produces only when he stops and uses his hands and arms rather than his feet.

At mealtime, put all your employees on the front line where they can be taking care of the customers.

Chapter 9

FOOD PREPARATION: HOW MUCH IS NECESSARY?

With the systems and techniques now available, more gains in productivity and operating economy can be made in the area of food preparation than any other. This is true of an existing facility as well as a new one. Innovations can be introduced at any rate of speed and can promote, not hinder, creativity in planning menus. Moreover, your guests need notice no changes except that the food and service are better, because what you have done in essence is to reduce the amount of labor required in the back kitchen and put more effort into the service out front.

The basic facts about food preparation are these: It requires relatively skilled employees who receive a higher average wage than food service personnel. And depending on the amount of on-premise preparation done, the kitchen area requires more building space and more expensive equipment than the service area, which is usually kept small and compact to save steps.

LIMITING AND BALANCING THE MENU

As in purchasing and storage, the more items handled, the more space and effort needed. Plan to change your menus often, then gradually cut down on the number of dishes you prepare by dropping the ones that don't sell. For example, customers will be more satisfied with one popular soup than with an assortment of unpopular ones. You can add variety to the menu by featuring a different soup for each day of the week.

Construct menus not only to vary the food but to distribute the work among the departments and balance the load for each employee. With daily menus you can even compensate for an employee's day off, since you can plan for his work to be lighter. Avoid overloading the preparation area by listing several different soups, a stew, meat loaf, and fancy potatoes on the same day; at least change the meat loaf to a chopped sirloin steak requiring no preparation.

Also remember that there can be breaks in the continuity of food preparation. Vegetables, for example, are best when cooked in small quantities; pastry when it is fresh-baked. Naturally there will be times when a particular vegetable or pie is not ready or when you have misjudged quantities and run out. Instead of naming all vegetables and pies on the menu, try simply listing fresh vegetables and fresh-baked pies. The servers can keep informed on what is available and tell the guests, who will be much happier than if they ordered dishes they cannot have. And you can forget about rushing to prepare another batch of baked acorn squash thirty minutes before the dining room closes.

MEAT COOKING

The effect of heat on meat is to coagulate protein juices, soften connective tissues, and develop extractives which produce flavor. Savings can be made in this most costly of all food categories if your cooks are familiar with proper methods of preparation.

Experimental work in many leading laboratories has proved that meat cooked at continuous low temperature, whether in the oven or in water, is tenderer, juicier, and more palatable, with a lower percentage of shrinkage, than under the old method of searing at high temperatures and cooking at medium. Prepare all meats except for steaks, chops, and other broiled or fried items at low heat throughout the cooking process.

Take advantage of the less expensive cuts that can be made into tasty dishes by braising, stewing, or simmering. Although these cuts are tougher, they usually have more flavor and when properly cooked will rank among the most popular entrees on the menu.

On some nights it seems as if everyone orders the complicated dishes like beef burgundy, and you run out at 7:30 P.M. Here again as with vegetables and desserts, don't frantically rush to make another pot; tell the servers that the item is out and that guests can choose from other entrees. Better still, use frozen beef burgundy to begin with; it can be thawed and heated in an instant.

Following are some general directions for meat cooking.

Braising

This method, in which meat is cooked by moist heat, is used for cuts that require moisture to bring out their full flavor and make them tender. The meat is usually browned in a very small amount of hot fat, then covered and cooked slowly in its own juices or in additional liquid such as milk, stock, or sauces.

Broiling

Broiled meat is cooked by direct heat over a charcoal grill or under a gas flame. The grill or broiler should always be pre-heated for 10 to 20 minutes before the meat is put to cook. The meat should be placed over the coolest area of the charcoal fire or 2" below the gas flame.

When fish is broiled under a gas flame, it should be 1½" below the flame.

Pan Broiling, Pan Frying, or Sauteeing

Meat is placed in a sizzling hot frying pan which has been rubbed with fat or suet from the meat. It should be cooked uncovered, without additional fat, at medium temperature. If fat cooks out of the meat, it should be poured off as it accumulates.

Roasting

Low-temperature roasting, a system developed many years ago but not widely used even today, reduces shrinkage and results in a better product. It yields more meat and saves on the crusting waste caused by the old-fashioned searing method, in which meats were roasted at very high temperatures. The idea was that the searing and crusting on the outside sealed in the juices, but this has been proved wrong. The fact is that searing increases the loss of juices, while the tough crust must be trimmed away. For successful low-temperature roasting, follow these steps:

1. Wipe meat with damp towel.
2. Rub well all over with salt.
3. Place in roaster, fat side up. Juices from fat will penetrate meat, enriching flavor and keeping roast moist because it bastes itself.
4. Insert meat thermometer so that bulb is in thickest part of roast but not resting in fat or next to bone—otherwise temperature registered will be inaccurate. Thermometer should remain in roast throughout cooking period.
5. Place in roasting pan in 300°F oven. (Exception: Start *beef* at 350°F for 45 minutes; then reduce heat to 225°F for the balance of cooking.) Do not cover. Cook to desired doneness, keeping oven constant and roast uncovered at all times. Remove and set uncovered in a warm dry place, or send to steam table for service.
6. A roast cooked to the *rare* or *medium* stage will continue cooking after it has been removed from the oven and let stand for service. Its interior has retained heat and the temperature will rise 10 to 15° over 45 minutes. In the case of *well-done* meat, there is little rise in the temperature of veal, pork, or lamb roasts after removal. But *well-done beef* continues to cook.

Temperature Chart for Roast Meats

(Temperature at which meats are removed from oven)

Prime ribs, medium	145°F
Prime ribs, rare	134°F
Beef, rare	134°F
Beef, medium	145°F
Leg veal	181°F
Leg lamb	181°F
Fresh ham	181°F
Pork loin	181°F
Cured ham	158°F
Roast turkey	170°F

NOTE: As a precaution against breakage of meat thermometer, use a meat skewer to make an incision for it.

Simmering

Meat is put into warm water that covers it during the entire cooking period. The temperature is kept at 180 to 210°F, or just below the boiling point of water. Occasionally bubbles form in the cooking water and rise slowly to the surface around the edge of the kettle, but the water should never bubble vigorously. The advantage of simmering over boiling (cooking at 212°F) is that the lower temperature produces a much tenderer meat with much less shrinkage.

Stewing

Stew meat is cut into cubes and browned on all sides. Then liquid is added and the meat is cooked at a simmering temperature until tender. The best meat for stews contains both fat and lean.

PREPARING AHEAD

Redistribute your preparation load by cooking food ahead of the day it will be used and refrigerating or freezing it on the premises. Many dishes that are popular but difficult to prepare, such as stews and various kinds of potatoes, lend themselves to this treatment. As shown in the following recipe, the great amount of work that goes into some best-selling items can at least be done during the off-hours rather than at the height of the rush.

Baked Stuffed Idaho Potato

	96 Servings	*192 Servings*
Idaho potatoes, approx. 1 lb. each	48	96
milk	2 qt.	1 gal.
salt	¾–1 cup	1½–2 cups
paprika	2 t	4 t
butter	½ lb.	1 lb.
pimiento, chopped	1 cup	2 cups
parsley, chopped	2 cups	1 qt.
egg whites	3 cups	1½ qt.

1. Wash and scrub potatoes thoroughly and bake in a 375°F oven for approximately one hour or until done.
2. When baked, cut in half lengthwise. Scoop out the inside and mash.

3. Add milk, seasonings, butter, pimiento, and parsley.
4. Fold in beaten egg whites.
5. Fill potato shells lightly with the seasoned mixture. Refrigerate. Just before serving, brown in hot oven.

Service: ½ potato

Another excellent specialty item, little thin pancakes, can be mixed and cooked in the afternoon on a griddle that would otherwise be idle. Store them in the refrigerator for service the following day.

Little Thin Pancakes

64 eggs
¾ cup salt
1⅞ cups sugar
1½ gal. flour
2 gal. cold water
1 gal. half & half cream

1. Beat eggs very light (high speed on Hobart mixer).
2. Add sugar and salt to eggs (set mixer on medium speed).
3. Measure flour, then sift.
4. Add water to eggs, sugar, and salt.
5. Turn mixer to low speed and add cream and flour alternately. Turn mixer back up to medium speed and let mix for 15 minutes or longer.
6. Place in covered containers in refrigerator until ready to cook (let stand at least 30 minutes before using).
7. Mix and whip mixture thoroughly each time before using. The longer this mixture stands and the more times it is beaten, the tenderer the cakes. The mixture may be thinned with half & half. Some flour requires more liquid. Do not thin with water.
8. Allow 3 oz. batter for each cake. With well-buttered grill at 400°F, cook till partially set, turn, and turn second time.
9. Remove from griddle, roll, stack rolls in a pan, and cover with a damp towel. Refrigerate.

Maple Butter

1 gal. maple pancake syrup
6 lb. butter

1. Cream butter in mixer until very soft and creamy.
2. Warm syrup till just lukewarm.
3. Add syrup slowly to creamed butter.
4. Mix well.
5. Place in covered containers in refrigerator until ready for service.

Pancake Service

3 thin pancakes, rolled
3 slices cooked bacon
2 no. 40 dippers maple butter

1. Place 3 rolled pancakes side by side on luncheon plate.
2. Top pancakes with 3 slices of cooked bacon.
3. Top bacon with 2 no. 40 scoops maple butter.
4. Place in radar oven for 5 seconds or under broiler until heated through. Serve sizzling hot at once.

By making the pancakes and maple butter in advance, you not only prepare a dish ahead when you are not busy but speed your service the next day. In the same manner, plan to have enough equipment and storage facilities so that special sauces can be made up in quantity and refrigerated for future use. It takes about the same amount of time to mix 10 gallons of french dressing as 1 gallon, so why not make the larger batch? It is this type of thinking and planning that yields the greatest gains in productivity and economy.

Freezing

Any restaurant offering quite a few specialties that are difficult to prepare can save so much money and time by freezing in quantity that the initial investment is worthwhile. The big expense, of course, is the freezer, which must hold a temperature of 30 to 40° below zero to protect food quality. Food frozen at zero or above develops large crystal formations, and the flavor is impaired.

Small freezers are on the market that will maintain the low temperatures needed for on-premise freezing. The model shown in Figure IX-1, for example, features a strong air blast of 35° below zero.

Figure IX-1. *Low-temperature blast freezer for on-premise freezing*

Tightly sealed packages are also necessary for a high-quality product. Unlike the large industrial packers, you will not be freezing in large quantities for long-term storage; but improper packaging can cause freezer burn and drying even in food stored for one or two weeks.

Individual sealed containers (portion packs) are probably not practical for most restaurant operations, since they require an expensive assembly-belt packing line to effect real savings. But there are many disposable pans of aluminum and even paper board available in all sizes. Food can be packed, sealed, frozen, thawed, heated in a convection oven, and placed, still in these pans, on the hot food table.

The correct temperature for storing frozen foods is *10° below zero*, not zero. And keep in mind that the longer any frozen food product is stored, the more likely the loss of quality. Use frozen foods as soon as possible and rotate them carefully in the holding freezer: *first in, first out.*

AUTOMATION AND SEMI-AUTOMATION

Investigate all equipment that can help in food preparation. Unless you have an extremely high sales volume it may not pay to buy automatic machines, but there are many semi-automatic ones as well as small attachments that will speed certain jobs. If you are cleaning your own shrimp, a small shrimp deveining machine will be more economical than slow and tiresome hand cleaning. Similarly, cutting up greens for a garden salad is time-consuming by hand but quick by machine.

PREPARING AND SERVING IN THE SAME AREA

There are several types of food service operation that can save steps and better utilize employees by arranging to prepare and serve in the same area. One is the eating place with low-volume sales, particularly when there are few high-volume peaks. The actual amount of sales that falls in the low-volume category depends on many factors, but it can be said that an establishment which operates a large percentage of the time with only one employee preparing and serving should combine the two areas as much as possible. In a luncheonette, for example, the same person can serve mid-morning stragglers while he is getting lunch ready. Similarly, operations with a simple one- or two-item service like schools and industrial cafeterias can benefit from consolidating these departments and using the same personnel in both.

USING FROZEN AND CONVENIENCE FOODS

Like anything else, frozen and convenience foods take getting used to. The gradual approach is best in most instances. Gradually or not, however, food service operators should be getting out of the food manufacturing business and into food selling. Usually they agree that this is a fine idea—for the other fellow.

Managers of school, hospital, and industrial feeding services are particularly apt to insist that frozen and convenience foods are not for them. Yet this group can gain more from ready foods than any other. Their facilities usually have simple one- or two-entree menus, definite serving times, and fairly exact information on the number of people to be fed. And because the operations are nonprofit, they cannot afford the skilled help needed to manufacture superior food.

Today neither a nonprofit establishment nor a moderate-sized restaurant can meet the rates commanded by a skilled butcher. If these places insist on cutting their own meat, they must use less skilled employees who cause waste through inexpert work. Likewise, experienced bakers are not only highly paid but very scarce, and many restaurants have gone so far as to hire a baker for a few hours a day. This is a good way to wind up serving stale bread and pastry.

Intelligent use of frozen and convenience foods reduces the number of employees, skilled and unskilled, needed and the amount of space required for storage and preparation. It lowers food costs because waste is eliminated, and it improves quality control because these foods can be bought to rigid specifications.

As a case in point, look at the following recipe for crab cakes.

Crabmeat Cakes

	17 2-cake servings or 34 1-cake	*51 2-cake servings or 102 1-cake*	*85 2-cake servings or 170 1-cake*
crabmeat, flaked and cleaned	2 lb. 8 oz.	7 lb. 8 oz.	12 lb. 8 oz.
onions, chopped fine	1 oz.	3 oz.	5 oz.
butter	4 oz.	12 oz.	1 lb. 4 oz.
bread flour	2 oz.	6 oz.	10 oz.
milk	1½ cups	1 qt. ½ cup	1 qt. 3½ cups
stale bread, chopped ⅛" pieces, crusts removed	8 oz.	1 lb. 8 oz.	2 lb. 8 oz.
eggs	2	6	10
worcestershire sauce	2 t sc.	2 T sc.	3 T sc.
cayenne pepper	⅛ t sc.	¼ t sc.	¼ t
salt	2 T	6 T	10T
parsley, chopped	¼ cup	¾ cup	1½ cups
sugar	1½ t	4½ t	2½ T
lemon juice	2 T	6 T	10 T

1. Saute onions in butter, but do not brown.
2. Add flour and stir until well combined. Add ⅔ of the milk to make a cream sauce. Stir until mixture thickens and has a smooth consistency.
3. Soak finely flaked stale bread in remaining milk.
4. Add beaten eggs, lemon juice, parsley, soaked bread, seasonings, and cream sauce to the flaked crabmeat and mix lightly.
5. Form into 2 oz. cakes using no. 20 scoop and shape cakes to ⅜" thickness.

Dip cakes in flour, egg batter and drain on wire rack.
6. Dip in finely sifted bread crumbs.
7. Dip in deep fat (325°F) for 2 minutes. They will be golden brown. Drain on unglazed paper. Salt lightly.

NOTE: After the crab cakes are breaded and ready to fry, they may be placed in single layers on parchment-lined trays and put in the refrigerator until ready to use.

If you use this recipe to prepare 85 servings of two cakes each, one employee must work approximately four hours, including cleanup time. At an hourly rate of $3 the cost of labor alone is 14 cents per order. And if he makes an error and the cakes have to be scrapped, the loss is yours alone.

Many restaurateurs who vividly remember the early frozen foods back in the late 1940s have refused to see what has happened since then. Yet the revolution has been colossal. With nitrogen, it is now possible to freeze at temperatures as low as 300° below zero. Packaging has become highly effective in protecting the product. The selection of both frozen dishes and processors is very wide, since many large restaurant chains have joined the regular food processors in putting their products on the open market.

Modern methods of handling and reconstituting also help ensure the quality of frozen food. A small, inexpensive indicator is available that automatically tells if a case of food has ever thawed before arrival. A great variety of efficient equipment has been developed for reconstituting frozen products.

One of the arguments against the use of frozen and convenience foods is that everyone will be serving the same dishes. But today the choice is large, and it is always possible to make your convenience foods distinctive by slight variations in seasonings, garnishes, and service methods. Even if only 50 percent of your menu is composed of these products, you will have more time to spend on standout features.

To close this chapter, here are some instructions for breading and cooking french fried shrimp which turn the dish into a specialty item. True, they are complicated, but they result in the finest shrimp anywhere. Saving time on the preparation of other foods and concentrating on an item like this may be the twist that will make your restaurant famous.

French Fried Shrimp

1. Clean the shrimp, leaving the tail.
2. Split the shrimp ¾ way to tail.
3. Remove the sandbag by washing in pan of water.
4. Soak the clean shrimp in milk ½ hour (½ pint of milk to 2 t salt).
5. Remove from milk and dip into flour (do not dip tail).
6. Dip in regular egg wash (8 eggs to 1 pint water).
7. Dip in crumbs (do not dip tail).
8. Place breaded shrimp in single layers on parchment-lined trays.
9. Be sure to separate the two parts of the split body when breading.
10. Fry in 325°F fat until golden brown.
11. Drain on paper towels to absorb fat.

Chapter 10

FOOD SERVICE: AN UNDERESTIMATED FACTOR

As discussed in Chapter 9, you can run a restaurant today with almost zero food preparation. But food service requires effort, and much of the current low productivity in our business can be traced to poor performance here. Providing good service is not nearly as complicated as it seems if you pay attention to its various elements, which are analyzed in this chapter.

CONSTANT SKILLED SUPERVISION

Lack of proper supervision is the main reason why food service is so bad in so many places. Skilled chefs, highly trained management, and all the skilled help in the operation should be in the food service area as much of the time as possible, especially during meals. At rush periods chefs and skilled cooks who are in the back preparing food and managers who are in the office pondering over last month's losses are not contributing as much to the business as they would if they were on the firing line.

Remember that the average restaurant is busy only 12 to 15 percent of the time it is open, because most people like to eat at mealtimes—from 12 noon to 2 P.M. and from 6 to 7:30 P.M. If you do not do business in these short periods, it is difficult to produce high sales. The manager should be on the spot helping to make the operation smooth, productive, and orderly. This does not mean that his place is in the dining room cleaning and bussing tables. If he is short of servers or cooks, he should work in the service aisle to expedite orders to the servers he does have. Much more can be accomplished by speeding the food to five or six servers than by having the manager act as one server. In Chapter 17 employee training will be discussed; here it is enough to point out that our weakest employee in most cases is the chef or manager who has never been formally trained, particularly in modern methods and systems.

To improve food service, management or the chef can do five simple things:

1. Check the entire service area carefully before serving times to make sure everything is in readiness to serve: the food on hand, the equipment functioning properly, and of course, the serving people at their stations. This is also an excellent time to test and sample the food to see that it is good.

2. As service begins, the top people should remain and see that all dishes are served attractively and at the right temperature.

3. When the rush really hits, top people can coordinate orders, acting as a liaison between cooks and servers. They can see that food is ordered correctly so that it all comes up for service at the same time, not piecemeal so that the steak is ready and getting cold because someone forgot to make the special salad plate. A good order coordinator can increase business 25 percent in a busy restaurant by smoothing out the food service. He can make sure that checks are properly written so the cooks can understand them. And he can time the placing of orders so that all dishes will come up when needed. If there are two guests at a table, it is poor business to serve one and tell the other that his order will be ready later. When the food is ready, the coordinator can summon the server and help to get him back to the dining area quickly.

4. The top people can step into weak spots where service is stuck, and often in a matter of minutes can have the operation running

smoothly again. Sometimes by merely shifting workers or bringing someone in from the dishroom, a manager can speed service and production.

5. With good supervision and control, the service area can be kept calm and quiet, and this in itself contributes to employee morale and improves the service. A frustrated, angry server will not treat the customers well.

FAST SERVICE

Regardless of the type of restaurant or the price level, food service must be fast. Many operators, especially those in the exclusive, high-check class, do not believe this. Yet even customers who wait patiently in line to be seated, dawdle over several drinks, and place their orders slowly want prompt service once they have ordered. Certainly it is to the restaurant's advantage to serve guests quickly, since its peak business occurs in a limited time. The faster the service, the greater the turnover and the higher the sales. Each seat costs so much and should produce a certain amount of sales per week, month, or year if you are to make a profit. And from the standpoint of the servers, most of their compensation comes from tips, so the more they can serve, the happier they will be. Since not all parties are big tippers, the steadiest income results from serving a number of parties.

HOT FOODS HOT, COLD FOODS COLD

Everyone in our business knows this, but few do anything about it. If the author had a dollar for every time he has been served cold hot food or warm cold food, he could have retired early. Butter plates and ice cream dishes are hot, entree service plates are stone cold. Actually, serving foods at correct and palatable temperatures requires only a few common-sense rules.

Hot Foods

Hot food serving units and thermotainers are not intended to heat foods but to hold them at designated temperatures (140 to 160°F, for example). If the foods placed in the service units are not at the right temperature, they will not be heated in time. Or if the holding unit is hot enough to heat them, it will be too hot to hold them without overcooking and drying.

Hot foods must be served on hot plates. Many restaurants make no provisions at all for heating plates or holding them hot for service. The majority have heating and holding units which are inadequate to take them through the entire meal, so that perhaps only the first hundred customers get hot plates.

If you are using a heated, self-leveling device (most hold 100 to 150 plates), realize that the plates are taken from the top. If you add plates that are not hot to this unit during the meal, you will not serve on hot plates. Make space if you can for several of these levelers and switch from one to the other during service. If this is not possible, provide an additional heated cabinet where plates can be heating prior to the time they are placed into the leveler.

Many operators depend on the heat from the dish machine to keep plates hot enough for food service. This is a poor system. If you have only a small number of plates and must wait for a few at a time to come from the final rinse, you will either run the legs off the dishwasher or cause constant delay at the hot food serving table.

Cold Foods

The same principles apply to serving chilled or cold foods except that the temperature is different. Serving refrigerators (pass-throughs or reach-ins) are not meant to chill food but to keep it cold for service. Salads, desserts, and juices should be already chilled when placed in them. The same applies to placing food on beds of ice for display or service: It must be cold when set into the ice.

Remember that small service refrigerators have large doors which are opened hundreds of times during meal service, and this brings the interior temperature up. Tests using timed recording thermometers on typical units show average temperatures of 50 to 60°F, especially during the serving period.

Though it is advisable to serve salads on chilled plates, few food service operations do because they are short of reach-in refrigeration. And because some managers think they can reduce breakage by operating with as few dishes as possible, plates for salads, butter, and ice cream have to be rushed into service from the hot final rinse of the dish machine, producing melted butter, soft ice cream, and wilted salads. If you do not have enough equipment to chill salad plates, at least have enough plates in service so that they can get down to room temperature.

The following attractive cold plates can be made ahead a few at a time and held in reach-in or pass-through refrigerators to speed service.

**Cold Sliced Chicken (or Turkey)
and Ham with Potato Salad
and Sliced Tomato or Vegetable**

½ oz. white meat of chicken or turkey
½ oz. dark meat
2 oz. canned ham, sliced
1 radish rose
⅔ cup potato salad
2 sweet pickle chips
3 slices tomato or vegetable
roll and butter
1 sprig watercress

1. Arrange 2 lettuce cups on one side of plate.
2. Fill 1 cup with potato salad, the other with slices of tomato or vegetable.
3. Place slices of meat on the other side of the plate.
4. Garnish with radish rose, watercress, and sweet pickle chips.
5. Serve a roll and butter.
6. Serve a 2 oz. portion of ham and 1 oz. portion of turkey.

Fruit Salad Bowl Topped with Sherbet

1 cup cubed lettuce, lightly salted
3 6 oz. portions of fresh fruits
1 no. 20 scoop of sherbet
2 T fruit french dressing

1. Place cubed lettuce in salad bowl.
2. Arrange fruit attractively on lettuce.
3. Top with sherbet and french dressing; garnish with watercress or mint.
4. In season garnish with fresh berries, pomegranate seeds, or avocado slices.

QUALITY FOODS COOKED RIGHT

For some reason food quality is the first corner that restaurants cut if profits are not adequate. Many operators think they are fooling the public when they lower the grade of foods they purchase, cut the size of portions, and omit ingredients, such as butter from sandwiches and eggs from sauces. This practice has hurt the entire food service business, especially in the past few years. When profits decrease, the right approach to the problem is not to skimp on food but to look for ways of increasing productivity and speeding service.

Many people wonder why restaurants often pay more for food than supermarket shoppers do. Offhand, it would seem that buying in larger quantities should reduce the cost. The fact is, of course, that the supermarkets are also buying in large quantities. But the most important reason is that commercial establishments need foods of higher quality and more uniformity than the housewife does.

Food served in restaurants must be prepared in advance and held for service, whereas the housewife cooks and serves immediately. Because commercial food is subject to this time lag it is often difficult to serve a quality product even when you have started with the best. Don't attempt to turn out good food with poor-quality ingredients. A cheap blend of coffee made fresh and served hot immediately will not taste too bad, but if the same coffee is held for any length of time and the temperature fluctuates, it will be unappetizing. Similarly, commercial foods must be uniform in size—cut and graded so that portions served will be alike. The housewife can buy lower-cost foods of varying sizes because she does not worry about serving the same amount each time.

Once you have started with quality products, use every known technique to cook and serve them right. Check the following suggestions against what you are now doing.

Proper Storage

The food service area should have adequate storage facilities at the correct temperatures. Reach-in refrigerators and freezers, which were discussed in Chapter 4 on food service equipment, are most important.

Correct cooking requires that foods be at a *certain temperature to start,* so be sure of this. If there is no reach-in freezer or it is not near the food service cook, he will leave the food out at room temperature instead of working from the freezer. To fry frozen french fried potatoes, for example, the instructions say to place the fries into the deep fat frozen for best results. But if the reach-in freezer is not near the fryers, the cook will put the frozen potatoes somewhere nearby in a hot place, which means that they will go into the hot fat thawed and produce an inferior product.

Correct Equipment

Like having good-quality ingredients to start with, the food service equipment must be right or it is difficult for anyone to produce good food. For example, if you are struggling with old or inadequate deep fat fryers, your fried foods will never make your reputation. If your fryers are undersized, you are frying in cool oil or fat and the product will be soggy.

Detailed Instructions

Once having developed your menu, work out the proper cooking instructions and service directions in detail and have them available for the cooks. What is more important, see that they are followed. There is a right way to serve every food, and it is the owner's and management's responsibility to find it. If you leave the procedures to the employees to work out on their own, you will always have trouble with food service.

The following recipes are given to show the care and detailed instructions needed to serve foods right.

Hard Cooked Eggs

1. Place eggs in pot with enough cold water to cover.
2. Add 1 T salt to each gallon of water.
3. Bring water to boiling point. *But do not boil.*
4. Hold in hot water on back of range for 15 minutes.
5. Drain hot water off at the end of the 15-minute period and cover eggs with cold water.
6. Peel eggs directly from cold water.

Egg Sandwich

1. Butter 1 slice bread and cover with sliced egg.
2. Cover egg with crisp lettuce.
3. Close with second slice of buttered bread.
4. Cut in two triangles.
5. Garnish plate with a piece of pickle.

Scrambled Eggs

1. Heat small frying pan and add just enough fat (about ½ oz. bacon fat or butter) to wet the surface of the pan.

2. Break 2 eggs in small bowl and beat with a fork to blend yolk and white slightly.
3. Add salt and pepper mixture to eggs.
4. When fat is hot but not smoking, add eggs.
5. Stir until eggs are just set but not dry or brown.
6. Garnish with parsley.

Service: 9" plate.

Grilled Chopped Steak or Salisbury Steak

1. Order the chopped sirloin or salisbury in ounces according to the size you serve: 4, 5, 6, 8 oz. portions, etc.
2. Place a small amount of fat on a medium hot griddle.
3. Salt and pepper steaks on the griddle.
4. Cook slightly; turn when steak is pink around the edges.
5. Cook other side until steak is cooked through but not dry.
6. Be sure to turn only once while cooking.
7. Do not press with spatula while cooking.

Service: 9" plate.

Automatic Timers

The food service industry has traditionally been laggard in spending money on equipment; it is easier to expect the cook to have a computer for a brain. The classic example has been the deep fat fryer with automatic lift baskets, which has been in existence for the lifetimes of most people in the business but is used on a very limited scale.

Most remodelings or new ventures exceed the original budget estimates, and as many cuts as possible are then made in the kitchen equipment. Top management, architects, and decorators reason that a good cook can produce a good meal on a coal stove. True, but we do not have this type of employee now, and the time has come to provide the best in equipment to produce good food. Make the cuts somewhere else.

Temperatures

This is an area too often left to the judgment of the food servers. Correct temperatures for certain foods should be established and controlled in equipment like fryers, griddles, broilers, hot food serving tables, thermotainers, heating or cooling dishes, refrigerators, and freezers. It is important to realize that even thermostats are not always accurate, especially if they are old. Check them from time to time.

Chapter 13 on equipment for the future has definite recommendations for equipment manufacturers on the problem of maintaining correct temperature. But here are some solutions that will help the food service operation now.

Deep fat fryers. The temperature of the fat must be right if good fried food is to be served. For frozen potatoes and frozen breaded items like shrimp and cutlets, fat should not be higher than 325°F or the food will brown before it is heated through. In several years of intensive testing, the author learned that modern fryers with quick heat recovery could be set at the one temperature of 325°F and never changed for all foods. This temperature coupled with automatic lift timing not only resulted in excellent fried products but produced enough savings on fat to pay for new fryers.

Most employees make two mistakes in operating deep fat fryers: (1) They overload the baskets, with the idea that if they pile food in more can be fried. Actually it is just the opposite; when the fryer is overloaded with cold or frozen food, the temperature of the fat drops considerably, and it takes much longer to fry. (2) They increase the temperature setting for the rush hours. They think that if they turn the fryer up to 425°F they will be able to fry more—which is true, but all they are doing is surface browning, not cooking the product through.

Griddle temperatures. Some new thermometers on the market will check temperatures on griddles, which need heat control as much as any other cooking device. Eggs and hot cakes, for example, require a lower temperature than meats. In cooking these products, you need two griddles, each set for the best temperature. When you get busy, see that employees do not turn the griddles up higher.

Broiler temperatures. These are hard to measure, and most broilers are incorrectly operated continuously at the top setting. If you have a broiler with ceramic coals, for example, it should be turned high at first and reduced as soon as the coals become heated. More restaurant fires are started by broilers than any other piece of equipment, and this is because they are usually too hot. Excessive temperatures also cause broilers to burn out much sooner than they would if operated correctly.

Holding units. Equipment used to hold food for service must be carefully checked. If the temperature is too high, the food will continue to cook; if too low, it will be cold when served or bacteria will grow.

All foods do not take the same holding temperature—creamed soups need a lower one than broth soups, for example. Besides temperature, humidity can also be controlled in many holding units to produce better food.

Temperatures throughout. The question of temperatures should be examined throughout the entire operation. Walk-ins must be at the right temperature, dish machine water for washing and rinsing have their correct temperatures, and good coffee cannot be made without water that is at least 205°F. Buy a few thermometers and do some checking on a regular basis—it is an easy way to improve your food.

Cooking in Small Quantities

One last simple rule: Heat and cook foods in small quantities often throughout the serving period. Of course, it is easier to prepare in large quantities far in advance of service, and some restaurants have the entire lunch or dinner ready to serve two or three hours beforehand. *No food can be good, cooked this far in advance.*

Set definite rules on when the food is to be prepared and in what quantities. One excellent way to control overproduction is to remove all large cooking vessels, including huge hot water bains-marie, so that employees are forced to prepare in smaller quantities.

CONSISTENCY IN FOOD AND SERVICE

The customer expects your food and service to be good every day, not just most days. He is not interested in your problems, even if the chef quit yesterday. It is discouraging to have a pleasant meal somewhere and return with a guest only to find that the food or the service is not as good as it was before. Organize your procedures and structure the employee situation so that you can maintain uniformity; don't depend on the skill of one or two employees who could leave and cause a drastic downturn in the quality of the food. Be consistent, too, in the portions you serve—not just to save money but so that your guests will know what to expect.

ATTRACTIVE-LOOKING FOOD

Sight is an important factor in the enjoyment of food. No matter how good an item may taste, if it does not look good, it will not please. Check your food before serving to make sure it looks appetizing. Plates must be clean, food neatly arranged, colors appealing, and attractive garnishes used to set off the entire dish. One drop of gravy on the edge of the plate ruins the appearance. Today there are many new chinas, casseroles, and other attractive serviceware to use for making dishes more tempting. Take some time to examine the food that is being served—start with the most popular items and see if you can't do something to make them even more attractive.

Using the following list of soup garnishes, for example, you can take a rather dull-looking soup and dress it up to add some interest.

Sliced stuffed olives. Try with tomato, green pea, and cream soups.

Toast squares with parmesan cheese. Dust 1 inch squares of toast with parmesan cheese and float on consomme, onion, green pea, vegetable, chicken gumbo, and cream soup.

Pimiento strips. Small strips of pimiento on cream of celery, green pea, cream of mushroom, and cream of chicken soup.

Green onion tops or chives. Slice very thin. Good with noodle, cream of chicken, chicken rice, clam chowder, cream of mushroom, tomato, and vegetable soup.

Good planning can make your food not only more attractive but easier to prepare, serve, and eat. The following recipe for an open club sandwich is superior in all these ways to the conventional double-decker held together with toothpicks.

Open Club Sandwich

2 slices white bread (toasted)
½ oz. whipped butter
1 cup lettuce (shredded)
2 oz. turkey (white meat only)
2 oz. thousand island dressing
2 strips cooked bacon (crisp)
2 medium slices tomato
2 slices egg (hard cooked)

1. Place one slice buttered toast in center of *cold* dinner plate.
2. Shredded lettuce on top of toast.
3. Turkey on top of lettuce.
4. Spread thousand island dressing over top of turkey.
5. Top the whole with strips of bacon crossed to form an X.
6. Cut second slice of buttered toast diagonally.
7. Place on opposite sides of open sandwich.
8. Place one slice ripe tomato on each half slice of toast.
9. Place one slice (center cut) of hard cooked egg on top of each tomato slice.

QUIET SERVICE

Most comedy skits about the restaurant business show noisy, confused service, punctuated with quarrels and broken dishes. Certainly food service employees are working under stress most of the time, and it is the job of management to organize the food service area and keep it peaceful. Not only is clatter disturbing to a guest, but he can sense confusion in the kitchen from the way he is served. If your servers are performing under difficulties or fighting with the cooks, they pass their unhappiness on to the person they come in contact with next: your paying guest.

ATTENTION TO SERVERS' PROBLEMS

"All waiters and waitresses complain," the manager says, without stopping to think why they do. His primary concern is still for the cook in the back or the cashier at the register rather than the servers. Frankly, it would be more important for his business to solve the problems of the servers.

First, the server is one of the few who have direct contact with your guest. Second, most of the server's income comes from tips, and if he is unable to give good service, he suffers financially. This is not true of the cook, cashier, or hostess, because they are paid a regular wage regardless of how efficiently they perform.

Think of these two factors when your servers are having difficulties, and do something to correct the situation. Chapter 3 on planning stressed the importance of proper service areas fitted with all the equipment needed to do a good job. Many restaurants are still carefully designing large kitchen areas where two people will work and then giving ten servers a tiny space to operate from.

USING UNSKILLED HELP

Other industries have learned how to utilize unskilled help by specialization, and we can, too.

Restaurant employees cannot be trained as well and as fast as they are needed, so that skilled help will not be available in the future. We must adapt to conditions as they are, not as we would like them to be. Operating with unskilled or semiskilled employees will require all the tools possible in the way of:

Automatic equipment
Timed equipment
Self-cleaning equipment
Equipment that is easy to clean
Timers
Correct small equipment like scoops, portion scales, ladles, etc.
Proper size and quantity of equipment to do a good job

In addition, instructions and directions for the service of food should be as simple and clear as humanly possible. This will make the on-the-job training easier so that unskilled employees can be used to good advantage.

The very name of our industry, food *service*, is an indication that the emphasis must be placed on this area, not on the manufacturing and preparation of food. Try turning your attention to the front of the house; service will improve, productivity will increase, and profits will rise.

Among the many examples of this transformation, consider the case of car service, which is still big business in many parts of the country. Years ago car hops were left to their own devices—they took the order, wrote the check, went to the kitchen area and called in each item, assembled everything at the same time, put it on the tray, and delivered it. With this system a good car hop could serve 35 cars in an evening of about 6 hours. Then someone decided to help the server with a new system: Pre-printed checks were pre-rung, and the server's order was put together on an assembly table while he was out writing more, so that he could pick up the completed tray and serve it without the old delay of paying for each. As a result, the average number of cars served jumped to 100 to 200 per car hop per 6 hours. A simple case of someone watching service and doing something to improve it.

It is interesting to note from productivity figures published in the trade magazines that the higher-priced operations do not lead the list for sales per employee per year. In most cases, it is the lower-check-average, fast-food establishments that clean up. These are operations which have been designed with great attention to service details so that there is no lost motion. They are places where on-premise preparation is at a minimum, and where all employees, including the manager, are out front at mealtimes.

Many chain operations have started their own commissaries to standardize product quality and save money on equipment, space, and labor in their many units. They have found, however, that another even more important gain resulted. When the preparation and manufacturing load became less in their units, and when all the employees including the managers began to spend more time and effort on the service, sales and profits began to increase.

Chapter 11

SANITATION: PLANNING CAN REDUCE THE WORK

The task of constantly maintaining a clean operation, which has long been one of the most difficult problems for food service ventures, is still prominent among the unpleasant jobs to be faced. It is true that the industry has better tools, equipment, and materials now, but the shortage of help has cancelled this gain. And in the future, food service operations must be cleaner than ever, not only because competition is keener and the public more selective but because old ideas and standards of cleanliness are changing in the face of growing concern about the ecology, pollution, and a cleaner environment.

Tomorrow, government agencies will be inspecting eating places much more carefully, and private groups and individuals will also be taking more interest. Environmental abuses, such as an inadequate exhaust system that throws fumes over the neighborhood, paper- and trash-littered parking lots, and trash areas with dirty cans of open garbage will not be tolerated. Dirty windows, peeling paint, or dirty carpets and floors, though these may not actually violate ordinances, will be noticed more by more people. It will soon be impossible for a restaurant to do anything but an excellent job of cleaning and housekeeping.

CLEAN AS YOU GO

This does not mean, in spite of advice given in much of the professional literature, that the food service operator should hire a night cleaning crew and set up daily and weekly schedules for accomplishing the various jobs. The cleaning crew approach is not only too expensive but unacceptable from the standpoint of effectiveness. The goal of good sanitation is to have the place clean and orderly at all times, not just when the night crew finishes work. Daytime employees will not keep their areas clean as they go when a crew is coming in to do the job anyhow.

The biggest positive step management can take in the field of sanitation is to make employees conscious of cleanliness. Keep at it until they accept as a basic rule the fact that the premises must always be clean, that there can be no excuse for dirty floors, counters, or tables, soiled or spotted dishes, glasses and flatware, greasy equipment, or messy rest rooms. Surprisingly, as soon as the cleaning crew is disbanded and the regular employees understand that they must clean as they go, the cleaning work becomes much lighter. When people know that they must clean up a mess, they see to it that the mess does not happen.

In a medium-sized restaurant with 35 employees, eliminate the all-night cleaning crew of two people; plan to have the cleaning done by the regular staff together with some professional help on the more difficult jobs (discussed later). Avoid hand work as much as possible by using self-cleaning and easy-maintenance equipment. With the proper layout and equipment, you can easily save the equivalent of 2½ full-time employees each week, with dollar savings of more than $10,000/year. And there are other advantages: The more often you clean, the easier the job (built-up dirt is hard to remove). Your place will be cleaner at all times. And employees can spend less time on work they hate and devote more to service—and increasing sales.

COOPERATE WITH HEALTH DEPARTMENTS

The second positive step in sanitation is to cooperate fully with all city, county, and state health departments and with the National Sanitation Foundation. Whether a new operation is being built or an existing one remodeled, the owner or architects should contact the local health department as early as possible to discuss the project and show plans and lists of equipment for the department's advice and approval. If changes are made as plans evolve, final plans should also be presented to the authorities for review. Many times if the health department is not contacted during planning or at the plan completion stage, an establishment will be ready to open but will be unable to get approval of the local authorities due to one or two planning oversights. In such cases, not only is an opening delayed but costly last-minute changes may be required to meet the health department requirements.

Cooperating with health departments means not only meeting design and layout requirements but following regulations from day to day, because the basic rules for sanitation have been developed over the years to protect the food service operator as well as the public. In fact, from years of experience the author recommends that employees be trained to go beyond the regulations; where food and feeding are concerned, it is impossible to be too clean or too careful. As a case in point, recent incidents of contaminated processed food received nationwide publicity and seriously damaged many businesses.

The following headline which appeared in *Nation's Restaurant News* (December 20, 1971) points up a trend: FLORIDA BILL WOULD ALLOW PATRONS TO INSPECT EATERIES' KITCHENS. The article reports that with the increase in the number of food service operations it is difficult for public authorities to make all the inspections needed.

Actually, it is time for the industry to assume responsibility for policing itself. Cleanliness in food service should not have to be forced on businesses; it is a top-priority requirement for success. True, there are unsanitary places doing business and making a profit, but the odds are much better for a super-clean establishment.

Following are some typical state board of health rules, together with a few notes by the author, to prove that these regulations are not dreamed up by some nut to make things difficult for you, but are good basic rules that must be followed in the food service industry.[1] Take time to read them; wouldn't you like to know that they are being followed in the next restaurant you dine in?

Purchase and Receipt of Food

"Food received or used in food service establishments shall be from sources approved or considered satisfactory by the health authority

---

[1]*Rules of State Board of Health, The Sanitary Code of Florida.* Chap. 170C-16, "Food Service."

and shall be clean; wholesome; free from spoilage, adulteration and misbranding; and be safe for human consumption."

"Poultry and meats received or used in a food service establishment shall be identified as having been officially inspected for wholesomeness and sanitation under a federal or state regulatory program."

"No food intended for human consumption shall be served, sold or offered for sale that is *unwholesome, adulterated, misbranded, unsafe or in any way likely to injure the public health.*"

Note: All this is so easy—easy to select reputable purveyors, easy to look for inspection stamps, to smell bad food. As mentioned in other chapters, a little device now on cases of frozen food even indicates whether the case has ever thawed.

Food Storage

"Perishable foods shall be stored at such temperatures as will protect against spoilage. All potentially hazardous foods shall be kept at safe temperatures (*40 degrees or below and 150 degrees or above*) except during necessary periods of preparation and service."

"Frozen foods shall be kept at or below zero degrees Fahrenheit except when being thawed for preparation or use. Frozen foods shall be thawed at refrigeration temperatures of 40 degrees Fahrenheit or below, or under cold running tap water or quick thawed as part of the cooking process."

"Food shall be stored above the floor on clean shelves, racks, dollies or other clean surfaces in such a manner as to be protected from splash and other contamination."

Note: Proper storage was covered in Chapter 8 on purchasing and storage. Simple safeguards include thermometers on refrigerators that will tell you at a glance if temperatures are right.

Food Preparation and Service

"Raw, unprocessed fruits and vegetables shall be thoroughly washed before use."

"Pork products shall be thoroughly cooked to heat all parts of the meat to a minimum temperature of 150 degrees Fahrenheit."

"Completed custard-filled and cream-filled pastries shall be refrigerated (40 degrees or below) promptly after preparation and held there until served."

"Ice-making machines shall utilize water from an approved source and shall be constructed, installed, operated and maintained so as to prevent the contamination of the ice."

"Individual portions of food once served to a customer shall not be served again."

Note: The four previous chapters have given ideas and procedures for the improvement of preparation and service. To their discussion of frozen and convenience foods it is worth adding here that these foods make the sanitation job much easier by eliminating the peeling, long preparation time, and work involved in making food.

Building Facilities

"All rooms in which food is stored, prepared or served, utensils are washed, toilet, dressing and locker rooms and garbage storage areas shall be well ventilated."

"The floor surfaces in kitchens and all the rooms and areas in which food is stored or prepared, utensils are washed or stored, walk-in refrigerators, garbage and rubbish rooms and toilet, dressing or locker rooms shall be smooth, non-absorbent material and so constructed as to be easily cleaned."

"Each food service establishment shall be provided with adequate and conveniently located toilet facilities for its employees and patrons."

"Adequate facilities shall be provided for the orderly storage of employees' clothing and personal belongings."

Note: Even though these rules come under the heading of good planning and design, there is no reason why an existing operation cannot be remodeled to incorporate them.

Equipment

"Approved facilities for manual or mechanical dishwashing of multi-use eating and drinking utensils. Suitable facilities shall be provided for removing food scraps and food residue from utensils including glasses before they are placed in wash water or wash compartment."

"For a hot water spray for final rinsing or sanitizing, the hot water system shall provide water at a temperature of at least 180 degrees Fahrenheit to the machine during all periods of dishwashing operations."

"Equipment shall be so installed as to facilitate the cleaning thereof and of all adjacent areas with the equipment in place, *unless the equipment is readily movable for this purpose."*

"Conveniently located sinks with running water, waste disposal units or containers or similar equipment for the washing, trimming and similar preparation of foods."

"All garbage and rubbish containing food wastes shall, prior to disposal, be kept in leakproof, non-absorbent containers which shall be kept covered with tight-fitting lids.'

Note: Proper selection of equipment is the key here. Chapters 4 through 7 furnish guidelines. If your operation is already in existence, see that you buy the right piece as it becomes necessary to replace equipment.

Employee Regulations

"No person while affected with any disease in a communicable form or while a carrier of such disease shall work in any capacity in a food service establishment."

"All employees shall wear clean outer garments, maintain a high degree of personal cleanliness and conform to hygienic practices during all periods of duty."

"Employees shall not smoke or use tobacco in any form while engaged in the preparation or service of food or while handling any utensils or equipment."

Note: Many operators say that employee regulations are difficult to police, but if you clearly spell out the rules and post them, there should be little trouble. These regulations do require enforcement and checking. It is like the argument that employees won't punch time cards, to which the answer is simple: then employees won't get paid.

Sanitation Procedures

"All walls and ceilings including doors, windows, skylights, screens and similar closures shall be kept clean and in good repair."

"Soiled cloths, linens, aprons, coats, and other uniform apparel shall be kept in suitable containers until removed for laundering."

"All parts of the establishment and its premises shall be neat, clean and free of litter and rubbish."

"Effective control measures shall be taken to protect against the entrance into the food establishment, and the breeding or presence on the premises of rodents, flies, roaches and other vermin."

"No live birds or animals shall be allowed in a food service establishment."

"Spoons, knives and forks shall be picked up and touched only by their handles. Cups, glasses and bowls shall be handled so that fingers or thumbs do not contact inside or outer surfaces."

"The use of steel wool for cleaning food contact surfaces is prohibited."

"Cloths used by waiters, chefs and other personnel for wiping food contact surfaces shall be clean and shall be used for no other purpose."

"The health authority shall inspect all food service establishments and other places where food is served to or prepared for service to the public as often as deemed necessary for enforcement."

Note: Like employee regulations, sanitation procedures must be simply and clearly spelled out for all personnel. Some of these rules are very easy to follow—for example, if steel wool is prohibited, see that there is none on the premises.

DESIGNING FOR SANITATION

When building, remodeling, or replacing, make sure the designer includes all the very latest improvements to help you with the job of cleaning.

Self-Cleaning Equipment

Buy self-cleaning equipment when it is available, and when it is not, check to make sure it is easy to clean. Use self-cleaning range ovens, convection ovens, easy-to-clean griddles. Install self-closing doors and drawers to prevent hand prints. Also buy multiple units, so one can be taken out for a fast steam-cleaning.

Mobile Equipment

Put everything possible on casters, including reach-in refrigerators and freezers so they can be moved for cleaning. Since it is possible in many areas to use gas, quick disconnects or long flexible connections, both gas and electric equipment can be bought on casters: fryers, grills, broilers, ranges, ovens, and the like.

Up Off the Floor

Mopping, scrubbing, or sweeping floors is one of the hardest tasks of all, so remove obstacles from the floor. Use mobile equipment and move it to allow a clean sweep in floor maintenance. Bring plumbing and electrical lines down from ceilings rather than up through floors. Cantilever pieces of equipment from the wall to do away with worrisome legs. And build rest rooms with everything off the floor—partitions, toilets, wash bowls, and urinals.

Easy-to-Clean Materials

Select easy-to-clean materials for floors, walls, ceilings, and equipment. Be careful about carpets in kitchens—they sound good and have some advantages, but ground-in food spills are almost impossible to remove.

Also select materials that do not show dirt and smears. Stainless steel, for example, though an excellent material for reach-in refrigerator doors, picks up unsightly streaks and prints which are not actually "dirt" but are very difficult to remove. Wood-grain vinyl-covered doors on reach-ins eliminate this problem and add color and warmth to the equipment.

Exhaust System

In addition to removing heat and fumes, a good exhaust system has a water spray to eliminate much of the grease before it gets into the air. The system should have removable grease filters that can be run through the dish machine daily. Once grease gets into fabrics and on surfaces, your cleaning job will be much harder.

Sinks Everywhere

Have plenty of sinks—hand sinks, utility sinks, mop sinks—located in the right places. The cost of sinks has decreased with new standard methods of manufacture, and nothing will help more to keep the operation clean than sinks located where employees will use them for wiping and cleaning. For example, unless there is a sink at hand where an employee can rinse the cloth he uses to wipe dining room tables, it will become dirty and greasy and leave unsanitary streaks. Similarly, a mop sink must be provided where mops can be rinsed clean after each use and then hung to air. Otherwise dirty, smelly mops will be used even in the public areas. These details of planning are very important if you expect people to do their jobs correctly.

Hot Water

Most food service operations have difficulties meeting sanitation as well as food preparation and service requirements for hot water because their hot water generating and transmission systems are not adequate. There are, of course, many hot water systems with various types of heaters and holding tanks from which your architect and his engineers can choose. The best way to protect against errors in selecting a system is to make sure you provide your architect with complete information on how much hot water will be needed to supply all the various points of use. In addition, the equipment specifications must also include the additional boosters needed for wash tanks and rinses on dish machines and pot sinks to meet National Sanitation Foundation requirements.

In general, it would pay to overspecify, rather than underspecify, on the hot water system because it is such an important part of the overall operation. And good sanitation and cleaning in all areas cannot be accomplished without enough hot water at proper temperatures.

Storing Cleaning Supplies

Provide convenient spaces for storing soaps, powders, paper towels, sweepers, brooms, and other cleaning supplies. This will encourage frequent cleaning and save on the expensive supplies and implements needed for ground-in dirt.

Garbage Handling

Don't leave garbage and trash handling to chance; study the best way to handle removal and storage, whether it be in cans or by compaction, disposers, incineration, or pulping. Nothing will drive guests away faster than a large pile of smelly trash on the parking lot, yet this is not an uncommon sight.

One excellent garbage handling system is to install a disposer large enough for all heavy food from the dining area, the remaining food from the automatic prescraper on the warehandling machine, and all trim and peelings from the salad and vegetable area. Combine this with a compactor to be used mornings in the preparation area for all boxes, cans, and containers and to be moved to the warewashing area at mealtimes to compact trash from the meal for disposal in small sealed containers.

Ventilation

See that the architect and his ventilating engineer provide good ventilation for the work and storage areas. Naturally there are very few air-conditioned kitchens, but some air movement can be arranged to relieve the heat.

Heating and air conditioning systems should have positive pressure in dining areas and some negative (exhaust) pressure in kitchens and service areas. It is a simple matter of balancing intakes and outgoes to prevent odors from going into the dining area and to bring a little of its cooler air into the kitchen, where it will be appreciated. Even in an existing operation, an experienced ventilation engineer can sometimes do much with minor adjustments to vents and louvers.

Mechanical Equipment for Cleaning

Get all the mechanical tools possible to help with cleaning chores. A good heavy-duty vacuum cleaner with attachments will save labor and even prolong the life of rugs and drapes. If you have large scrubbable floor areas, a machine that scrubs, rinses, and dries may be practical. A small, manual carpet sweeper with revolving brushes is excellent for a quick brush-up job in the dining room during mealtime without disturbing guests. Steam and pressure cleaners can be considered for cleaning equipment, carts, and shelving units. And although in the past we swept parking lots by hand with large push brooms, it is wise today to use a power machine that will do a good job in a short time.

Professional Cleaners for Some Jobs

To assist with the day-to-day cleaning work, hire professionals for some of the larger tasks such as window cleaning, lawn and shrubbery maintenance, cleaning outdoor signs, carpet cleaning, periodic thorough cleaning of walls and ceilings, ventilation duct cleaning, and service for repair, maintenance, and cleaning of air conditioning and heating ducts and vents. Although the regular monthly charges may seem high, these are difficult jobs to include in your routine schedule and in most cases cannot be done as well or cheaply by your staff.

For example, an experienced window cleaner will do a faster and better job than one of your own employees who is not trained and does not have the proper equipment. And for the average restaurant, regular carpet cleaning is best placed in the hands of professionals. If you have a very large volume food operation with qualified maintenance and cleaning personnel, it pays to have a scrubber vacuum machine. However, unskilled workers can do great damage, since too much liquid will produce rotting and destroy an expensive carpet. The average operator should remove spots often and vacuum frequently, but leave the deep cleaning to carpet specialists.

Burnishing Silver

If you use silver, place the burnisher in the warewashing area near the place where flatware is sorted. Instead of burnishing all the silver each Thursday night (which is a difficult task and does not keep it bright from day to day), put tarnished pieces into the burnisher as they are found, and burnish several times a day. This will give you much brighter silver at the same time that it does not seem like such a huge job.

Shelving

Reach-in refrigerators and freezers that use small half-size plastic trays instead of wire shelves are much easier to clean. The trays can be washed in the dish machine, and, with the trays out, it is a simple matter to wipe the box. Similarly, solid removable shelf units for storage areas are easy to clean and stay cleaner from the start, since spills cannot leak from top to bottom.

These suggestions, though they do not exhaust the possibilities, show how much can be done to simplify the seemingly impossible task of keeping clean. With proper planning, good equipment, the use of professional help for the large jobs, and a constant clean-as-you-go program, your sanitation problems can be greatly reduced and your establishment much cleaner at all times.

Part IV

PLANNING FOR GROWTH AND CHANGE

Chapter 12

MOVING TOWARD AUTOMATION: CONSIDER WHAT'S AVAILABLE NOW

Soon after World War II, some leaders in the food service industry recognized the need for more automation, and started research and development on a limited scale. Several problems arose immediately, however.

BARRIERS TO AUTOMATION

First, although the food service industry in total is a huge business, it is made up of hundreds of thousands of small components. Only a few chains had the money for R & D, and most of them chose to invest it in expansion instead. Second, there is little uniformity in our business. Most eating places prepare, serve, and operate differently, and this makes automation difficult. Car manufacturers, in contrast, turn out different cars but can use the same assembly methods and adopt the same automation techniques. Third, food service equipment manufacturers did not want to invest a lot of money in new automatic equipment. The models they already had were selling, and they were not getting any strong requests for new ideas from either the operators or the design and layout people. There was a definite need for improvement, but no one wanted to stick his neck out.

The few attempts to bring out new automatic or semi-automatic equipment were not met with much enthusiasm. For example, automatic lifts for fryers were made many years ago, but to this day they are not widely accepted. The author remembers helping to put together the first shake freezer and the terrific effort involved in getting a manufacturer to consider producing it. The food service industry did not accept even the semi-automatic approach to the equipment and labor problem, and today many operators are still doing everything by hand. An example is the simple racks used for washing glasses and cups, which were intended not only to carry the glasses and cups through the machine, but to transport them out to the service area. Probably half of all restaurants are still washing in these racks and then transferring each glass and cup to a tray to be carried out to the service stands. Of course, the extra work, handling, cost, and breakage are staggering, but the ancient procedure persists, both because the glass and cup racks are considered expensive and it has been decided to buy only a few of them, and because the designer usually forgot to allow enough space for them on the serving stands or to provide places to put the empty racks.

A few years ago there arose a great hue and cry about automation. Most speeches, articles, and seminars within the industry made it the central theme, and many expensive pieces of equipment began to appear for eliminating handwork. Everyone thought that the problems of labor and productivity would be solved, but the automation cry died away like the earlier efforts to get a special minimum wage law for the food service industry and the drive to train thousands of skilled cooks who would offset the need for any sort of physical or equipment help. Now the time has come to take a realistic look at automation in our industry and develop a sensible approach.

Automation for Food Manufacturers

The degree of pure automation in a given technology depends upon the volume of business done. Any industry with volume sales can afford automatic equipment—not only the initial investment but the high maintenance costs.

This brings us to the food manufacturing companies, which are producing frozen and convenience foods for restaurants on a large scale. Previous chapters have emphasized that all operators should be using these ready foods in order to get out of the food manufacturing business and concentrate on food serving: The more they do, the more automation the food manufacturers will be able to pay for. And as the manufacturers grow larger and more automated, the better the products they can produce while lowering costs (or at least, holding the cost line). Indirectly, all the small operators who cannot afford expensive automation will benefit.

Semi-Automation for Food Service

Chapter 13 on equipment for the future describes types of equipment and methods that will be needed in the food service industry as current trends shape future necessities. For the time being, let's concentrate on semi-automation, making full use of what already exists that will boost productivity and service. The sooner we learn that there is no single miracle item to solve our problems, the faster we will advance. Little improvements, like the proper use of cup and glass racks to avoid rehandling, can add up to give positive results on a large scale. Analyze your operation carefully; if you introduce only five or six small changes each month, the first year of effort can make a great difference.

SEMI-AUTOMATIC EQUIPMENT

The following list brings together a number of semi-automatic aids, most of them described in other chapters, that are designed to reduce hand lifting, hand carrying, walking, stooping, bending, and other tiring motions. Many are not expensive, but remember that before buying anything in the equipment line you should make sure it is suitable for your own operation. For example, cutting machines are available that will chop cases of lettuce in seconds, but they are not practical for small- or medium-size places. Also study the equipment and talk with other users to find out the problems of maintenance: taking apart, cleaning, putting together, and repairing.

Not all the items listed are new—many have been on the market for years—but most restaurants are not taking advantage of them. Often they are bought for new ventures and then not used because handling procedures are left up to the employee, who decides to do the job in his own way. Here again, it is management who must see that people use the equipment and use it properly. If you purchase a clean dish cart (and you should), see that it is put in action to take hundreds of dishes around to the points of service at one time; don't let the busboy go on carrying 20 or 30 dishes in his arms. Too many of the good ideas in our business die on the vine because employees decide they are not workable and management does not want to rock the boat.

Hand truck. A simple, inexpensive two-wheel truck with handles that will enable a man to take several cases at a time from place to place without straining.

Four-wheel flat bed truck. An inexpensive way to transport heavy items like garbage cans and large bags of flour and sugar.

Three-shelf utility cart. Small and inexpensive, but a great help in the kitchen for going to and from storage areas for supplies. One trip with this cart will save many steps.

Power lot sweeper. Parking lots in most food service operations are either swept by hand with a push broom or not cleaned at all. Nothing hurts business like a dirty parking lot or untidy entrance, so consider a power sweeper that will make this job easier and keep the exterior neat and clean.

Power floor scrubber. Hand mopping, brush scrubbing, hosing down, and rinsing are unpleasant jobs and do not always produce good results. If you have large floor areas, consider machine scrubbers, buffers, and other such equipment.

Portable pressure or steam cleaners. Many practical units of this type are available that not only reduce some of the hand labor but do a better job of sanitizing. They are excellent for cleaning shelving, trucks, dollies, work tables, and many other items.

Portable power conveyor belt. For any operation with a multi-floor problem, this unit can save a great deal of time and effort. Belts are adjustable for angle and speed and will bring cases down as well as take them up.

Gravity conveyors. Here is another standard product widely used in many industries but seldom applied in food service work. These conveyors differ from the power-driven belt or link belt in that they are not mechanical. They can be on wheels or rollers, and by slanting or tilting them, the tray or box will move along on its own. Naturally, they are much less expensive than power belts with their motors and washing devices. A simple roller-type gravity conveyor can be used in nursing homes and hospitals to form an inexpensive tray make-up unit: As one dish is placed on it, the tray can be pushed to the next station for the next item, and so on until it reaches the end of the line. Conveyors can also take products to and from storage areas or can transport trays and boxes of soiled dishes to warewashing areas. These standard wheel- or roller-type conveyors come in sections that can be taken apart for easy cleaning.

Pot washing machine. For years this has been considered suitable only for very large operations, but the time has come to eliminate hand pot washing from every food service establishment, large or small. Chapter 13 on equipment for the future suggests measures that will enable all eating places to afford machine pot washing.

Rack washers. For the larger institutions like hospitals, schools, and cafeterias, a rack washer could perform many chores now being done by hand. Carts, trucks, shelving, pots, and pans all can be washed automatically and thoroughly in this unit.

Compactor. A recent development in our field and one that is gaining more recognition each day. Not all the problems in using it have been solved, but it takes the nightmare out of handling trash and garbage. Make sure the compactor you choose will do the job you want done, and, if possible, install it at the source of the waste to avoid rehandling.

Bus carts. One of the oldest aids in our business, and one that should be used more to avoid the hand carrying, walking, and breakage now evident in so many dining areas. These carts are being made in attractive designs and colors to hide most of the waste and soiled ware they carry.

Serving carts. Why is it still common practice for the server to come into the dining area carrying a huge tray of plates of food that cannot be set down without help? Why can't we use a small multi-level service cart on casters, cover the attractively arranged plates and platters of food with stacking covers, stack them neatly on the serving cart, add other items like salads and hot breads, and wheel the entire load into the serving area and up to the table? There it can be neatly and easily served without a weight-and-balancing act.

Conveyors to take full racks of dishes into and out of dish machines. Excluding the many round warewashers now being produced, conventional dish machines and tables should be equipped with simple conveyors to ease the job of pushing or lifting heavy racks into the machine and pulling them out. It is hard to imagine any conveyor-type dish machine not having roller conveyors, especially at the clean end so that the racks of clean ware do not have to be pulled, pushed, and lifted to a place where the ware can drain before being sorted and stacked. It is not a matter of large sums of money, because the power conveyor in the machine will push the racks out on the roller conveyor.

Automatic pre-rinse (or pre-scrap). In any operation needing a two-tank conveyor dishwasher, an automatic pre-rinse (pre-scrap) should always be added. If the volume of business requires a machine this large, you cannot afford to scrap soiled ware by hand. And it is important to remove scraps before putting the ware into the wash tank or it will not come out clean. If disposers are not prohibited by code, the pre-scrap should be operated with fresh water and a disposer. The cost of the additional water is nowhere near the labor cost of constantly emptying screens and cleaning spray arms and nozzles. Naturally, the pre-wash can be activated by the rack so that the water and disposer operate only when a rack is in position.

Dollies for racks of cups and glasses and clean dish carts. As Chapter 6 emphasized, all warehandling areas regardless of size should have these. Space can be reserved for them under the soiled and clean dish tables. By providing a place to put the clean ware quickly, reducing rehandling, and making it easy to distribute ware back to the service areas, these units greatly reduce labor, steps, and breakage.

Product levelers. Spring-loaded levelers that bring dishes, trays, pans, racks, and so on up to work height as the previous item is removed should be utilized whenever feasible in terms of cost and space. They are available in many sizes for many different items and in models that are heated or refrigerated. Levelers can be expensive but, when properly used, they substantially speed service and save labor.

Automatic fryer lifts. These should be used in all operations regardless of the price. They are most valuable in the small place where one cook is trying to do all jobs, because the fried shrimp will be removed from the hot fat in 2½ minutes, even if the cook is at the other end of the kitchen.

Automatic sandwich grilling. Although this is a relatively minor item, an automatic sandwich griller is another aid to productivity and a better product.

Automatic toasters and roll grills. Be sure you have enough automatic toasters to serve a fresh piece of toast. Many operations must prepare the toast ahead to keep up with the demand. If you butter grill rolls for sandwiches, by all means invest in an automatic roll grill. Not only will this give you a uniform product, but it will prevent the cook from serving rolls that are barely toasted.

Timers of all kinds. Invest in all the timing devices possible on all kinds of equipment. Remember that you will be working with fewer employees in the future.

Automatic egg boilers. An old-timer in the food service industry. If you do breakfast business, buy one.

Automatic self-cleaning equipment. After the domestic market started with self-cleaning ovens, the commercial field began to follow suit. Cleaning equipment is a hard job; automate it wherever possible.

Ice maker-dispenser. The automatic ice maker is widely used and the maker-dispensers are gaining ground. Besides speeding service, dispensers ensure sanitation and prevent accidents. Although health regulations call for the use of scoops, most ice is actually put into glasses by hand or by dipping the glass into the ice. Should the glass crack, chip, or break, someone may be injured.

Automatic defrost. Here is another area where the commercial field has lagged far behind the domestic market. Units with this feature, however, are now being produced even for ice cream cabinets. Insist on getting automatic defrost equipment; not only is there a great deal of labor involved in unloading and removing frost from freezers with warm water or heaters but the quality of the frozen food is affected. Also, heavy layers of frost are usually chipped off with tools which damage the walls of the freezer.

Automatic evaporators for condensers. For reach-in refrigerators these are now in general use. They eliminate the need for drains, save the constant work of wiping up the water from the bottom of the refrigerator, and make it possible to have refrigerators on casters for mobility.

Automatic coffee maker. Good coffee demands correct water temperature for brewing, consistent brewing time, and correct temperature for holding. An automatic coffee maker, whether the bottle or urn type, is a must.

Temperature controls. If thermostats are available, by all means use them and pre-set against unnecessary change.

Automatic wash exhaust hoods. Systems that utilize a constant water spray for removing grease, smoke, and odors are worth investigating. In addition to doing a better job in carrying away impurities, they protect against costly fires.

Self-closing drawers and doors. Drawers and doors should always have recessed pulls and magnetic closers, since these reduce maintenance, save on refrigeration, and prevent accidents. In the near future perhaps more freezer drawers will also be available.

Waste disposers. If permitted and feasible, disposers should be used in preparation and warehandling areas to eliminate all garbage handling possible.

Automatic liquor dispensers. Gaining in use for bar establishments because of the control and ease of operation.

Automatic carbonated beverage systems. Excellent for bars and regular service. Convenient stations can be placed where needed to speed service and serve beverages at the right temperature.

Change makers—pre-set and computer-registers. Progress in this field of control has been rapid. Investigate machines that print check items, do the addition (including tax), compute the change, and give accurate counts of items sold.

Ice cream freezers. Both the automatic shake and ice cream freezers are well known in the fast food industry, but few service restaurants have taken advantage of machines like this. Much can be done with them to serve an array of desserts easily and profitably. Examine the manufacturers' folders, which show some of the attractive desserts possible.

Many operators are slow to adopt semi-automatic features like the ones listed in this chapter because they mean a change in old routines and arouse some resistance from employees. Other managements object to the price, although the initial cost increase is often insignificant compared with the additional cost of operating an old hand model for years. Actually, operators and many designers do not keep up to date on the latest advances. The easy road is to continue using what has been used in the past, even though this does little to solve contemporary problems.

The next time you build, remodel, or replace equipment, take time to investigate new equipment and methods. If you had only the items listed above (and many more are available), your profits would be larger, your service would be faster, and, most important, the quality and consistency of your food would be higher. Every time the chance for human error goes down, quality goes up.

Now that labor and all other costs have risen sharply, we can expect more action in the field of automation or semi-automation. Keep your mind and eyes open from now on for new ideas, systems, products, and equipment. The trade publications are an excellent source for finding out what is new; equipment shows also give operators and owners a chance to see and discuss a host of products. Local restaurant associations could perform a valuable service if they would devote one meeting every few months to an open discussion of new products and ideas.

While you are looking for new equipment, don't forget to check on frozen and convenience foods in the future. You may find that they can save you from investing in that new piece of production equipment or even enable you to discard something you are now using. A recent article in a trade magazine indicates that sales of frozen foods will grow 53.1 percent in the next three years to a total value of $12.3 billion.[1] Now is the time for us to take a good look at what we are doing, stop complaining and dreaming, and move ahead with other industries.

---

[1]"Frozen Foods Will Grow 53.1% by 1975 to a Total Value of $12.3 Billion." *Quick Frozen Foods*, March 1972.

Chapter 13

EQUIPMENT FOR THE FUTURE: WHAT WE NEED

There is a great need for new equipment, systems, methods, and devices in the food service industry. We must have automatic, semi-automatic, and labor-saving equipment to offset shortages in our employees' numbers and skills. The efforts in this direction over the past 20 years have been hit or miss, with a lack of enthusiasm from operators, designers, and equipment manufacturers. When the brief spurt of automation did hit, many new devices were quickly designed and manufactured without much thought. They turned out to be too expensive and impractical for use, and at this point the manufacturers lost most of their desire to try anything new. Much like the convenience food program in the 1950s and 1960s, the automation drive fizzled out.

OPERATORS AND MANUFACTURERS: GIVE A LITTLE

The first step is to establish a dialogue between the industry and the equipment designers and manufacturers. The author got started in the design and layout business while working for a large food service chain which had an expansion program underway. The new restaurants were not doing the job, for the simple reason that the operators did not understand the plans and blueprints, while the designers knew nothing about food service. Unless a designer has actually worked in restaurants and seen the operating problems over a long period of time, it is difficult to come up with plans that will be practical under many different circumstances. Most of the automatic equipment existing today can only be used for one particular type of establishment or by very large volume operations that can afford high investment and maintenance costs. For the future, we need new equipment which is:

Versatile. So that it can do more than one type of job in more than one place.

Mobile. For flexibility and ease of cleaning.

Less expensive. A $5,000 automatic broiler is fine, but it cannot be purchased by medium-sized and small ventures.

Easier to operate. The highly skilled design engineer may think his machine is simple, but he should go out into the field and see whether unskilled help can use it.

Easier to clean. Most equipment today is very difficult to clean because of bad design or poor choice of materials.

Fewer loose parts. Manufacturers today provide technically written instruction manuals telling the restaurant employee how to take the machine apart to clean it. If it has a number of separate pieces, he is likely to put it back together wrong or lose some of the parts.

Easier to repair and maintain. Even if a machine does an excellent job, it becomes a problem if a local service man cannot repair it easily and quickly.

Self-contained. Units that are self-contained are easily moved from place to place and save the cost of running expensive lines.

More compact. With fewer employees, food service areas are getting smaller. Equipment must also get smaller without losing capacity.

More complete packages and systems. Inefficiency in the dishwashing area, for example, is rarely caused by the machine (most are oversized) but by the supporting equipment and tables. Similarly, a slicing machine is much more useful if it is on a mobile stand, so the manufacturer should include a good stand as an accessory. In fact, he should show the slicer on this stand.

Fewer models. The variety of models on the market today not only confuses the designers and operators but increases the price of the machines. With fewer models and variations, it will be possible to mass-produce and lower prices.

Less weight, effort, lifting, drudgery. It is time to design these features out. Manufacturers should take a look at the employees of today—the mighty men of brawn are gone.

The slow progress in the improvement of equipment for the food service industry cannot be blamed on operators or manufacturers alone but on both, and both sides need to do something about it.

Operators

1. *Recognize the need for better equipment* to solve problems of productivity and service in the future. Certainly better-trained employees will help, but improved equipment is essential to improve the quality of the product served.

2. *Change the "too expensive" attitude.* Many operators who still think in the terms of the low wage era are turning down excellent pieces of equipment that would save many times their cost. Years ago, for example, the job of going through guest checks and tabulating the number of items sold was done by the servers, whose hourly wage was next to nothing. Today there are many fine electronic registers that will record counts as checks are rung, eliminating the now expensive manual counting.

3. *Accept standard models.* Responsibility for the great diversity of models on the market rests not with the manufacturers but with facility designers and operators, each of whom seems to have some little idea about equipment that he thinks is all-important. The variety of layouts, systems, and methods demanded is still causing models and variations to multiply each year and costs to increase as well because most pieces of equipment being sold are almost custom models even though they are listed in catalogues.

For instance, try specifying and ordering what should be two simple pieces of equipment that by now should have become standardized and mass-produced: reach-in refrigerators and ranges. Reach-in refrigerators come in all sizes and shapes; they are self-contained or remote-controlled; there are several electrical choices and many choices of doors, drawers, colors, materials for the interior and exterior, casters or legs, evaporators, drains, lights, shelving, slides for many types of pans and trays, and freezer position; there is even a choice of warranty on the condenser. The same confusion exists in the selection of a range, and as discussed in Chapter 6, there are many unnecessary sizes and lengths of dishwashers too.

4. *Be willing to test equipment* in an intelligent and fair manner. It is management's responsibility to decide what new equipment is needed within a given price range, determine the best place and use for it, see that it is installed correctly, and thoroughly instruct employees on the reason for the machine and on how it is to be operated, cleaned, and maintained. Finally, give the equipment a fair trial; adjustments may be needed and the employee may not like the machine at first, but allow time and follow up to see that it is being used correctly.

Equipment Manufacturers

1. *Spend more time in the field* and more time learning exactly what is best for *the most operators.* Many pieces of equipment now being produced were requested by one operator.

2. *Reduce the number of models and variations.* Every manufacturer is trying to get 100 percent of the sales and market. Perhaps there would be more profit and fewer headaches in getting 50 percent of the market with a good standard model.

3. *Do everything possible to instruct the user* in operating the equipment. The more we get into automation and semi-automation in the food service industry, the bigger the teaching job will be. Get the instructions and directions down to the level of the people who will be using the machine.

4. *Think in terms of packages and systems.* If a machine lacks support equipment, it will not perform right. Even if the manufacturer does not himself produce the support piece, he should make it available or recommend it to the user.

5. *Plan equipment with cleaner lines.* Design smoother surfaces with fewer bolts, handles, and other projections that make wiping difficult. Chrome trims and raised-letter names only add to the sanitation problem. Perhaps existing mastics can be used instead of so many nuts and bolts.

6. *Produce lighter-weight equipment.* With convenience foods, smaller packaging, and less weight to throw around, equipment can be easier

to handle and less expensive to build. We no longer throw quarters of beef on tables or 30 and 40 gallon pots on range tops. A few operations may continue to do this, but they should design their own heavy-duty equipment instead of expecting everyone to suffer high costs.

IDEAS FOR NEW EQUIPMENT

The following list of suggestions and ideas should be of interest to both operators and manufacturers. Most of the items named are small things, but they are important to anyone faced with the everyday task of serving food. Some are in existence now; all should be, and should be available in standard models.

1. Deep fat fryers that are easy to clean and compact, with rapid heat-up time and recovery. They should be equipped with a filtering device that is easy to use (lifting and pouring large pots of hot grease is not the most desirable task). The hot fat should swirl or circulate around the product so that the food does not have to be shaken to achieve even cooking. Baskets should be lightweight and easy to empty, eliminating the need to pound the basket on the table to get the product out. If the recovery is fast, the temperature can be pre-set at one heat (preferably 325°F). In addition to being compact, fryers should be inexpensive so that multiple units can be purchased for ease of cleaning and savings on fat. Last but not least, they should *all* have automatic basket lifts.

2. An automatic broiler or grill 6 to 8 feet long that will take all sizes of meat and cook both sides at once. Speed should be adjustable and we should be able to put the product on at various points to get rare, medium, or well-done food. The machine should produce a minimum of flame, smoke, and spattering grease. It should be easily cleaned without being taken apart, and it should be versatile enough so that it can be used to cook products for all meals including breakfast.

3. In addition to the small cutters now available for slicing vegetables such as tomatoes and onions, it would be valuable to have a hand-operated cutter for dicing green salad. It should be small, simple to operate, and machine-washable.

4. It is time someone invented a new mop without all those strings that wrap around every leg, then devised a method for wringing it without backbreaking effort, and finally, built a simple shower-type unit to rinse it clean.

5. An inexpensive lift-up-door type of pot and pan washer. Hand

pot and pan washing cannot be a part of our business in the future.

6. As explained in Chapter 6, for many operations there is a possibility of building a combination dish and pot washer. One expensive machine could then do two jobs.

7. As much as possible, temperatures should be pre-set or controls designed so that temperatures cannot be easily changed.

8. A minor point: We would all appreciate having the name plate with the model number and utilities on the front of a machine where they can be found and read easily.

9. All freezers, especially reach-ins, should defrost automatically. A start has been made on ice cream cabinets, but this feature should be standard across the board. As discussed in Chapter 4, freezer drawers are needed badly, since below the 36" level it is very hard to bend down and reach into a freezer or refrigerator compartment. These drawers should be deep and have good capacity.

10. A caster that moves easily in all directions without strain. In addition, casters should be made to set back under the equipment, out of the way, so they won't collect all the dirt and grime. Designers should remember that equipment on casters does not have to be 6" off the floor, so perhaps most of the caster could be recessed.

11. All the automatic timing devices possible.

12. Instead of the timeworn glass sneeze guards on the front of self-service or buffet equipment, which are difficult to clean and not very effective, why not an air curtain to block the spray from sneezing and coughing?

13. Work tables should have a simple, clean design, especially under the top. Drawers should be standard stainless steel pans that can be easily pulled out for machine washing. There should be no fixed undershelves (so that mobile equipment can be used underneath) and legs should be equipped with casters. Speaking of details, provide a small pair of slides under the top for a plastic cutting board.

14. Simplified exhaust hoods and systems that are self-cleaning and require no filters. So much progress is being made in the extraction of grease and odors that it is time to go all the way and eliminate the need for ducts. Use all the heat that escapes to pre-heat the hot water.

15. No handles on doors and drawers; recessed pulls only.

16. No latches on refrigerator doors; magnetic seals.

17. Self-closing doors and drawers.

18. All sinks should be equipped with a knee or leg pedal; no more protruding spigots that add to handling and cleaning problems.

19. Levelers for items like cups, glasses, and dishes that do not destroy all the top working space so badly needed in compact serving areas.

20. Portable hot and cold food service units with levelers that are self-contained. The units can be heated or cooled by special plates that are dropped in just before service.

21. Equipment should be designed so that more mistakes in specifying can be corrected in the field without returning the entire unit. For example, doors should be interchangeable so that the swing can be adjusted on the job. It should be possible to change electrical characteristics in the field—say, from 208 volts to 240 volts.

22. Mobile compactors designed to be used on the spot. Filling a can and then taking the can to the compactor is not labor-saving.

23. As explained in Chapter 6, dish tables should be designed and produced as a standard item instead of custom-designed for each installation. By this time we certainly know what is needed for the proper handling and washing of dishes.

24. In designing for the future, think in terms of using more vertical as opposed to horizontal space. We need compact work areas that are efficient and strong, whereas by constantly adding to the horizontal, we are making the areas larger and harder to use.

25. Cooking equipment that works faster so we can handle more business, yet improve food quality by doing more cooking to order. For example, a griddle that cooks both sides at once will reduce cooking time and speed service. In cafeterias it could reduce the need to cook so much so far ahead.

26. A china service plate that stays hot longer. Perhaps this can be achieved with a built-in metal disk.

27. Service carts that fold or nest.

Notice that most of the items on this list are not complicated and costly to build, but simple things that will greatly improve food service at little expense. The important thing for designers and manufacturers to remember is that in the future, *we must adapt the equipment to the help, not the help to the equipment.* If employees do not want to wash pots and pans by hand, arrange it so that they don't have to.

Briefly, the equipment in demand for the future will be self-contained, mobile, limited standard models, less expensive, functional and versatile, and easy to clean and service. If we are locked in by old-style fixed and expensive equipment, there will be little chance to make the changes that will be necessary.

Chapter 14

REMODELING AND EXPANSION: POINTS YOU SHOULDN'T OVERLOOK

The timely topic of remodeling has two aspects: remodeling an existing operation to improve decor and service, and remodeling an existing building to start a new operation. The first is of prime importance to all operators. There are some famous landmark restaurants that go along from year to year with the same decor, but even they periodically repaint and repair, and many have added modern kitchen and service areas in the back. Experience shows that in almost every instance remodeling and redecorating improve business. If the rest of the facilities are also modernized correctly, profits improve, too.

As for starting a new venture today, it pays to consider remodeling an existing piece of property. Not only is the cost of a new building very high but good locations are difficult to find. A restaurant that has failed may still be in a favorable situation and may have profit potential if it is given a well-planned remodeling job and a new face.

Some failures, of course, will never be able to make a comeback; this is a matter for careful study. The important thing to realize is that it will take more than a sign reading "Under New Management" to put a loser back in business.

The remodeling approach is popular in many lines of work: Old homes have been turned into successful office buildings, for example, and groups of small businesses have been combined into attractive shopping areas. In investigating properties to remodel, remember that a successful food operation, too, can be made from a place that was not formerly a restaurant.

REMODELING FOR HIGHER PROFITS

Whether you are remodeling to improve an existing operation or to start a new one, the first step should be to hire a food service consultant who has had experience in remodeling. In a short time he will be able to tell whether the project will pay and whether there are adequate facilities and enough space to do a worthwhile job. Get someone to evaluate the plans from all angles because an equipment house or salesman will think in terms of the new equipment, an architect will think in terms of the building exterior, a decorator will think in terms of the furnishings. It is best to have an overall study made of the feasibility before engaging these other specialists.

To pay for itself, remodeling should improve the service. Since business will usually increase after any kind of remodeling, make changes that speed the service as well as changes that refurbish the public areas. Otherwise, the increased patronage will be a problem rather than a blessing. Also see that enough improvements are made to increase volume and profits so that the remodeling will pay for itself in a reasonable length of time. For example, you might relocate and modernize the warehandling operation to reduce steps, motion, and man-hours. Or try changing the location of the serving kitchen to increase the speed of service and produce faster turnover. Even the addition of adequate service stands in dining areas will help the servers give better service.

Keep major structural changes to a minimum. Study your plan carefully to reduce the amount of electrical, plumbing, and other major alterations. A qualified consultant will work out several alternatives to the preliminary plans and in many cases come up with solutions that will cost far less. It is much cheaper to make several drawings and get the right answer than to start work on the first idea that someone has.

Good plans of the existing structure are necessary to show the designer where the columns are located, where the main electric panels are to be found, and many other facts that must be known before work starts. If no plans are available, pay to have some made before you get involved in a costly project that might never pay.

Also carefully check local building codes. In a case mentioned earlier, an operator who had taken over an existing restaurant learned too late that local regulations demanded a much larger septic tank system for the type of establishment he was planning to open, and this increased the cost of the remodeling by an unexpected $15,000. Such mistakes are being made frequently. Their worst consequence is that the budget for the whole job must be cut, and the reductions are usually made in the back of the house. Without proper equipment and serving facilities it is even more difficult to make enough profits to pay for the remodeling.

Improve conditions for the customer. A new carpet, new draperies, and expensive art on the wall are fine, and the guests will appreciate them. But if you can provide more comfortable seating, better climatic conditions, less glare, less noise, more attractive rest rooms, easier check paying procedures, and quicker parking, customers will be even happier.

To increase volume, improve all departments. One of the most common errors being made now in the food service industry is the rush to add another dining room because business is good and there is a standing line. This is an excellent idea, provided the new dining room is not located hundreds of feet from the service area, and provided the other facilities are improved to match the new seating. If not, the result of remodeling is simply that customers wait at the tables for service rather than in line. Experience shows that people will complain less in line than they will after being seated; once sitting down they expect to be served. Another outcome of poorly planned seating expansion is that there are several closed-off stations of tables because of lack of servers. This, too, makes guests angry because they cannot understand why they should wait in line with all those empty tables.

Aim for minimum investment. The less you can spend to effect a good remodeling, the better. This is the main reason for considering a former restaurant or existing building for a new venture. Examine your budget and cost projections carefully and make sure that they are within your monthly costs; don't make the mistake of projecting future sales and profit increases too high to justify the high costs of remodeling.

Include new miscellaneous equipment. Often this part of remodeling is forgotten when the budget is being established, yet as discussed in Chapter 7, small equipment can be essential to the success of the operation. The effect of a newly redecorated dining room is impaired by worn-out china and glasses; the efficiency of a new warehandling system can be cancelled without enough glass and cup racks; the faster service needed to increase sales will not materialize when servers must constantly search for equipment because there is not enough of it.

Stay open during remodeling. A rule derived from years of experience with many kinds of remodeling jobs is to stay open even on a limited scale, if at all possible. Or if it is necessary to close, make the closing time as short as possible. With the amount of good competition that exists today, it is too easy to lose regular customers and too difficult to get them back.

Another fact about remodeling that may surprise the inexperienced operator is that customers will be very interested in what is happening, and many will come more often just to see the progress of the job. It is the old sidewalk superintendent principle; something in all of us makes us enjoy watching things being built.

One of the best ways to manage staying open is to plan the remodeling in stages. For example, a new warehandling operation that is to be located in a better position can be installed first and then the old one removed. You can even install an entirely new kitchen in stages without closing. A limited menu can be offered for the period, with a note on the menu and on a sign in the lobby that you are remodeling.

Make customers aware of the remodeling. Tent cards on the tables, signs outside the building and in the lobby, a note on the menu, an explanation by employees—all will keep your customers informed during this trying period. Several operators have even hung the decorator's detailed designs for the new decor in the lobby. Despite some hardships, most guests are glad to know that the place is being upgraded, especially if they are regulars. Of course, you will get some cranky comments and suggestions, but these, too, show that people are interested.

Don't just replace—improve. In replacing old equipment, investigate to see if better versions are available. For example, one of the new convection ovens will do faster baking and roasting in a smaller space. New fryers are more compact and have faster recovery, so that you may be able to use two new models instead of three old ones you now have. And the space you save on smaller new equipment may enable you to get some other advantages without enlarging the building. The same applies to replacing tables and chairs in dining rooms. As explained earlier, all four-seaters produce about 55 percent efficiency, while deuces that can be moved apart or together to take care of large parties will produce about 90 percent. Study your present seating plan before buying new furniture and you will be able to have a more effective seating arrangement that will increase sales and take care of parties of all sizes.

Put money in sales areas. This has been emphasized throughout the book; the paying customer *never sees that "prize" kitchen* in the back but only what exists in his areas out front.

Don't do half a job. New draperies with the same old dirty rug just emphasize the bad condition of the rug. In running restaurants back in the leaner years, we did not dare ask the boss for new dining room furnishings. Instead, we would ask for new draperies, and he would approve. After they were hung, he would immediately see that the tabletops needed replacing to do the draperies justice. After the tops were installed, it would be evident that the rug did not come up to the draperies and tops; so little by little we got the complete job done.

IMPROVING EMPLOYEE FACILITIES

Years ago help was plentiful, and this was reflected in restaurant designs and planning. Now the situation has changed, and facilities for the employees are becoming increasingly important. These include:

Lockers. No matter how small, at least they provide a place to store valuables and avoid loss.

A place to eat and have a smoke. If your dining areas are partitioned, perhaps your servers can eat out there before or after the meal period. But what about the people in the kitchen? They should at least have a table and some chairs.

Toilets and hand sinks. These are part of the standard code in most areas, and they should be.

Some place to rest. No matter how small, a place to take a break and have a cup of coffee makes a big difference to morale. It should be away from the public area, because customers do not understand that the employee is having a deserved break. If service is not good, they will complain about everyone sitting around doing nothing. Even supervisors do not always know that an employee sitting in the dining room has earned the rest period.

Some space for management. This means a place for the phone, for necessary papers and forms, for some quiet to do the bookwork, and for some privacy to talk to employees. Most owners are against office space for managers because they fear the manager will spend all his time there and not be on the job. This is faulty reasoning; with modern reports and figures, the owner can quickly judge the manager's performance without worrying about his loafing in the office. If you have ever tried to do bookwork in a hot kitchen, or talk over a phone that is next to the dishwashing machine, you will agree.

Part V

MAXIMIZING THE BENEFITS OF GOOD PLANNING

Chapter 15

MERCHANDISING: PHYSICAL ELEMENTS

Most restaurants, including the chains, do so little advertising that there are few statistical guidelines to help the food service operator get the most for his merchandising dollar. Certainly the way to start, however, is to run a fine restaurant with good service, tempting food, pleasant surroundings, moderate prices—everything that leads to enjoyable dining. Lacking these features the most expensive signs, spectacular advertising campaigns, and elaborate menus mean nothing.

The whole point of merchandising should be to increase the customer count. Many restaurants, including chains, are fooled by slight increases in sales dollars that have been caused by price hikes over the past few years. Often these hikes have driven people away, and a decrease in the customer count is a sign of trouble ahead. In today's expanding market, all eating places should be continuously increasing the number of people served. As Seattle restaurateur Peter Canlis, quoted in *Nation's Restaurant News*, has said, "We do not need higher prices, we need more customers."

The idea that price increases can overcome declining business and decreasing profits, though it may be valid for products like cars and homes, is unsound in the food service industry. People have built-in sales resistance to restaurant prices. Meals are sold for cash, not on the installment plan, and once they are consumed there is nothing to show for the money. When considering a price rise, first investigate every other way by which profits might be improved.

Another caution: Before embarking on a promotion campaign to attract more customers, be sure you can handle the extra traffic. Everyone has been lured to a restaurant only to find that it has run out of the advertised special or that the service is bad because the place is overcrowded. Add to your staff and facilities in advance, or you will drive away some of your regular customers as well as new ones.

Many successful operations have spent little or nothing for promotion; they simply did a good job on food and service. Their growth came mainly from word of mouth, which is still an excellent way to increase volume. If your building is a little run-down, the food not all it could be, and the staff on the weak side, spend your money first to correct these things. In most cases business will pick up without any promotion drive, and because the increase in customers is gradual you will have a better chance of holding them.

Once you have provided pleasant surroundings, delicious food, and excellent service, then look into other forms of merchandising. There are two main types: on-premise promotion and off-premise promotion. It is best to start on the premises, because this approach usually produces more lasting results. Advertising campaigns are expensive and can create tremendous temporary impact business that is difficult to handle. The following discussion treats elements of on-premise promotion in detail and touches briefly on off-premise merchandising.

THE SIGN

Fortunately, we are coming to the end of the era of the giant sign that in many cases cost as much as the building. Although the sign company will still try to sell you one like this, it is better to select a moderate size that is in good taste. Keep your message brief; remember that traffic moves fast today, and a long spiel in six-inch-high letters is difficult to read at 50 miles per hour. The sign should feature your name; then, in large letters, something like "Restaurant" to indicate that you are in the business of serving food and are not an undertaker or an antique shop. The sign should also show that you are "Open," "Closed on Monday," "Serving Breakfast," or whatever, so that the new or impulse eater will know whether to drive in or come back another time. Don't make him park his car and walk up to the front door, only to find that you do not serve breakfast on Thursday morning.

Keep the sign simple and attractive, with a minimum amount of reading, in large letters. Stick to moderate size and cost. Realize what a sign is for: a "quickie" type of merchandising mainly for the new customer (your regular customers probably couldn't tell you whether you have a sign or not). Finally, stay away from outdated slogans like these:

Under New Management
Steaks and Chops
Seafoods
Home Cooking
Fine Food
Open Twenty-Four Hours
Truck Drivers Welcome

THE EXTERIOR

Much can be done in exterior building design to attract attention and show that yours is a place for serving food. In some locations the sign itself can be a part of the building. If you have intentions of expanding or becoming a chain, identifying features can be incorporated in the façade (as in the case of Howard Johnson's orange roof). Or the design of the exterior can indicate the interior motif, whether it is nautical, modern, or planned on some other theme.

Although the exterior should be appealing in order to act as a merchandiser for you, in general it is best to avoid the spectacular or outlandish building design. Even though they might attract attention, odd features have not proved successful for the average eating place, nor do they fit well into the community.

THE LOBBY

Your entrance or lobby can serve to promote the restaurant and highlight certain features. Again, hours and days of operation should be posted here, and your menu can be attractively displayed so that guests waiting for a table can examine it and perhaps make their choice in advance. Or if there is nothing they like and the price range is not suitable, they can leave without all the time and trouble of being seated.

Awards and special features, pleasingly arranged to fit the general decor, can also be displayed in this space. Many operators use their lobby and cashier areas to sell other items such as gifts and packaged foods, and, if this is well handled, it can be a focus of interest to your customers and a welcome source of extra income. Whatever you do with the entrance or lobby, see that it looks good, because it is what your guests see first and last.

THE MENU

The menu is your most important tool and should be closely tailored to your operation. Owing to various menu award contests, which are much like the kitchen design awards that stress appearance instead of practicality, many restaurateurs give excessive attention to menu design. Your main interest in the menu should be in how well it merchandises for you rather than in how it looks to someone who has never seen what you are doing.

A good menu conforms to the physical setup of your particular establishment. Don't use a moderate-priced, high-volume type of menu if your kitchen is not equipped to produce a lot of good-quality food in a short time. Don't feature fried foods if you have one old fryer that turns out grease-soaked food. If you are designing a new restaurant or remodeling, study the menu first and go over it carefully with the food service consultant or designer before making the layout and selecting the equipment.

It is not necessary to spend great sums of money for expensive backs or menu holders and four or five color-run interiors. Large chains can do this because they order by the million and can reduce the cost per menu. For very little expense the small operator can put out an attractive menu that will do the same job. In fact, the inexpensive menu is much more practical because it can be changed often.

Changing the Menu

If a menu cost him a lot, the operator tends to use it too long so that it becomes dirty and frayed and makes a bad impression on the customer. The less expensive menu that can be replaced frequently is best for this and many other reasons.

Here are some of the advantages of changing menus often.

1. Customers appreciate it, particularly when they are regulars. It is tiresome to come in month after month and see the same old menu.

2. Seasonal changes are desirable not only to take advantage of foods in season but because appetites change with the seasons.
3. Prices must change with changes in the wholesale market. In fact, it may be necessary to drop certain items from the menu at times because their cost is out of your particular range.
4. Sales tabulations, which should be made regularly by every food service operation, will show certain items that are not selling, and these should be dropped from the menu as soon as possible.

When you change the menu, reposition key items to regulate sales. There are certain spots that attract the eye first (one is the upper left, because we all read from left to right and top to bottom). These are the places to put your specialties that are profitable and easy to serve.

The Menu Cover

The cover is the least important part of the menu and should be simple, tasteful, and printed in one color to reduce the cost. Too often the greatest amount of money is spent for the cover, a cost allocation which is hard to understand when all service manuals say that the menu should be placed in front of the guest open, with the cover down. Few customers ever see the cover and those who do are usually not interested, since they came to eat, not look at a printer's artwork.

Dirty Menus

The problem of dirty, tired-looking menus, which seems almost universal, is mostly caused by seating people at tables that have not been cleaned from the last party. Not only must the new guests face the soiled dishes and tabletop but the menu is placed in the dirt that is left. This should *never* happen in any food service establishment! If a table cannot be cleaned and made ready for the next party, do not use it.

Another cause of soiled menus is the lack of sufficient menu holders. These should be conveniently located where servers will put menus so that the host can pick them up for reuse. Without holders, menus are thrown on service stands and on trays of soiled dishes.

The so-called washable menu, which is laminated or plastic-coated, is not necessarily a good investment for the average operator. Not only does the expense make him reluctant to change the menu but the service staff has the task of washing the menus. If they don't perform this job regularly and do it correctly, the menus look as unappetizing as any other dirty ones.

Menu Items

How many items should your menu carry? This difficult question is best treated on an individual basis from experience and study. Spectacular success stories about restaurants like pancake or roast beef houses that serve only one or two items can be balanced by sad tales about the failures of the same kinds of places. If you are already in business, it won't take long to discover what items are your most popular, and you will be able to develop just the right menu for your needs. If you are new, study the potential market and the competition, start with a moderate approach, and be ready to make adjustments.

Naturally, the long menu with hundreds of items is not practical today. The experienced help to handle it is not available, and the difficulties of preparation and service will reduce sales per hour to the point of no return. Design your menu for balance and variety, but limit it to what you can handle and serve well from your physical setup. From time to time you can change to other items so guests do not have that same-old-menu feeling.

Years ago a successful chain presented a new menu for each meal. Total number of items on any one meal was 26 to 30, including beverages—a very limited selection. However, because of the frequent change, customers regarded the menu as always new and interesting. By serving only a few items at each meal, the company could make and serve them well. For example, instead of trying to prepare and store five or six salad mixes for sandwiches, the chain featured one salad mix sandwich each day, and the mix was fresh and delicious because it had just been made. Remember that the fewer items you can serve and handle and still do a large-volume business, the more profit you will make. But this should be a long-range goal that you work toward gradually, testing your market and customers to find the best combination.

Layout

Obviously menu size will be determined by the number of items it contains. For the layout, follow these suggestions: First, use a type that is clear and easy to read. Main entrees or your main items should be in large type, because a great many people have trouble reading small print. Second, organize items so that they can be found readily. If a customer wants a sandwich, it should be easy for him to spot the section listing sandwiches. Third, avoid long descriptions and unnecessary repetition. These give the menu a crowded look; your printer will tell you that it will be more attractive with some white space. For example:

> Delicious Char-Broiled Hamburger done to your taste on a butter grilled roll with crisp lettuce, slices of ripe tomatoes, crisp onion slices and our special home-made dressing.
>
> Delicious Char-Broiled Cheeseburger done to your taste on a butter grilled roll with crisp lettuce, slices of ripe tomatoes, crisp onion slices and our special home-made dressing.

can be reduced to:

> CHAR-BROILED HAMBURGER on grilled roll, lettuce, tomato, onion and dressing ....
> WITH MELTED CHEESE ....

Not only will the last version take up less space, but putting the hamburger in large type makes it easier to find and sells it better. Descriptive explanations are a waste; why would anyone claim to serve anything other than a "ripe" tomato or "crisp" lettuce?

To further unclutter the menu and help your employees, avoid long lists of minor items. For example:

Beverages

> Coffee — Hot Tea — Iced Tea — Iced Coffee — Milk — Buttermilk — Chocolate Milk — Hot Chocolate — Cola — Root Beer — Orange Drink

Both the public and your servers know the standard drinks; it should not be necessary to name them. Similarly, if under "Juices" you specify orange, grapefruit, tomato, prune, apple, pineapple, V-8, cranberry, and so on, you are wasting space on items which most people don't want and which you don't have refrigerator space for anyhow. Also, as Chapter 9 pointed out, long lists of vegetables and pies present hardships for guests, servers, and cooks. Invariably the one item the customer selects is out, and he must start all over again. The menu should simply say "Vegetables" and "Fresh-Baked Pies," and servers can be notified which ones are available.

Prices

With today's high costs, the old system of marking up so many times cost or of maintaining a certain fixed percentage cost of food is no longer a practical pricing policy. Many operators have devised new methods of merchandising with moderate prices that produce high volume and high profit at the same time. The industry as a whole needs to take a good look at merchandising and pricing systems and develop a more workable one.

As stated earlier, it is better to make 5 percent net profit on $500,000 than 10 percent net profit on $100,000 sales. Other retail industries learned this lesson years ago and put it to good use. There is a huge potential market composed of people who would like to eat out more often, but the food service industry has failed to adopt methods that will make volume business possible. One successful restaurateur commented recently that he is very happy to earn one dollar on each steak dinner—and he has net profits to prove that he is right.

When you think of merchandising, don't forget price. The idea that price does not make any difference has never been true and probably never will be in the food service business.

Diets and Health Foods

Unless you intend to specialize in either diet foods or health foods or both, do not emphasize them on a regular menu. Many restaurants have a popular Slim Jim plate at lunch for the man who thinks he is dieting, but it has always been difficult for any food service establishment to tell the customer what he should eat. Years ago a very successful chain failed because the owner began to force health foods on guests. Our concern for the customer's health should confine itself to serving fresh, high-quality foods free from contamination, bacteria, and foreign objects in clean and sanitary surroundings. This is a full-time job.

OTHER ON-PREMISE IDEAS

Several other on-premise merchandising techniques are very effective without requiring large investments.

Food Displays

In lobbies or entrances to dining rooms, displays of such foods as raw steaks, fresh fruits and melons, and beautiful desserts can boost sales and underline the fact that this is the entrance to an eating place. Displays must be fresh and attractively arranged, however; nothing hurts business more than a tired-looking or messy assortment of food.

Exhibition Cooking

A major asset in some restaurants is a service kitchen out front that is decorated in appealing colors, fitted with easy-to-clean materials which are kept spotless, and staffed with neatly dressed cooks. Diners enjoy watching the action, and locating the kitchen in the dining area saves steps and speeds service.

Attractive Food

When plates or platters and certain specialties are beautifully arranged, other guests who see them will order the same thing and increase your sales. Cultivate "flair," with attractive serving dishes, special attention at the table, and carts or trays of salads and desserts. Good food well presented is its own best merchandiser.

Clip-Ons and Tent Cards

Although these are helpful if used right, avoid having too many of them. Be sure that they are well designed and that they actually say something. A tent card that reads "Enjoy Thanksgiving Dinner with Us!" doesn't mean much; it should give your Thanksgiving menu, the price, your serving hours on Thanksgiving, and your telephone number for reservations. Never have more than one tent card on the table at once—and make sure it is clean.

The purpose of clip-ons is to sell specials or leftovers; confine them to this. For example, if you feature fried chicken in your restaurant, the livers will accumulate, and a clip-on will do an excellent job of selling the amount you have ready to serve. Then it can be removed.

Personal Selling

As the only direct contact between the restaurant and the customer, your servers should be trained to merchandise for you. Be sure they are familiar with all the foods you sell, with your specialties, with dishes to recommend for fast service, and with your high-profit items. A little time spent with servers each day will result in more satisfied customers.

For example, coffee is the most expensive beverage you have (because second and third cups are served free) and the most time-consuming for the guest to drink, especially if he has more than one cup. Yet when they take the beverage order, most servers will say "Coffee?" Certainly in hot weather they ought to be saying "Iced Tea?" since this is the most profitable drink you can serve. Also, if the customer can have all the coffee he wants at no extra charge, why can't he have some more iced tea without being charged for the second glass? Similarly, in one chain that served complete dinners, coffee and milk came with the dinner, but if a guest wanted a cola drink, there was an extra charge. Why? The cola was much cheaper than either coffee or milk, and few if any guests drink more than one soft drink at a sitting. Often your servers can suggest improvements of this nature from their knowledge of customer requests.

Place Mats

Here is an article put directly in front of your guest that can do a lot of selling. In fact, it can be used as a menu to speed service as well as promote your specials. At breakfast, for example, the menu printed on the place mat is already in front of the customer when he is seated, and, by the time the server reaches the table, the guest will often be ready to order. There is no reason why the same device cannot be used for lunch and even dinner. Under this system the menu will always be clean because each guest gets a fresh one.

Place mats are also excellent for merchandising desserts, drinks and cocktails, and special events. As long as you are paying for the mat, investigate the possibility of using it as a merchandiser.

Aromas

Most operators do everything possible to hide the smell of food, including some good smells that could help in merchandising. If you feature hot breads, why not have a trace of the wonderful aroma of fresh-baked bread in the air? In one restaurant the doors of the bread-baking ovens do open directly into the dining area. Nothing smells good as fresh coffee beans being ground, and another restaurant keeps the coffee grinder out front. Sizzling bacon is one of the best morning smells there is. Perhaps we should look into aroma as another on-premise merchandiser—after all, we are selling food.

OFF-PREMISE PROMOTION

After you have put your house in order and developed methods of on-premise merchandising, you may want to explore off-premise techniques. These include advertising through radio, television, newspapers, billboards, local school papers, and the yellow pages of the phone book.

Actually, the phone book is a special case. Even before construction of a restaurant starts, it is advisable for management to check with the telephone company not only about private and pay phone service but about the printing date for the next directory. Make sure your restaurant is included because this can be an important source of business. Most people, especially when they are strangers in town, consult the directory for places to eat, so get listed as soon as possible.

If you wish to embark on a program of advertising and promotion, take the following steps:

1. Make sure the operation is ready to handle the new business well.
2. Study your profit and loss picture with your accountant and set up a budget for advertising.
3. Go to a good professional advertising agency with all the facts and work with them on the best program for the money you have to spend. We all know that it is fine to be on color TV, but only a few of the big chains can afford nationwide coverage on a consistent basis.

A good agency can recommend various programs to get you the most for your dollar. These may be in highway signs, radio, or newspapers, depending on your local picture. One thing to remember is that advertising must be well done over a period of time. Repetition is the key; one small ad in a newspaper one week followed by a small radio blurb the next is not effective. A little money scattered about on an irregular basis is a waste of money.

In your local area it may pay to belong to some civic associations and perhaps to award small trophies for various local activities—prizes of free dinners, for example. Many local restaurants sponsor bowling teams. This type of local promotion is not costly and will do much to spread your name.

In conclusion, to repeat the main point of the chapter: Everything you do to publicize your establishment will help business, but the best and surest road to success is to do a good job. Most of us have a tendency to ignore or play down word-of-mouth advertising, but it is a powerful force that can make or break you.

Chapter 16

MEETING COMPETITION: MORE THAN PRICE IS INVOLVED

A restaurant's competition can come from many sources: other food service operations; the home, including the backyard barbecue; supermarkets; and other units in the same chain. It can also come from the restaurant itself, in the sense that you may be your own worst enemy. (As a well-known food service consultant recently said: "Our industry's poor performance is now our biggest competitor.")

No one in the restaurant business should fear competition, but we all must recognize what we have to face and do something about it. Just coasting along, hoping that something will happen to the competition or that customers will happen into your place, is not enough. You must stay in a good competitive position at all times because customers are creatures of habit, and, once they are lost, it is very difficult to get them back.

Some years ago the executives in a successful chain made it a practice to dine out in another restaurant at least once a week and report on what happened. The reports were studied, and the good ideas were adopted by the chain. In addition to this kind of shopping around, it is advisable to actually meet your competition—visit their places, make yourself known, and invite them to come to your establishment. There are very few secrets in our business today, and an exchange of visits and ideas can be beneficial to both parties. Being on friendly terms does not mean the end of hard competition, but it helps to find out what is going on in the world outside your own four walls.

THE NEW CUSTOMER: FIRST IMPRESSIONS

Is the outside of your building inviting—clean, freshly painted, with the sign in good repair and the planting in good shape? These are the first things a new customer will notice. Your regulars will concentrate on the food and ignore a shoddy exterior, but, to be successful, a restaurant cannot exist on its present set of customers; it must constantly strive to get new people to come. Papers on the parking lot, chewing gum on the sidewalks, weeds in the lawn, dirty windows, and peeling paint will lose a lot of potential business.

Once inside, the new guest casts a critical eye on the entrance lobby and the dining area. How does yours look? Dirt or litter on the floor, dirty dishes on the tables, noise, confusion, employees who are smoking, odors, a temperature that is too hot or too cold, poor lighting, and dirty walls create a bad first impression that is hard to overcome. As for untidy rest rooms, they can discourage people to the point where they will not even enter and try your food. The next time you come into your place, pretend you are a guest arriving for the first time and carefully note all the things that could be corrected or improved. Or have someone do it for you and give you an unbiased report. Even the parking lots in many food service operations either have no painted lines at all or are badly laid out. Drive in some day, and, instead of going to your reserved space, try some of the other places to see how the customers feel.

After you have looked your establishment over with the eyes of a new customer, try dining there as guest. Invite a friend or business associate, and approach the dining area to be seated as though you were a guest with a party. Note how long you must stand in line, what the greeting is like, whether the table and menu are clean or dirty. Is the table well set? Do you have water? Observe the service to others around you and note how quickly and well your order is taken. Perhaps you can get the server to turn it in to the kitchen without saying "This is for the boss." Time how long it takes for the order to be served and then check the food. This will help you find out what is happening to the regular guest—the one who pays the bills. Don't assume that you and your employees are doing a fine job; sometimes managers can assume themselves out of business.

STUDYING THE COMPETITION

In visiting the competition, be sure you include the most successful operations in your own class. If you are in the fast-food field but always eat out at swank places, naturally you will find that you cannot match all the elaborate things they do. Remember what you are set up to do and stay in your own backyard unless you are deliberately trying to move up to the next class. Recognize the type and level of your own place and make it the best in its field.

Competitive Pricing

When studying a competitor, note carefully his price structure and the values he gives. Get his menus and compare their prices with your own, taking into account the size and quality of his portions. With the exception of a few famous gourmet restaurants, reasonable prices are an important requirement today for success in the food service business. Make sure you are within the right range for your type of establishment and your particular locality (what is called "reasonable" in one city may be considered high in another). Lately many operators have been led astray by the idea that increased prices will solve their problems and bring in high profits, only to learn that volume business also has much to do with the amount of dollar profit. Too much emphasis has been placed on increasing percentages when the prime objective should have been dollars. People are forced to pay higher taxes, higher utility costs, and higher prices for their cars, but they can and do avoid higher menu prices by staying home. Know who you are feeding and what they can afford; don't reason that you sell X number of some item and can raise the price Y amount in order to make that many more Z's because it doesn't work.

The Home and the Supermarket

Food service operations must compete not only with each other but with the home and the supermarket. Years ago we could rely on air conditioning to bring in business during hot months, but no longer.

In fact, homes are generally more attractive and more comfortable than they used to be, and today they are equipped with backyard broilers, color TV, and a wonderful assortment of frozen and convenience foods for the housewife. To visit one of your really big competitors, stop in at a modern supermarket and look at its array of ready foods. Today supermarkets are cooking meats and chickens, baking pies, and preparing many other foods for the little woman to take home and serve with ease and speed. Years ago, washing dishes was such a chore that the housewife would eat out just to avoid it. Automatic dishwashers, throwaway pans, self-cleaning ovens, and bags to roast in are formidable competition today. Anyone who can reach into a freezer and read directions can turn out good food with a minimum of labor.

It is up to the food service operator to make it a pleasure to eat out, and this means not only providing an enjoyable atmosphere and good service and food but doing it so that it doesn't cost an arm and leg. In cities that have quite a few moderate-priced restaurants more people eat out more often.

Also recognize that getting the "family business" means satisfying all its members, from the tiniest tot to mother and dad. Forget to take good care of the children, and you can be sure that the parents will go elsewhere the next time. Fail to please the woman, and the couple will switch to another restaurant. Little things like bad lighting that shows up wrinkles or a waitress who is too friendly with the man will lose a lot of business in a hurry.

Self-Competition

Some operations are their own competitors in the sense that it is possible to develop merchandising programs which create competition from within. Recently a fine restaurant featured a complete luncheon for a dollar—a price that was way out of line with the rest of the menu. The featured dish could not have produced much profit, nor was it quick and easy to serve. Naturally, an item with a very low price attracts business away from the rest of the menu. In the same way a menu that offers prime ribs of beef and chicken at the same price will cause a stampede for the roast beef.

Self-competition can also occur in chain operations where an expansion program is not carefully studied. Sometimes the units are located so close together that they must fight each other for customers. Friendly rivalry between a chain's units can be helpful, but not a struggle for survival.

Individual vs. Chains

The competition between individual operations and chains has recently grown, owing to the advent of franchising. Despite their increasing numbers, however, chains are still a small part of the total food service picture. Private individuals should not be discouraged. In fact, several articles in the trade publications have recently pointed out that privately owned and managed operations seem to be gaining again, and this is a good thing. The work that the chains have done is to be admired, but we still need the private venture to provide balance and create new ideas. The well-run, privately owned restaurant can compete with the best of the large chains in both volume sales and profits. Although the chain has some advantages, it also has liabilities: a supervision problem, large overhead costs, and lack of flexibility. Even in the best of chains the quality of the individual unit is only as good as the manager hired, and owner-management is usually more interested in doing a good job. And whereas a unit of a chain must operate within a rigid format, the individual enterprise can adapt quickly to special situations and take advantage of local features.

Contrary to common belief, central purchasing on a large scale does not always produce magical savings. In its centralized purchasing the chain sets up rigid specifications to maintain a level of quality throughout the operation. This means that a chain unit may be paying more for products than the individual who can shop around and quickly alter his menus and merchandising to take advantage of market conditions.

Although it has been predicted that the big chain will gradually take over the food service industry, I think that the good individual operation will continue to compete with any chain in any location.

Competition for Employees

Another form of competition is the battle for competent help and experienced management. Not only are food service enterprises competing with each other for employees but other industries raid our ranks for our best people. The restaurant business is not in a good bargaining position, because wages per hour are relatively low; the work is difficult physically, involving lifting, walking, and many hours on the feet; total hours are long and include evenings, weekends, and holidays; and fringe benefits are minimal.

These factors explain our high turnover, which leads to snowballing costs that make us fall even further behind. According to *Nation's Restaurant News* in September, 1971, 60 percent turnover is a good rate in the food service industry. Facts cited were:

> An average restaurant with 30 employees will lose $9,000 a year because of turnover.
> Loss of an unskilled employee can cost $100; a skilled worker $1,000, with a $300 average for all employees.
> Restaurant turnover averages well over 100% annually reaching rates of 300% to 500% (as compared with 4.6% for manufacturers and 6.1% for food manufacturers).

It is time to investigate new avenues of employee relations to solve this very serious problem. As stated before, the main reason most restaurants do not have proper employee facilities like rest rooms, a place to eat, lockers, kitchen ventilation, and many other small items which could increase comfort is that operators have a negative attitude: why spend the money, when the help won't stay anyway?

During World War II there was a haunting rumor of a company that paid employees very well, bought them expensive shoes which were comfortable to work in, gave them excellent food, and provided many other unheard-of benefits. It was even whispered that this operation charged no more for its product and had a unit cost lower than its competitors.

Recently a large chain in Europe set out to restructure its organization to try and pay the same hourly rate as car manufacturers. It succeeded, essentially by reducing the number of employees through a little automation and a lot of cuts in the hours of operation for table service. Careful study showed that the chain could make money with table service for only two hours at lunch and two at dinner, and management was willing to make the change.

A report mentioned earlier cited a study of 13 table service restaurants that average 20 hours a day. If we continue on this road, we will never be in a position to compete for competent help. Added to the problem of staffing and scheduling for long hours is the difficult task of training swing or relief help to replace employees who are off. The swing job is not only difficult to learn but very unpopular.

Many well-managed restaurants are finding it profitable to serve one meal a day, close one day a week, and even shut down for vacation at the slowest time of the year. Total sales may be lower but dollar profit is much higher. Start taking hourly sales readings in your own place; you may be surprised at the great number of dead times.

In the food service industry competition can help every operator involved. A successful manager once explained that he preferred a location close to the best restaurants in town, not away from them. As he saw it, even if he just got their overflow, he would be better off than he would in a lonely spot away from the action. In many localities all the best restaurants are grouped together, and it works because customers learn to go to this one area. A related point is that if a town has several good eating places the residents will eat out more often.

Never fear good competition; get in and compete. Don't try to be as good as the next one—make sure you are better. Start by thinking more of your customer and what you can do to please him. Make sure you know what is going on in your dining room and your competitor's, and remember that the bigger they are, the harder they fall.

Chapter 17

EMPLOYEES: MAKE THE MOST OF YOUR MANPOWER

So much has been written about this area of the restaurant business that the conflicting theories cancel each other out and food service operators tend to avoid reading any of it. No attempt will be made here to explore the work that has been done in personnel psychology, motivation, and other fields of expertise, important though these may be in arriving at any overall solution to the manpower problem. The approach in this chapter will be a practical one with definite suggestions about what an operator can do now to reduce turnover.

In restaurants with only 35 employees, turnover costs exceed $12,600/year, or 13 percent/month, according to a recent study by the National Restaurant Association and the federal government.[1] This and other reports, including statistics on the low average dollar sales

[1] *Labor Utilization and Operating Practice in Table Service Restaurants.* Government Printing Office, Washington, D.C., 1971.

per employee, indicate that the personnel problem is central to our industry. Unfortunately turnover and training costs are hidden; if they did show up on the profit and loss statement action would be taken immediately.

MANAGEMENT AND TOP MANAGEMENT

As one reason for the lack of motivation and high turnover rate in our business, the study cited the reluctance of restaurant operators to train their employees. This is the clue to the first practical step we can take to start making the most of our manpower. And the way to do it is to begin at the top and work down; some of our main troubles today have developed because we have people at the head of the industry who do not know enough about food service. Unless we train good top management, training programs for cooks and servers are a waste of time.

At the operating level too, management must be more carefully chosen and trained. The working manager of a food service enterprise must be able to lead (not boss) people, must know the various jobs, and must be skilled in conducting constant on-the-job training. Periodic training programs are worthless, because at current rates of turnover a group of cooks trained this week may be completely replaced by a new crew the week after next. To get a manager who is competent in these functions, select him according to facts of performance, not because he went to college or has X years of experience or is recommended by someone who says, "He's a good manager."

Look at the types of operation he has managed (the head of a high-priced establishment will not usually fit into a fast-food venture).

In addition to his gross sales figures, check to see if he had increases in volume over several years of operation.

Examine sales per employee per year in some of his former restaurants to see how efficiently he managed.

What have his rates of turnover been? Any applicant with a poor record in this respect is not a good risk.

Once a manager is hired, top management should check his performance regularly using such guidelines as sales increases, sales per employee per year, turnover percentages, and profits. It is possible to go into any operation and make an excellent short-term showing that collapses in the long pull.

It is up to top management, however, to provide a reasonable financial structure for the operating manager and his employees to work within. If the structure is such that a profit will be difficult to make or maintain even under expert management, there will always be employee problems. And few prospective managers will admit when applying that the proposition made to them is not feasible.

Another responsibility of top management is to make sure the establishment has the proper layout and equipment to do the job. The study mentioned earlier pointed out that considerable savings are available through more efficient restaurant designs; an experienced management force does not shave the budget in this area.

Finally, it is no secret that the food service industry is not a leader in dollars paid per hour, but top management should make every effort to pull rates up in order to compete in the labor market. Management should also see that earnings among various groups within the operation are fair and equitable. Food service businesses have been trying for years to hire employees for less money to do more difficult work under conditions worse than those in other industries. Perhaps the computers will help to solve many of these problems in the future—by demonstrating, for example, that it is better *not* to remain open 20 hours a day, seven days a week, trying to be all things to all people at all times.

A STABLE WORK FORCE

Anyone who has had experience with exit interviews learns that there are innumerable reasons for resignations, most of them minor. It seems natural to assume that the majority of people quit because of the money, but this is not true. Interviews show that many other things can be done to make employees more contented. The following is a list of practical suggestions for the management that aims to create a more stable work force.

Inexperienced Help

1. Face the fact that most replacements in the future will be inexperienced. Stop the wishful thinking about great numbers of people being trained for our industry, accept what is available, and gear the operation for on-the-job training by the manager. Several of the large chains have hired inexperienced people for years and have given the public good service.

2. Even after employees are thoroughly trained, see that they do

not slip into bad work habits. Supervision of their performance should include the simple dollar sales per man-hour measurement, checked daily or even weekly. A percentage wage cost figure does not reveal operating efficiency, but by using dollar sales per man-hour, comparisons between restaurants can be made.

3. Simplify the entire operation for the person being trained and the person doing the training. Limit the menu so that less food has to be prepared. In training employees give clearer instructions; use photographs and everything else that will help. Revise checks so that they require no writing, no adding, less bookkeeping. Every improvement that makes the job easier reduces turnover.

Reducing Fatigue

4. Concentrate on relieving pressure and tension—on making the operation smooth and quiet without the usual bickering and noisy confusion. Turnover among servers is particularly high, and much of it is due to the fact that they have so much difficulty in getting the food and serving the guests. The customers become angry, the cooks quarrel, and the server walks out in disgust.

5. Lighten the drudgery. The study cited earlier reported that 27 percent of the workday is spent walking—and this includes all employees, not just the servers. Years ago a chef told the author, "You'll make it in this business if your feet and back hold out," and he was certainly right. However, time and motion studies show that no one is producing when he is walking, and if our employees are walking 27 percent of the time, no wonder our productivity is so low and they are so tired. Other industries learned this long ago; they set up production lines and analyzed the product flow to create work stations and reduce walking. Today it is possible in our industry to eliminate most of the hard work and walking with the right layout and equipment. All we need is to do it.

6. Plan so employees can sit to work. In other businesses work stations are arranged so that most people can work while seated. Many of the jobs in the food service industry can be done sitting down, but often they are not, except in places like the large food processing plants. If it is possible for an employee to sit even for part of the time, arrange it.

Employee Meals

7. Scrap the old restrictive type of employee meal program; the more restrictions, the less cooperative the help. If handled with intelli-

gence and understanding, employees' meals should present little problem. A person can eat only so much, and in most cases it is a waste of effort to have each employee write a check to be filled by the cook unless management is going to take time to supervise and tally the orders.

The best approach is, first, to provide a definite space and definite times for employees to eat; second, establish the number of meals per shift for the employees; third, let them have a choice of as many items as possible within reason. It is difficult to know why many places will not permit cola drinks because these cost about half as much as coffee or milk, and a sweet drink tends to reduce what a person eats.

Naturally there are foods on the menu that cannot be served to employees because of excessive cost or the time and effort needed to prepare them. A steak that must be cooked to order will probably not even be on the menu for the manager. Beer or spirits for employees are also a no, for obvious reasons. If management explains the thinking behind these rules, however, people usually cooperate. Another good rule is that all employees should eat what they put on their plates.

Physical Conditions

8. Provide some simple accommodations for employees:

An enclosed and air conditioned office where the manager can do his work and discuss things in private with employees and others.

Convenient employee rest rooms.

Lockers and dressing rooms where they can store their valuables and change clothes.

A place away from food preparation areas where they can take a break and smoke.

Good first-aid supplies and simple medications that they can use for minor troubles.

A regular or pay phone they can use for making or receiving important calls.

A full-length mirror for employees so they can check uniforms.

9. Not many kitchens are air conditioned nor will they be in the future, but provide at least some ventilation. In most kitchens, "make-

up" air is introduced for the exhaust systems so that air is not taken from the dining areas. Make sure this is not cold air in the winter or hot air in the summer blowing down some employee's neck.

10. Falls in work areas are one of the major causes of injury in the food service industry. See that floors are dry, that drains are in the right places, and that dangerous areas are protected with no-slip strips.

11. Reduce noise levels with acoustic materials as well as with good management that eliminates shouting and arguing. It is most tiring to work in a noisy place for very long.

12. See that the light level in work areas is adequate, since poor lighting can cause inefficiency, fatigue, and accidents.

13. Provide the physical conditions and equipment that will enable you to make use of part-time people, older people, and even the handicapped. These workers can assist in solving many scheduling problems.

14. Since servers must depend on tips for the biggest part of their earnings, and they are the employees who have direct contact with your paying guests, see that they have a chance to do a fine job. Perhaps a few mobile service carts would help them to carry out and also to serve large parties. And as described in Chapter 15 on control and profit, their work is made more pleasant by the pre-printed check that has only to be marked quickly with a dot.

Schedules

15. Spend time on work schedules to see if you cannot help certain employees who have difficulties, such as small children, at home. Recently the author visited a hospital that had a serious nurse shortage, yet enforced a rule that all nurses had to work a full shift and only at certain hours. As soon as the rule was changed, more help became available.

16. Restaurants in a town in Greece have an interesting system for working on weekends. Each restaurant has to close every fourth Saturday and Sunday, which gives the employees some weekends off. Weekends are rotated so that only one restaurant is closed at a time and customers still have places to eat. This plan enables every place to make up the lost sales on the other three weekends when it is open and someone else is closed. Perhaps some such system of rotation could be introduced in your community to overcome the problem of working nights, weekends, and holidays.

Benefits

17. Try to provide all the fringe benefits, such as hospitalization, that are possible. It is time to start thinking positively—perhaps the more we give, the more we will get.

Many more items could be added to this list of practical things that can be done to help employee relations and reduce turnover. It was the management, not the employees, of a certain car manufacturer that first reduced the working day to eight hours. Rumor has it that not only did production increase per work hour but the company saved even more money because the number of mistakes decreased.

It is time for the food service industry to take a hard look at the employee problem and do something definite about it. It is fine to talk about motivation and incentive, but let's also do all the things we can do and can afford, and see where we get—it may be far.

Chapter 18

CONTROL AND PROFIT: SOME HELPFUL PROCEDURES

Profit is the name of the game, and our title here is "Control and Profit" because the chances for profit are drastically reduced if you don't have control. In the food service industry, renowned for erratic profit performance, control is not our long suit. This is obvious from the great fluctuations in our quarterly reports and the wide variations in menu prices from place to place for the same item. Many restaurants today are trying to make up for lack of internal control by raising prices, a practice much like blackmail in that once you start, it is difficult to stop until it is too late. Yet our put-out-the-fire type of management is not intrinsic to the food business; we have the tools to keep control and produce steady profits if we would just use them.

Someone once asked Willie Mays how he had mastered the whole range of skills in baseball. He said:

"It's simple. They throw the ball, I hit it. They hit the ball, I catch it."

216 RESTAURANT PLANNING

Like Mays, let's take a simple approach to the problem of control and see how the monster can be cut down to size. Instead of getting into technical terms like "double entry," "depreciation," and "amortization," we can divide the problem into six simple categories that will help management improve control and profits:

1. Establish a reasonable financial structure.
2. Get what you pay for.
3. Get paid for what you sell.
4. Maintain security.
5. Aim for volume sales.
6. Remember that accounting is a tool of management.

Nothing here is really difficult or complicated. And systems and machines are available today that end most of the time-consuming drudgery involved in accounting and control. This approach is not intended to create do-it-yourself accounting; everyone in business needs an experienced accountant, whether full or part time. But if you improve your job of record keeping, your accountant and tax man can give you better service and your whole operation will gain.

A REASONABLE FINANCIAL STRUCTURE

Many food service ventures never have a chance because of faulty projections and unreasonable costs that cannot be met no matter how efficiently management performs. Great competition developed some years ago for toll road restaurants that were being built for lease to existing operators, and many unlucky winners contracted to pay such high rents (based on percentage of sales) that they were in trouble before they started. One of the problems in our industry is that not all owners, managers, and investors understand the food business and the profit structure. Chapter 1, Why Start a Restaurant? mentioned that many people think restaurant profits run as high as 50 percent. They don't. Although operations differ widely, here is a rough guide to cost distribution:

Percentages of Sales

Cost of food	42%
Salaries and wages	30%
Other expenses	14%
Total operating expense	86%

In this projection only 14 percent is left for rent, interest, taxes, nonoperating expenses, and profit—which means that you should be careful in setting up a food operation. If you have one or more of the following, there will be trouble: excessive investment in land, building, or equipment; above-normal rent; high land lease; high labor costs; above-average maintenance costs; more expensive food due to the area or transportation. Any such unusual built-in costs must be recognized in the beginning and methods for compensating devised.

Effective methods for cutting costs, however, do *not* include reducing portions and quality of the food, hiring "cheap" help, raising prices, cutting maintenance to the bone, stopping all advertising, or downgrading management and supervision. These are the easy solutions to an earlier mistake, and the worst part is that they do usually produce a sudden improvement and make someone a hero overnight. But the public can't be fooled all the time; the volume of business soon begins to drop, and the going starts to get rough.

1. Avoid falling into this situation by being careful in the conception stage.

2. If you are already in it, recognize the problem and get professional help. Rather than ruin the business, you may be able to restructure your situation in order to reduce some of the high fixed costs.

GET WHAT YOU PAY FOR

Although this sounds so simple, it is nevertheless one of the largest areas of loss in the food service industry. Most operators think of checking purchases only in terms of the food bought, but there are many other pieces to the problem.

Food and Supplies

To begin with the obvious, provide the tools and facilities to account for merchandise received. Have a covered space inside or outside the building (not the same as the storage area) where goods can be unloaded for checking. Remember that you and your own help should put the merchandise away.

The unloading area should have an accurate scale. Naturally each item does not have to be weighed, but be sure you spotweigh as well as count items.

All delivery slips and invoices should be clearly written, priced, and totaled. If a supplier refuses to do this, get a new supplier. Check the delivery ticket against your order copy for both quantity and price quoted so you need not spend time going through them later. If there is an error, better to have it corrected at once by the deliveryman.

A well-planned receiving area is near the office, and every well-equipped office should have an electric adding machine. Once you have checked quantities and unit prices, run a quick tape on the adding machine. Before the deliveryman leaves, you should be finished with the invoice so that it is ready to be entered.

Employees

Strange as it may sound, you are buying and receiving this service so check employees' efficiency. The first step is to install an electric time clock with cards for each week. This not only eliminates the guessing game each night about who worked when, but makes it easy to compute the payroll. The standard objection to the time clock is that employees will not use it, and the standard answer is that you should get employees who will.

Naturally, it is impossible to supervise everyone all the time, but a weekly sales per man-hour figure (total sales divided by total hours taken from the payroll sheet or time cards) provides a reliable early warning. If the figure drops, it is time to begin checking on the production of individual employees or certain shifts. Because we cannot afford all the supervision we would like, such danger signals tell us when and where to use management time.

The accompanying chart demonstrates how the sales per man-hour figure is used for control. Suppose that your projection (budget) requires a 28 percent (of sales) payroll to give you the profit you need. As shown on the chart, if your average hourly wage is $1.80, you must produce $6.42 in sales per man-hour, which comes to $128.40 if you have 20 employees. Get hourly register readings; then you can quickly establish sales per man-hour and look it up on the chart to determine your productivity. In fact, you can spot the exact periods where you have fallen short of the goal.

Contracts and Agreements

Sometimes in the hectic rush of starting a business, agreements for pest control, window washing, lawn maintenance, water softening, and so on are made in a hurry and not even recorded. It is an excellent move to get these services lined up; just be sure to check later and see that you are receiving what you pay for.

Have a folder in the office listing the services with their prices and specifying what is to be done when. Then use a calendar and keep

Sales per Manhour Needed to Produce Certain Wage % of Sales

Average hourly wage rate	24%	25%	26%	27%	28%	29%
1.20	5.00	4.80	4.62	4.44	4.29	4.14
1.30	5.42	5.20	5.00	4.82	4.64	4.48
1.40	5.84	5.60	5.38	5.18	5.00	4.82
1.50	6.24	6.00	5.76	5.56	5.34	5.18
1.60	6.66	6.40	6.16	5.92	5.72	5.52
1.70	7.08	6.80	6.54	6.30	6.08	5.86
1.80	7.50	7.20	6.92	6.66	6.42	6.20
1.90	7.92	7.60	7.30	7.04	6.78	6.56
2.00	8.34	8.00	7.70	7.40	7.04	6.90
2.10	8.74	8.40	8.08	7.79	7.50	7.14
2.20	9.16	8.80	8.46	8.14	7.86	7.58
2.30	9.58	9.20	8.82	8.52	8.22	7.94
2.40	10.00	9.60	9.24	8.88	8.58	8.28
2.50	10.42	10.00	9.62	9.26	8.92	8.62

a record of performance. In addition, check the quality of the work to make sure you are getting good service. As regards advertising you contract for, whether it is via radio, television, billboards, or something else, make sure that it appears.

Shop Around

Many operators become "married" to their suppliers, which can be a costly way of doing business. Shopping does not mean bargain hunting, but it is a good idea to look around once in a while to be certain you are getting good value. Many managers have an aversion to checking up on people for fear someone will complain about not being trusted, but getting what you pay for has nothing to do with distrust; it is just sound business practice.

GET PAID FOR WHAT YOU SELL

Here is another big leak that drains profits. For years it has been a tedious job requiring many man-hours to verify guest checks and duplicates. As labor costs rose, less time was devoted to this function and the losses from both errors and petty theft rose, too.

The ideal solution would be to set up systems and procedures that eliminate the checking and prevent the leaks, and, fortunately, machines are now available that can do this work automatically. For example, the pre-printed check with overlay shown in Figure XVIII-1 can be marked with a simple dot, eliminating the job of teaching servers how to write a check and saving time on order taking. The order is then pre-rung by placing it in a machine (Figure XVIII-2) which prints the items and quantities out clearly for the kitchen. The same computer can even control the bar.

After the party has been served, the server puts the check back into the machine and presses the total button. In a matter of seconds each item is priced correctly, the tax is printed, and the bill is correctly added. When the guest pays, the transaction can be handled by either the server or the cashier and requires only a change drawer instead of a register. This saves lines waiting for checks to be rung.

The computer will also count selected items as they are being rung and give you a total of how many were sold in the meal period. And at the end of a shift of a meal, it will report the total sales of each server.

Every operator who learns what this machine will do wants to get one immediately—until he hears the price. For a restaurant with high volume the computer-register can take as long as six months to pay for, while a moderate-volume enterprise may need eight to twelve months. The best course is to investigate this and other systems carefully to make sure the one you select fits your operation. If you have a very busy house with many servers, for example, a pre-ring register where each girl must ring each item might slow service.

In general, the most desirable system features pre-printed checks, a minimum of ringing, no writing, and no manual adding.

As discussed in the magazine *Institutions,* the use of computers like the register machine is spreading.[1] A dinner house chain that has several hundred seats in the dining room, together with bar and lounge areas and oyster bars, has installed one to relieve servers of arithmetic chores during busy hours. Its computer-register both frees them and saves the 1 percent of sales that is usually lost by errors in calculation. A different use of computers is reported by a coffee shop chain which has turned bookkeeping and control tasks over to an off-premise computer center. The chain's profits are up 2 percent because better control has reduced food and labor costs by 1 percent each. In these and other ways automation can save man-hours and increase the accuracy of the work done.

[1] Pat Dando, "Who Said Computers Aren't for You?" *Institutions,* January 15 1972.

CONTROL AND PROFIT: SOME HELPFUL PROCEDURES 221

Server	Persons	Table No.	Date		
NO. IN PARTY		WAITRESS		QTY	PRICE
NO. IN PARTY			①		
Chicken Soup			②		
Onion Soup			③		
Shrimp Cocktail			④		
Chop Ch Liv	Herring		⑤		
Fruit w/Shbt			⑥		
Tom Juice			⑦		
Cheese Cake	Stwbry Sh Ck	Parfa ⑧			
Pastries			⑨		
Ice Cream			⑩		
Tea Sanka Milk Pot Pouring			⑪		
Coffee			⑫		
Share A C		Salad	⑬		
Prime Rib	R MR M W	⑭			
Extra Cut	R MR M W	⑮			
CHILDS PRIME RIB	R MR M W	⑯			
Chopped Steak	R MR M W	⑰			
CHILDS CH STEAK	R MR M W	⑱			
Steak Kabob	R MR M W	⑲			
Filet Mignon	R MR M W	⑳			
NY Strip	R MR M W	㉑			
Baby Back Ribs			㉒		
Ribs & Chicken			㉓		
Lamb Chops	R MR M W	㉔			
Boneless Chicken			㉕		
CHILDS CHICKEN			㉖		
Medlins of Beef	R MR M W	㉗			
Chicken Livers			㉘		
Beef & Lobster	R MR M W	㉙			
Sirloin Tips Saute			㉚		
Steak & Peppers			㉛		
Calf's Liver	R MR M W	㉜			
Filet of Dover			㉝		
Roast Duck			㉞		
Pork Chops			㉟		
CHILDS PORK CHOP			㊱		
Stuffed Shrimp			㊲		
Fried Shrimp			㊳		
CHILDS FRIED SHRIMP			㊴		
Florida Snapper			㊵		
Lobster Tails			㊶		
			㊷		
Baked Pot St Pot Peas Carro			㊸		
Wild Rice Mushrooms			㊹		
		.25	㊺		
		.75	㊻		
		1.00	㊼		
		1.10	㊽		
		1.10	㊾		
		1.25	㊿		
		1.50			
CHECK NO.	LOCATION	SUB TOTAL			
061218		TAX			
		TOTAL			
061218	LOCATION	TOTAL			

Figure XVIII-1. *Pre-printed check to be used in computer–register*

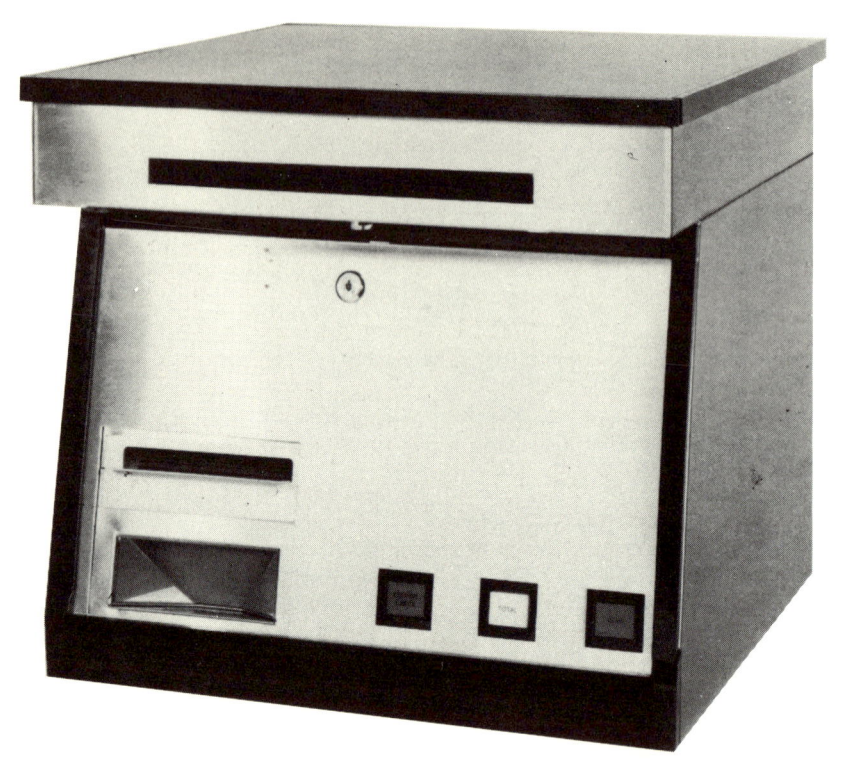

Figure XVIII-2. *Computer–register eliminates writing, ringing, and adding*

SECURITY

This is the easiest and least expensive leak to stop, so pick up a few percentage points here in a hurry. The food service industry may be behind other industries in many departments, but in pilferage it is up near the top. Following is a list of suggestions to help pull it down.

Put good locks on all doors in the building and storage areas. Know and check on everyone who has the keys.

Allow only authorized persons in nonpublic areas. There have been many cases where people entered restaurants and walked away with equipment and other valuables without being questioned.

Keep rear doors locked at all times except for authorized entrances and exits. If this is a fire exit, it can be inexpensively equipped with a special lock that will permit emergency exits.

Lock main storage areas (refrigerated and nonrefrigerated) as much of the time as possible. As explained, these were not meant for working out of, and after meal periods they can be secured.

Allow no packages into or out of the premises. Make this a very strict rule for employees.

Have a good safe secured into the floor or wall. This area should be well lighted even when the building is closed.

Keep inventories as small as possible and keep items (particularly small ones) in their cases as much as possible.

Watch garbage cans. One of the easiest methods to get food and other items out of a restaurant is to conceal them in the trash and garbage containers taken out back. Check these from time to time—or use a compactor, since it is difficult to smuggle out anything after it has been compacted.

Locate cashier in a good position for keeping an eye on check paying and on people going in and out.

Although a security system is relatively easy to establish and maintain, most operators seem to assume that no one is going to steal from them. The best way to reduce pilferage is not to check up on people continually but to remove temptation. One of the reasons for the amount of pilferage in our industry is that we are dealing in products which can be used by everyone. Years ago, a chain switched from using small packages of ground coffee to grinding whole-bean coffee only when coffee was to be made. The change saved the company an unanticipated 5 percent on the use of coffee, because the whole beans are no good without a grinder. Don't stick your head in the sand about pilferage—recognize that it exists and do something about it.

VOLUME SALES

This book has emphasized many times that high volume means higher profits, a fact that the advanced chains recognized years ago because they had the money and personnel to make in-depth studies of profits. As a result, chain operators set minimum yearly sales figures for their units and dropped those which fell below the minimum as soon as possible. The ideas this book has advanced on how to speed service, put less effort into making food and more into serving it, design the best layout, and buy proper equipment all have one goal: to increase sales volume and produce more profit. As explained repeatedly, it is better to make 5 percent net profit on $500,000 in yearly sales than 10 percent on $100,000.

Preceding chapters have also emphasized that price increases, which have been epidemic recently throughout the industry, usually cut into sales and have a negative effect on profits. Operators are taking a hard look at their sales today and changing their ideas about markups and traditional guidelines like the rule stipulating that the purchase cost of food must not exceed 30 percent of the selling price. Times have changed; take another look at your own operation and do everything possible to increase total sales to raise dollar profits. Most of the thinking in the past has focused on percentages, but it is the dollar profit that counts.

There are several side benefits to being busy in addition to making more profit. Many employees derive much of their income from tips, and if business is slow, their income is small and they do not stay. A busy operation with full dining rooms and perhaps even a small waiting line makes an excellent impression on the new guest since it indicates that the food and service must be good. Contrary to logic, a busy operation will run better and smoother than a slow one because employees are keyed to a fast pace and tend to work better and give better service. High-volume sales also yield enough money for proper management and proper maintenance; it is like the old saying, "The rich get richer!"

ACCOUNTING IS A TOOL OF MANAGEMENT

Accounting used to be considered a separate part of the food service operation—something strange and mysterious that gave the score, which might come as quite a shock at the end of the month. After inventory was taken, say on October 1, the primary role of accounting was to tell us on October 15 how we had fared in the month of September. Although this information might be timely for stockholders and the IRS, it was a little late to be used for making corrections and improvements. If there was a loss, it was difficult for anyone to remember back four or five weeks to understand what had happened. It is much like asking a server after four or five days to explain what has become of a missing check, whereas the average person cannot remember what happened today.

A previous section, Get Paid for What You Sell, pointed out how modern systems can help restaurants achieve better control and eliminate much of the tiresome work we have been doing for years.

Naturally, not every operator or even every chain can afford computer accounting, but today there are simpler systems that also save time and effort. The one outlined here is not a matter of theory alone; it has been tested and proved in many operations.

This system eliminates monthly inventories of the kind we now know, in which each bit of food and even the salt in the shakers is counted and tediously priced. Naturally, it will be necessary to take an inventory at the end of the operating or calendar year to close the books, but not every month.

Instead, a partial inventory is taken on a slow day at the beginning of every week, the day before weekly orders are placed for food. It covers only *unopened* cases of food in refrigerated, frozen, or plain storage, and it can be used to compile the food order for the next day. This is what we mean by making accounting a tool: as long as you must take inventory, take it at a time when the same work is needed for the food order.

Form A-102, Weekly or Bi-weekly Order and Inventory, furnishes a quick and simple inventory record and doubles as a guide for placing orders. As you progress, you can look back on the same sheet to see what you ordered last week. For example, on February 24, 1972, you had one full unopened box of hamburgers. Sales were running about $2,000 per week, and since you knew from experience how many boxes it takes to do various amounts of business and had already entered this in the columns marked Pars, you ordered 5 boxes to bring the supply up to the 6 boxes needed for another $2,000 week. When you had received these cases the previous week, you had quickly marked the $20 invoice cost on each. This $20 cost times one case gives a $20 value for the item on 2/24/72. It is obvious how fast the inventory can be taken and how easily the order can be made up at the same time. This procedure not only prevents ordering too much but ensures that you will order enough not to run out.

Note that at the time of delivery the receiver uses a marking pencil to write the price on each case as the deliveryman brings it in. Your own employees should put away the food in the proper storage areas (following the first-in, first-out system) stacked in the cases with name and price showing. Priced, extended, and corrected delivery tickets or invoices are then filed (and other expense items like paper and laundry can also be put on file).

The cost of food is quickly figured at the end of each week by adding the previous week's closing inventory value to the total value of all food purchased for the week (taken from the invoices and delivery

LOCATION: RESTAURANT X MGR: JOHN DOE

A-102   WEEKLY OR BI-WEEKLY ORDER AND INVENTORY

DESCRIP.	ITEMS LOCATION:	UNIT	DATES 7/24/72 ON HAND	ORDER	ON HAND	ORDER	ON HAND	ORDER	ON HAND	ORDER	ON HAND	ORDER	PRICE	VALUE DATE 2/24/72	VALUE DATE	VALUE DATE	VALUE DATE	VALUE DATE	PARS $2000	$3000	$4000
80/4 OZ.	HAMBURGER PATTY	BX.	1	5									20.00	20.00					6	10	14

A-101   WEEKLY OPERATION RESULTS

MONTH: __FEB.__   YEAR: __1972__   LOCATION: __RESTAURANT__   MGR: __JOHN DOE__

A. WEEK ENDING	1. FOOD INVENTORY	+	2. FOOD PURCHASES	–	3. FOOD INVENTORY	=	4. COST OF FOOD SOLD	5. SALES $	6. % FOOD COST	7. PAYROLL $	8. % PAYROLL	SALES INC. OR DECR. PREVIOUS WEEK	SALES INC. OR DECR. LAST YEAR
FEB 3	JAN 28 200		1500–		100–		1600–	4000–	40	1000–	25	+150	+350
FEB 10	FEB 3 100		1600–		200–		1500–	4500–	33	900–	20	+500	+50
CUMULATIVE 2 WEEKS							3100–	8500–	36	1900–	22	+650	+400
CUMULATIVE 3 WEEKS													
CUMULATIVE 4 WEEKS													
CUMULATIVE 5 WEEKS													

INSTRUCTIONS:

A. Week ending: use full weeks as much as possible
1. & 3. Inventories: unbroken cases of frozen or canned foods only—take this near "order" day so same inventory can be utilized for ordering
2. Total of all food invoices for week—see that all suppliers price and extend delivery tickets

1. + 2. – 3. = 4. Cost of food sales
4. ÷ 5 = 6. % food cost
7. Total dollar payroll for week
7. ÷ 5. = 8. % payroll
Sales inc. or decr.—compare sales each week
8. Use whole numbers only—no cents or fractions

_____ MGR.

tickets); computing the value of the bulk unopened case inventory taken; and subtracting the dollar value of the bulk inventory from the total dollar value of the previous inventory and the food purchases made during the week. Divide this cost of food by the total dollar sales for the week and you will have a food cost percentage. Naturally, these figures can be totaled to find monthly or period results. Also, since most operations pay weekly, it is a simple matter to total the payroll and divide by the total weekly sales to arrive at a percentage for the payroll.

The sample figures in form A-101, Weekly Operation Results, show how to arrive at these figures. The food industry totals in columns 1 and 3 come from form A-102, Weekly or Bi-Weekly Order and Inventory. Sales figures are easy to get, and payroll costs are determined by running a total from the payroll sheet. Note that only dollars are used—forget the cents and figure everything to the nearest dollar to save a lot of time. If you wish, you can add other information such as the sales increase or decrease compared with the previous week and with the same week last year. Other invoices for laundry, paper, detergents, and so on can also be added and divided by sales to give a weekly figure for these expenses.

For your accounting records the 13-period system is recommended in preference to the 12-calendar-month system used by most firms. Calendar months can vary from 28 to 31 days, and one month may have, say, five Sundays. These irregularities throw off comparisons, whereas 52 weeks divided by 13 periods gives 4 equal weeks, or 28 days, to a period, with days of the week evenly distributed.

Many will argue that the simplified accounting system described here is not as accurate as the monthly inventory system. From experience in many operations, however, the author can promise that it is. Furthermore, it gives you three operating expense figures to use each week for control: food cost, labor cost, and the cost of supplies. As explained, the weekly bulk inventory will also help with ordering. Purchases and inventory should be held to a minimum for many reasons, and these can easily be watched on accounting forms like the two shown here. In addition, utility costs should be checked each month so they can be kept in line. Since fixed charges like taxes, insurance, rent, and depreciation are more or less noncontrollable by management, other costs should be monitored on a red flag or warning basis. If payroll costs, purchases, or food costs jump in one week, *investigate immediately;* that is why we need figures fast.

Most operations cannot afford to be without the new systems and work savers available today. If your volume is low and you install control, profits will increase and you will have money to use for remodeling or promotion to increase volume and really make money. It is the negative approach that hurts most businesses—the idea that nothing can be done to help. On the contrary, you can do much to reduce expenses, eliminate tedious work, and give your key people more time to spend on the key function, food service.

INDEX

INDEX

Accessibility, 26–27
Accounting, 199, 224–28
Adding machines, 218
Address, 24–26
Advertising agencies, 199
Advertising and promotion, 16, 189, 199, 219
Aerial photographs, 30
Air conditioning systems, 161, 203
Airports, 6, 14, 15
Aisles, 40, 41
Alcoholic beverages, 14
Amusement centers, 6
Architects, 29, 145, 154, 160
    kitchen design and, 57, 58
    layout and, 42, 44, 45
Aromas, 198
Ash trays, 108
Associations, restaurant, 22, 172

Automatic equipment, 11, 59, 78, 88, 134, 145, 150
Automation, 33, 134, 165–73, 174, 177

Baby seats, 41, 96
Back kitchens, 50, 51
Baked stuffed Idaho potato recipe, 130–31
Bakers, 135
Baking, 62
Banquettes, 41
Bargains, 113–14
Baskets, fry, 63, 178
Benefits, employee, 214
Bids on equipment, 44–45
Billboards, 24, 28, 219
Bins for ingredients, 101
Booths, 40–41, 184
Bowling teams, 199

233

234 INDEX

Breakeven sales level, 9
Braising, 128
Braising pans, 74
Breakfast business, 33
Breaking-in period, 9
Broiler man, 62
Broilers, 52, 56, 59, 60, 62, 74
   automatic, 158, 178
   temperatures of, 145, 146
Broiling, 62, 128, 191
Buffets, 14, 15, 34
Building codes, 4, 42, 183
Buildings, restaurant, 4, 9, 38, 81, 156, 202
Bureau of Labor Statistics, 22
Burnishing machines, 95, 98, 162
Bus carts, 169
Bus pans, 104
Bus terminals, 6
Butchers, 135
Butter service, 105
Butter spreaders, 103

Cafeterias, 52-53, 124, 134, 169, 180
California, 21
Can openers, electric, 101
Canlis, Peter, 189
Cans, trash, 80, 100, 152-53, 223
Car manufacturers, 165, 206
Car service, 150
Carbonated beverage system, 172
Carpet cleaning, 161
Carpet sweepers, 161
Carpets in kitchens, 159
Carts, 96, 169, 180
   service, 105, 169
   utility, 74, 168
Cashiers, 149, 223
Casseroles, 148
Casters, 55, 60, 158, 179
Chains, restaurant, 39, 113, 136, 150, 165
   advertising and, 189, 191, 199
   competition and, 201, 204, 205, 206
   opening a restaurant and, 12-13, 17, 23
Chambers of commerce, 23
Change makers, 172
Check holders, 104

Checks, guest, 112, 150, 176, 213, 219-20
Chefs, 50, 57, 138, 139
Chicken, cold sliced, and ham with potato salad recipe, 142
China, 9, 35, 96, 113, 148, 180
   ordering, 97-100
Chinese food, 33
Choppers, 74, 95
City planning departments, 25, 26
Clean dish carts, 168, 170
Cleaners, professional, 161-62
Cleaning, *see* Sanitation
Club sandwich recipe, 148
Codes, local, 90, 170
   building, 4, 42, 183
   planning, 20, 28-29
Coffee, 147, 171, 197-98
Cold cabinet, 122
Cold food serving units, 65, 180
Compactor, 80, 91-92, 160, 169, 180, 223
Competition, 8, 16, 201-7
   location and, 20, 29
Computer-registers, 172, 220
Computers, 19, 30, 111-12, 220, 225
Condensers, 171
Connections, utility, 70, 95, 158
Consultants, 9, 30, 67, 182
   food service planning and, 36, 37, 42, 54
Continental breakfasts, 15
Contracts, 218-19
Controls, 3, 10, 215-29
Convection ovens, 61, 62, 133, 158, 184
Convenience foods, 36, 49, 115, 134-37, 167
   equipment and, 51, 61, 112-13, 173, 174, 177
Conveyors, 168-70
Cooking methods, 33, 35, 88, 142-47
   meat, 127-30
Cooking units, 56, 180
Cooks, 112, 149, 166
Coolers, walk-in, 115, 117, 118, 119-23, 125
Cooling dishes, 146
Costs
   operating, 35, 68
   property, 8-9, 20, 27

Counter service, 34
Covers, plate and platter, 106
Crabmeat cakes recipe, 135–36
Credit, 9
Cup and glass racks, 107–8, 166, 170
Custom-designed equipment, 42, 54–57
Cutting boards, 100, 179
Cutting machines, 78, 167, 178

Decor, 41
Decorators, 45, 145
Defrost, 171, 179
Designers, 58, 67, 158, 166, 175, 183
    equipment and, 42, 44, 51, 95–97, 180
Desserts, 72, 141
Deuce tables, 41, 184
Diet foods, 196
Dining cars on trains, 15
Dinner business, 21, 33
Dishes, *see* China
Dishwashing, *see* Warehandling
Dispensers, 101, 106–7, 172
Disposable pans for freezing, 133
Disposers, 80, 85, 90–91, 93, 160, 170, 171–72
Dollies, 170
Drains, 95
Drive-in restaurants, 28
Dry storage, 123, 125
Dump pans, 52–53, 63
Dunnage racks, 115, 123, 124

Eating habits, 30
Ecology, 152
Egg boilers, 59, 171
Egg recipes, 144–45
Egg sandwich recipe, 144
Electric kitchens, 55, 57–58, 158
Electrical connections, 95, 159
Electrical work, 45
Employees, 10–11, 49–51, 149–51, 157, 208–14, 218
    expansion and, 12, 13
    facilities for, 185–86, 206, 212–13
    food service planning and, 31–32, 59, 69
    hiring of, 11, 205–6
    training of, 9, 11, 39, 51–52, 150, 209–11

    turnover of, 10, 80, 205–6, 208
    unskilled help as, 149–50
Engineering work, 44
Engineers, 55, 58, 160, 161
Environment, 29–30
Epoxy-based paints, 70
Equipment, 3, 4, 156–57
    automatic, 11, 59, 78, 88, 134, 145, 150
    choosing, 42–45, 58–65
    cleaning, 161
    custom-designed, 42, 54–57
    food service, 49–78
    future needs and, 174–80
    miscellaneous, 95–108, 183–84
    standard, 42, 53, 54–57, 69, 176, 180
    storage, 119–24
Equipment houses, 113
Evaporators for condensers, 171
Exhaust systems, 152, 159, 161, 171, 179, 213
Exhibition cooking, 197
Expansion, planning, 11–13
Expense accounts, 21

Fabricator-supplier, 55
Family business, 41
Fast foods, 14
Fat, filtering, 100–1
Fatigue, 212
Features, 33, 35
Fiberglass, 43
Filtering fat, 100–1
Fires, 56, 146, 171
Fire protection, 20, 28
First-aid supplies, 212
Flatware, 35, 79, 96, 113
    dispensers for, 106–7
    ordering, 97–100
Flite type of machines, 87, 89–90
Floor maintenance, 158–59
Floor scrubbers, 168
Florida, 154
Food, 33, 142–43, 196
    fast, 14
    pre-packaged, 36
    prepared, 88
    ready, 51
    serving, 138–51, 155–56

See also Convenience foods; Food preparation; Frozen foods
Food displays, 196
Food preparation, 67–68, 126–37, 155–56
  equipment for, 49–78
  layout planning and, 33, 36, 38
Food service, 138–51, 155–56
Four-seater booths, 41, 184
Four-wheel flat bed trucks, 168
Franchises, 6, 7, 11–12, 15–17, 205
Freezers, 56, 59–60, 74, 132–33, 146, 171
  ice cream, 172
  low-temperature blast, 133
  reach-in, 143, 158, 162, 179
  shake, 166, 172
  storage, 115–23, 125
Freezing, 132–33, 136
French fried shrimp recipe, 136–37
Fringe benefits, 214
Frozen foods, 32, 134–37, 155, 167, 173
  equipment planning and, 49, 51, 69
  reconstitution of, 60–61, 62, 117, 136
  storage and, 112–13, 115, 132–33
Fruit salad bowl recipe, 142
Fruits, 155
Fryers, 101, 144, 158, 178
  automatic lifts for, 166, 170, 178
  baskets in, 63, 178
  cooking temperature of, 145, 146
  layout planning and, 52, 54, 56, 59, 60, 63

Garbage, 81, 100, 156, 157
  disposing of, 90–93, 160, 169, 223
Garnishes, 147–48
Gas connections, 95, 158
Gas kitchens, 55, 57–58
Glass racks, 107–8, 166, 170
Glassware, 9, 35, 79, 96, 113
  ordering, 97–100
Gravity conveyors, 168–69
Griddles, 62, 145, 146, 158, 180
Grilled chopped steak recipe, 145
Grills, 52, 56, 59, 62, 158, 178
Grocery sales, 12
Growth, planning for, 163–86
Guest checks, 112, 150, 176, 213, 219–20

Hand trucks, 168
Handling techniques, 124
Handling trucks, 119
Hard cooked eggs recipe, 144
Health departments, 153–54, 158
Health foods, 196
Heated food cabinets, 122
Heating dishes, 146
Heating systems, 161
High chairs, 41, 96
Highways, 20, 24
Hiring employees, 11, 205–6
Holding units, 146–47
Hospitalization, 214
Hospitals, 90, 124, 169, 213
Hostesses, 41, 149
Hot food serving units, 62–63, 64, 140, 141, 145–46, 180
Hot syrup dispensers, 106
Hot water, 159–160, 179
Hotels, 6, 15
Hours of employment, 11
Hours of operation, 33, 59
Howard Johnson chain, 191
Humidity, 147

Ice, 141
Ice cream, 21
Ice cream cabinets, 171, 179
Ice cream freezers, 172
Ice maker-dispensers, 156, 171
Ice pans, 65
In-flite feeding, 12
Incinerators, 92–93, 160
Indiana, 21
Industrial feeding, 12
Industrial plants, 6
Infrared lamps, 64
Institutions (magazine), 220
Insurance, 28, 96
Inventories, 9, 112, 113, 223, 224–25
Investments, 4, 8–9, 18, 73–74, 183

Juices, 141, 195

Kitchens, 32, 42, 126, 154, 212–13
  equipment and, 49–65, 100–4
  staffing, 50–51
Knife sharpeners, 103–4

INDEX

Ladles, 103–4, 108, 150
Lawn maintenance, 161, 218
Levelers, 64, 141, 170, 180
Lighting, 41
Liners, trash can, 100
Liquor dispensers, 172
Liquor license, 29
Lobbies, 191–92, 196, 202
Location, 8–9, 13, 16, 19–30
Locker rooms, 156, 185, 206, 212
Locks, 222–23
Low-temperature blast freezer, 133
Low-temperature roasting, 88, 128–29
Lunch business, 21, 33
Luncheonettes, 134

Maitre d', 41
Managers, 138–40, 149, 151, 185–86, 209–10, 211
Manufacturers, 81, 82, 87, 165–67, 174–80
Maple butter recipe, 131–32
Market potential, 3, 20, 23–24
Marriott, J. Willard, Jr., 31
Mays, Willie, 215–16
Meals, 20, 24, 115, 212–13
Meat, 155
  cooking, 127–30
Meat thermometer, 129
Menu holders, 192, 193
Menus, 64, 97, 112, 115, 127
  equipment choice and, 51, 53, 59, 67–69, 76
  layout planning and, 33, 34, 36, 53
  merchandising and, 191, 192–95
Merchandising, 76, 97, 189–200
Microwave oven, 61
Minimum wage law, 11, 166
Mirrors, 212
Miscellaneous equipment, 95–108, 183–84
Mixers, 74, 78
Mobile equipment, 43–44, 53, 69–70, 158, 175, 180
Mops, 159, 178
Motels, 6, 12, 14–15, 24
Multicounters, 112

National Restaurant Association, 22, 208

National Sanitation Foundation, 153–54, 160
Nation's Restaurant News, 10, 154, 189, 206
Necessary supplemental operations, 6–7, 13–15
Neighbors, 20, 29
New Orleans, 7
New York City, 21
Nitrogen, 136
Noise level, 41, 149, 183, 202, 213
  plastic equipment and, 98, 100, 104, 106, 107
Nonslip trays, 108
Nonstick pans, 100
Nursing homes, 169

Offices, 212, 218
Ohio, 21
Oklahoma, 58
Operating costs, 35, 68
Ordering, 96–100, 108
Ordinances, 93
Ovens, 61–62, 74, 78, 158
Overhead, 12

Package units, 43
Paints and painting, 70, 73
Pan broiling, 128
Pan frying, 128
Pan racks, 115
Pancake houses, 22, 194
Pancake recipe, 131–32
Pans, 9, 100, 104, 133
  washing, 79, 124, 169, 178–79
Parking lot sweepers, 161, 168
Parking lots, 20, 21, 26–27, 28, 183, 202
  cleaning of, 152, 160, 161, 168
Pastry, 127, 155
Pest control, 218
Philadelphia, 21
Place mats, 198
Planners, 29, 30, 34–37, 45, 76
Planning codes, 20, 28–29
Plastic equipment, 43, 98, 100, 104, 106, 107
Plate and platter covers, 106
Plate heaters, 63–64, 141
Plates, *see* China
Plumbing, 45. 159

INDEX

Police protection, 20, 28
Pollution, 92, 152
Polynesian food, 33
Population, 21–23, 30
Pork, 155
Portable units, 43–44
Portion control, 101, 103–4, 147
Portion scales, 103, 150
Pot washing machines, 169, 178–79
Potential for growth, 20, 23
Pots, 9
    washing, 79, 81, 87–90, 124, 169
Poultry, 155
Power companies, 57, 58
Pre-packaged foods, 36
Pre-scrap tanks, 83, 85, 88, 160, 170
Prepared foods, 88
Pressure cleaners, 161, 168
Prices, 4, 21, 189–90, 196, 203
Product levelers, 64, 141, 170, 180
Professional cleaners, 161
Profits, 4–5, 203, 215–29
Projected sales, 33, 34, 53
Proofers, 122
Property, 8, 9, 20, 27–29
Pulping of garbage, 90–91, 160
Purchasing, 33, 36, 68–69, 111–25, 154–55, 205

Quarry tile floors, 70
Quartz ovens, 61

Rack washers, 124, 169
Racks, 71–72, 74, 96, 119–22, 124
Radio, 199, 219
Railroad stations, 6
Ranges, 56, 60–61, 74, 97, 158, 176, 177
Reach-in freezers, 143, 158, 162, 179
Reach-in refrigerators, 4, 59, 65, 125, 141, 176–77
Ready foods, 51
Receiving scales, 119, 217
Receiving supplies, 114–15, 154–55, 217–18
Recipes, 10
    baked stuffed Idaho potato, 130–31
    cold sliced chicken and ham with potato salad, 142
    crabmeat cakes, 135–36
    egg sandwich, 144
    French fried shrimp, 136–37
    fruit salad bowl, 142
    grilled chopped steak, 145
    hard cooked eggs, 144
    little thin pancakes, 131–32
    maple butter, 131–32
    open club sandwich, 148
    Salisbury steak, 145
    scrambled eggs, 144–45
    soup garnishes, 148
Reconstitution of frozen foods, 60–61, 62, 117, 136
Refrigerators, 44, 45, 56, 59–60, 62, 74, 146
    cleaning of, 158, 162, 171
    reach-in, 4, 59, 65, 125, 141, 176–77
    serving, 141
    storage and, 116, 118, 143
    walk-in, 68, 147, 156
Registers, 172, 220
Remodeling, 39, 76, 115, 118, 154, 181–86
Reopening an unsuccessful restaurant, 7, 17–18
Repair service, 44, 175
Resort hotels, 15
Rest rooms, 40, 42, 159, 183, 202, 206, 212
Restaurant associations, 22, 172
Roasting, 88, 128–29
Roll grills, 59, 95, 170

Safes, 223
Salad bars, 35
Salads, 72, 78, 85, 141
Sales
    breakeven level of, 9
    projected, 33, 34, 53
Salesmen, 6
Salisbury steak recipe, 145
Salt and pepper shakers, 108
San Francisco, 7
Sandwich grills, 59, 95, 170
Sanitation, 152–62, 175
    equipment and, 53, 69, 70–71
Sauteeing, 128
Scales, 103, 119, 217
Schedules, 213

School papers, 199
Schools, 124, 134, 169
Scoops, 103-4, 108, 150
Scrambled eggs recipe, 144-45
Seating, 38, 40-41
Security, 222-23
Self-cleaning equipment, 53, 59-62, 70, 150, 158, 171
Self-closing doors and drawers, 158, 171, 179
Self-contained equipment, 42
Self-service restaurants, 14, 24, 34
Semi-automatic equipment, 59, 78, 177
Semi-automation, 134, 167-72
Septic tanks, 90
Servers, 112, 127, 139-40, 149, 197-98
Service, type of, 33-36
Service areas, 38, 81, 104-8
Service carts, 105
Serving areas, 134
Serving carts, 169
Serving utensils, 33, 35-36
Sewage, 20, 27-28
Shake freezers, 166, 172
Shelving carts, 119
Shelving units, 96, 115, 123-24, 162, 169
Shopping centers, 22
Short-order cooks, 50-51
Signs, 24, 28, 161, 190-91, 202
Silver flatware, 9, 98, 162
Silver sort carts, 90
Simmering, 130
Sinks, 60, 85, 88, 157, 159, 179, 185
Slicers, 71, 95, 103, 175-76, 178
Snack bars, 15, 21
Sneeze guards, 179
Snow pans, 65
Soak sink carts, 88
Soak tanks, 80
Soup, 148
Speed limit, 20, 26
Spoons, 103-4, 108
Spreaders, 103-104
Sprinkler system, 28
Stainless steel, 43
Standard equipment, 42, 53, 54-57, 69, 176, 180
Standards, 8
Starting a restaurant, 3-18

Steak houses, 58
Steam cleaners, 161, 168
Steam tables, 62
Steamers, 61
Steel wool, 158
Stewing, 130
Storage, 69, 111-25, 143, 155, 160, 222-23
Storage racks, 119-22
Supermarkets, 143, 201, 203-4
Supervision, 138-40
Suppliers, 113, 219
Supplies and deliveries, 20, 29, 33, 36, 111-25, 217-18
Sweepers
  carpet, 161
  parking lot, 161, 168
Syrup dispensers, 106

Table service, 34
Take-out service, 34
Telephone company, 199
Telephones, 212
Television, 199, 219
Temperature control, 171
Temperatures, 179, 202
  cooking, 143, 145-47
  dishwashing, 80, 156
  frozen foods, 133
  roast meat, 129
  served food, 64-65, 140-41
  storage, 155
Tennessee Valley Authority, 58
Thermometers, 65, 104, 129, 146, 147
Thermostats, 146, 171
Thermotainers, 64, 140, 146
Tile walls and floors, 70
Time clocks, 218
Timers, 59, 77-78, 145, 150, 170-71, 179
Tips, 149, 213, 224
Toasters, 95, 170
Toilet facilities, 156, 185
Toll roads, 6, 13-14, 15, 24
Tomato slicers, 103, 178
Tourism, 21, 24
Trade magazines, 22, 172
Traffic, location and, 20, 25, 26

240 INDEX

Training programs, 9, 11, 39, 51–52, 150, 209–11
Trains, dining on, 15
Transportation centers, 6
Trash, 81, 90–93, 169
Trash cans, 80, 100, 160
Tray carts, 124
Tray stands, 105
Trays, 101, 108, 162
Trucks, 119, 124, 168, 169
Turnover rates, employee, 10, 80, 205–6, 208

Universal Kitchen Motor Unit, 74
Unskilled help, 149–50
Utility carts, 74, 168
Utility companies, 57, 58
Utility connections, 70, 95, 158
Utility racks, 71–72, 74

Vacuum cleaners, 161
Vegetable slicers, 103, 178
Vegetables, 85, 127, 155, 195

Ventilation, 44, 45, 160–61, 206, 212–13
Volume, sales, 59, 115, 223–24

Wages, 11, 218
Waiting line space, 40, 41–42
Walk-in refrigerators, 68, 147, 156
Warehandling, 79–94, 156
　large operation of, 87
　machines for, 81, 87, 147, 160, 169–70, 175, 179
　medium to large operation of, 83–85
　small to medium operation of, 82–83
　temperatures for, 80, 156
Waste disposal, 71, 157
Water, 95, 159–60, 179
Window washing, 161, 218
Work tables, 179
Working conditions, 11

Yellow pages, 199

Zoning codes, 28